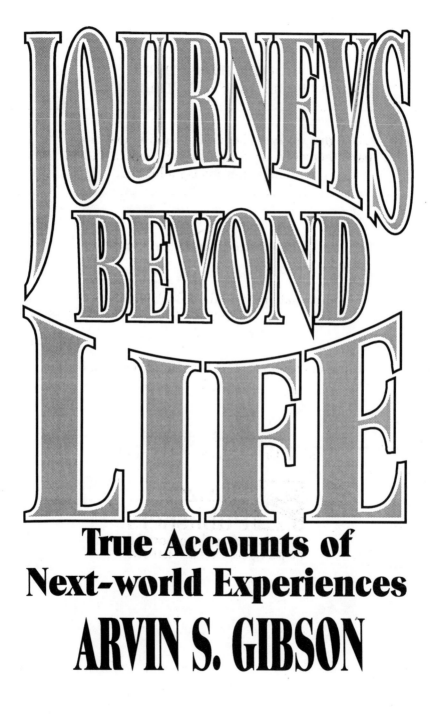

JOURNEYS BEYOND LIFE

True Accounts of Next-world Experiences

ARVIN S. GIBSON

First Printing, September 1994

International Standard Book Number
0-88290-508-2

Horizon Publishers' Catalog and Order Number
2012

Printed and distributed
in the United States of America by

Horizon
Publishers
& Distributors, Incorporated
P.O. Box 490 Bountiful, Utah 84011-0490

Acknowledgments

This book would not exist save for the efforts and encouragement of many people. First among those is the marvelous lady, Carol Gibson, whom I somehow was wise enough to marry forty-four years ago in Berkeley, California. Carol continues to be my right arm. She assisted with the many interviews in the research for the several books I have written, and she offered helpful comments throughout the effort.

Duane Crowther initially encouraged me to conduct the research for this work, and he suggested the idea for this book. His encouragement—and courage in offering to publish another book on near-death experiences—were vital in getting me to continue with the substantial effort necessary to complete this book. He, and his people at Horizon Publishers and Distributors, contributed much to the finished product.

Rose Mari Finter labored to improve my grammar and writing style. Her careful attention to detail helped me avoid embarrassing mistakes.

Marian Bergin, a clinical psychologist practicing in the Provo, Utah area, assisted me in a difficult technical area. She provided the scientific material needed to better understand an issue of importance to the book.

Several people read drafts of this work and offered helpful comments. Included in that group are: Norman and Helen Herzinger, Janice Ridges, Pat Pexton, Grant Bishop, Randle King, Fred Beckett, Bill and Leslie Starkweather, Bill English, Leanne Mayo, and Sid Stepehenson. I am grateful for their diligence in using their expertise to make suggestions for improvement.

The Utah Chapter of the International Association for Near-Death Studies (IANDS of Utah) was a fertile source of help. The officers of that group were supportive of my effort, and many of those selected for interviews came to my attention during local IANDS meetings.

Without the freely offered experiences by the many people Carol and I interviewed, there would be no book. These people touched our lives in ways that cannot be expressed by a simple thanks. They changed the way we thought about those things we cherish most. Their unselfish giving of themselves, often under significant emotional strain, helped me to better understand the Near-Death Experience (NDE) phenomenon. Their stories should provide sustenance to many people.

3

Of special interest is the account in this book of the experience of Howard Storm, who was a Professor of Art from Northern Kentucky University at the time that he had an extensive NDE in 1985. Howard Storm is now Pastor Storm in the United Church of Christ, and he generously agreed to allow us to include a rather complete account of his NDE in this book.

My sons, Craig, Aaron and Dale Gibson, and their wives, Janis, Sue, and Lori; and my daughter, Leah Gibson, provided encouraging support. They reviewed early drafts of research materials and suggested interesting areas for investigation.

All of us doing research in the near-death field are indebted to those pioneers that initiated the research work and first brought it to the attention of the world. Foremost among the early researchers was Dr. Raymond A. Moody, Jr., in his book *Life After Life*. Other pioneers in the field included Dr. George G. Ritchie and Dr. Kenneth Ring. Dr. Ring was one of the founders of the International Association for Near Death Studies (IANDS).

Journeys Beyond Life is primarily the result of my work and my judgment. In exercising that judgment I attempted to do the research and to present the material in as accurate a manner as possible. It is my fervent desire that the material so presented will provide others with the same feelings of love, wonder, and hope which I felt as I listened to people tell of their experiences. May this book prove to be a source of knowledge and understanding to all who read it.

Arvin S. Gibson

Contents

Foreword

Arvin and Carol Gibson first came into my life in 1990. Arvin had manuscripts under his arm and we talked publishing. I learned he had recently retired as a power-company executive.

It was particularly exciting when I learned of his interest in near-death experiences. I gave side-line encouragement as he and Carol undertook research—locating and interviewing many dozens of individuals who had received out-of-body experiences. Their work was done with precision, care and careful insight. Two books with numerous penetrating insights on life after death were produced: *Glimpses of Eternity* and *Echoes From Eternity*. A third book, an autobiographical work entitled *In Search of Angels*, also contained profound near-death experiences.

Arvin has been a significant force in the founding and sustaining of a state branch of the professional society for the study of NDEs: the *International Association for Near Death Studies* (IANDS of Utah). This has given him continuing access to individuals with other significant near-death experiences. He is systematically gleaning knowledge and insights that add to the growing body of knowledge on this important subject.

Journeys Beyond Life explores many new areas of research in addition to reinforcing numerous previous findings. These areas include premonitions of impending disasters, the palpable nature of spirit beings, the life-review experience, spirit-being travel, how spirits re-enter their mortal bodies, spirit-world reception of those who commit suicide, and miraculous healings. Other areas include returns to mortality to complete life's designated purposes, the nature of knowledge possessed by spirit beings, continuing body functions even though the spirit has left it, evil beings who influence out-of-body spirits, visits to mortals by spirit beings, the intense emotions felt by spirit beings, experiences with Christ, knowledge of future world events granted to spirit beings, and much, much, much more!

One of the most valuable aspects of *Journeys Beyond Life* is the statistical analysis of the experiences reported. The numbers provide perspective on many of the more-publicized elements of near-death experiences. Does everyone who goes beyond mortality experience the "tunnel"? Not by any means! Out of the Gibsons' samples, only 21.6% did so. Does everyone

11

encounter Deity? Only 26.5% did so, with 18.1% asserting that they actually saw the Lord.

But their figures provide a host of other insights—60.2% saw a brilliant light while out of their bodies; 55.4% saw people during their experiences, with 39.8% knowing the people they encountered and 27.7% recognizing they were relatives. Almost two-thirds of the interviewees heard a voice or voices. Just over a fifth of them described beautiful landscapes, but less than a tenth saw buildings. A tenth experienced a life's review, while a third of them received significant new knowledge during their out-of-body experience. A tenth of them heard beautiful ethereal music.

Even more intriguing are the stats on the overwhelming emotions the interviewees experienced during their NDEs. Forty-seven percent told of all-encompassing love; almost the same number spoke of experiencing a deep, abiding peace. Twenty percent spoke of feeling warmth. Negative feelings were reported also, with 12% experiencing fear and 6% feeling intense remorse.

As a publisher, and also as an author of a significant work concerning life after death and spirit-world experiences,[1] I recognize that *Journeys Beyond Life* is a major work—a scholarly contribution to the rapidly expanding topical area that is of vital interest to almost every person on earth. The book is clearly one of the finest in the field, and it is clear that it will experience rapid acceptance on both the scholarly level, the general reader level, and in book stores across the nation and beyond. I feel privileged to have been a participant in its publication.

Duane S. Crowther
Senior Editor,
Horizon Publishers

---

[1] *Life Everlasting* (Salt Lake City, Utah: Bookcraft, Inc. The book is currently in its 31st printing.)

INTRODUCTION

A Marvelous Experience

. . . I found myself walking . . . in a completely different sphere. It was beautiful beyond description and we were walking on a path. . . . It was a different world than this one. . . . As we walked along the path I noticed a profusion of flowers and trees. They were of a wider variety, and they had many more colors than on earth—or maybe it was that I could see more colors than on earth, I'm not sure.

. . . I noticed someone on the path ahead of us. As we got closer to the individual I could see and feel that he was a magnificent person. I felt overwhelmed as I looked at him. He was bathed in light. [My guide] asked if I knew who that was, and I answered yes. It was Jesus Christ.

When we got close to the Savior, I felt a tremendous love emanating from him. It's hard to describe, but you could feel it all around him. And I felt a similar enormous love for him. I fell at his feet—not because I thought about it, but I couldn't stand. I felt an overpowering urge to fall at his feet and worship him.

. . . As I knelt there at the feet of this marvelous being I became conscious of my past life being reviewed for me. It seemed to occur in a short period, and I felt the Savior's love during the entire process. That love was . . . well, it was everywhere. And it was as if we could communicate with each other without speaking. After a period the Savior reached down and I knew I should stand. As soon as I stood, he left.

[My guide] next led me to a city. It was a city of light. It was similar to cities on earth in that there were buildings and paths, but the buildings and paths appeared to be built of materials which we consider precious on earth. They looked like marble, and gold, and silver, and other bright materials, only they were different. The buildings and streets seemed to have a sheen and to glow. The entire scene was one of indescribable beauty.

. . . There was a feeling of love and peace. On earth there always seems to be something . . . you know how things bother you here.   There's always some problem troubling you—either it's health, or money, or people, or war—or something. That was missing there. I felt completely at peace, as if there were no problems which were of concern. It wasn't that there were no challenges. It's just that everything seemed to be under control. It was such a wonderful feeling that I never wanted to lose it.

And there was the feeling of love. Love from . . . from Jesus Christ. It emanated from him, and it was all around; it was everywhere. . . .

This astonishing experience was related to me by my father, Marshall Stuart Gibson, when I was a young man. He only told the experience a few times in his lifetime; each time was a spiritual event.

The event described by my father occurred in 1922 while he was working in Bingham, Utah for Western Union, and was the result of a massive heart attack. My mother, my grandmother, and my aunt were present during the attack.

Dad recounted this experience when I was a young man attending the University of California at Berkeley, and during a period when I was struggling with some of my beliefs. I was profoundly affected by his, and my mother's, descriptions of what had happened. I knew that my parents never lied, and it was obvious that they were convinced the experience had been real.

Why This Book?

Numerous books have been written about individuals who have had Near Death Experiences (NDEs) in which they apparently left their body or had some other unusual experience related to approaching death. The sheer volume of such books, as partially delineated in the bibliography, attests to popular interest in the subject. My own interest stemmed from my father's description of what had happened to him, and from the corollary description of the event from the point-of-view of my mother.

My father died in 1963, and in 1978 I read Dr. Raymond Moody's book "Life After Life."[1] Later, I read Dr. George Ritchie's "Return from Tomorrow."[2] Both books detailed experiences of people who had supposedly died, left their bodies, and later returned to life. Some of the accounts were remarkably similar to what my father had, years before, told me. In later years I read most of the books listed in the bibliography.

In reading the literature on NDEs, I felt that Dr. Raymond Moody and Dr. George Ritchie provided a significant service—through their pioneering work on NDEs, and through the publication of these experiences. By announcing to the world the existence of the NDE phenomenon, and by showing that different events had many elements in common, and were not as rare as previously supposed, they caused the scientific community to treat the subject with the serious attention that it previously lacked.

Other investigators quickly followed the lead of Dr. Moody and expanded upon his work. The resultant investigations included studies from other countries,[3] critical analyses of the recorded events,[4] statistical studies,[5] historical studies,[6] semi-successful attempts to recreate NDEs through hypnosis,[7] and even application of experimental drugs to determine whether NDEs could be duplicated in the laboratory environment.[8] The Gallup organization, based on a survey, estimated that there are eight million Americans who have undergone NDEs.[5]

Most of the studies were conducted in such a way as to enhance their credibility in the scientific world. One book, in fact, used the word *scientific* six times in the first two pages as if, in so doing, the author could assure others of his objectivity.

Interestingly, despite the fact that NDEs are spiritual by their very nature, few authors have attempted to correlate the experiences with Christian and Jewish religious teachings and literature. Raymond Moody and George Ritchie, both religious men, acknowledged the spiritual nature of the experiences. Dr. Maurice Rawlings in his book *Beyond Death's Door* showed the correlation between Christian Biblical scriptures and NDEs,[9] but most investigators do not follow his example.

In 1990 my wife, Carol Gibson, and I began interviewing subjects through advertisements and other means who claimed to have had NDEs. In the period from 1990 through 1994 we interviewed in excess of one hundred people. Our major objective was to determine, through our own research, what patterns might be evident from listening to the participants, and to record the experiences in as open and complete manner as possible. We were particularly interested in documenting spiritual experiences in the Christian tradition.

How the Research was Conducted

Three types of research were conducted for the book: 1) seeking and obtaining first-hand accounts from individuals who had undergone NDEs or analogous experiences; 2) reviewing much of the available literature on NDEs; and 3) reviewing and comparing events from NDEs to determine particular patterns that became evident from the research.

Since others have performed statistical work on the fraction of individuals undergoing NDEs who proceeded into out-of-body situations, or "core experiences" as they have been defined in some books,[10] no attempt was made to repeat those analyses. Rather, we screened out, ahead of time, those individuals who did not proceed from an NDE into an out-of-body, or as a minimum, an unusual spiritual experience.

To find suitable candidates we used two methods: referrals from friends, relatives, and associates; and advertisements in local papers and publications. Both methods were fruitful. Indeed, the respondents could have been multiplied many times simply by continuing the effort for a longer period.

In soliciting candidates to interview, no attempt was made to screen for religious or non-religious beliefs. The only criterion that had to be met was that the candidate had undergone some type of NDE, or other incident, which led to an out-of-body or related spiritual event.

The interviews were conducted in my home or in the home of the respondent, except for one which was conducted by telephone. Where women were involved, my wife, Carol Gibson, was usually present.

All the interviews were taped, later typed, and forwarded in draft form to the respondent. The respondents then made changes that they felt were appropriate to correspond more closely to their memory of what happened.

Some of those interviewed preferred to be recognized with their true identity; others preferred a pseudonym. For those desiring complete identification we used their full names; others desiring anonymity were assigned a pseudonym for a given name, with no surname.

To assure complete coverage of the subject those interviewed were first asked to give background information about themselves and the incident. Then they were asked to tell, as completely as possible, what had happened to them. We had previously prepared a check sheet with pertinent questions that were to be covered before the interview was complete. By reviewing the check sheet as the interview proceeded we were able to ascertain where desired topics had not been covered. We then asked questions, in as open-ended a manner as possible, to cover the desired issues.

I have frequently been asked two questions concerning the interview phase of the research. These are: "What was the motivation of those responding to your advertisements?" and, "How do you know they were telling the truth?"

Regarding the first question, of all those responding, only two individuals asked if there was a fee involved. When I explained that we couldn't pay a fee, otherwise people might be accused of fabricating a story for money, the individuals quickly understood. The primary motivations that people had for responding to our queries were threefold: to talk to someone who was sympathetic to what they had to say; to find out about others who had had similar experiences; and to help others by sharing what the respondent knew about death.

One lady put it this way: "For many years I thought I was the only one who had experienced anything like this." Another said: "When I first tried to explain what had happened, my doctor, my friends, and even my husband, implied that it was a dream, a hallucination, or I was crazy. I stopped telling others until recently."

The second question, concerning whether or not the individuals were telling the truth, is interesting. The very nature of the experiences was such that they were anecdotal and unique to the individuals involved. We, of course, observed the individuals during the interviews, and in essentially all the cases they were emotionally moved when they reached certain points in the interviews. Some could hardly continue as they relived the experience in their minds.

The demeanor of the people during the interviews was that of persons who had undergone a profound experience, one that affected their understanding of who and what they were, and one in which there was no need to embellish the reality or truth of what they had experienced. They knew what they had experienced and they could not, or would not alter the facts to suit other peoples' preconceived notions of what might have happened. For this, and other reasons, we became convinced that the individuals, whose experiences are included in this book, were telling the truth and their experiences were real.

The other phases of research for this book involved reading the available literature on NDEs, marking appropriate sections of books for later reference; and tabulating the research results of the observed patterns.

In a particular phase of the research I received a copy of a tape covering the experience of Howard Storm, who was then a Professor of Art from Northern Kentucky University.[11] The taped experience was so unusual and so extensive that I transcribed it into a written experience. With Professor Storm's kind permission I have included much of his experience in this book.

How this Book is Organized and What it Contains

The chapters immediately following this Introduction contain printed accounts of the interviews of respondents largely as they were recorded on tape. The interviews are reported, including background information, in their totality and with as much detail as is practical. In some instances considerable background information is given, either because the information is directly pertinent to the experience, or, equally important, because it adds to a better understanding of the individual. The reader can review the interviews without the interjection of editorial comment and can thus obtain a better feeling for what the respondent was saying in the setting of the total experience.

Of the slightly more than one hundred people that Carol and I interviewed, we have selected thirty-two complete first-hand accounts for inclusion in the book. Selected quotations from other accounts have also been included. Those full accounts that were selected were chosen for their general interest value.

The last three chapters in the book (Chapters 19, 20 and 21) provide an analysis and overview of the preceding material. Chapter 19, *Are The Stories True?* is written to answer continuing questions concerning the reality and authenticity of the stories in the book. The statistical data reviewed in Chapter 20, *Patterns and Parallels,* provides a rather complete analysis of the available data from our research. References from other NDE books are also cited where appropriate. Chapter 21, *Universal Messages*, is just that; namely, an exposition of the final messages and thoughts gleaned from those that we interviewed.

Chapter 1

TWO LEFT—ONE CAME BACK

Eloise Weaver

Background and an Early Experience

Eloise Weaver was a short, cheerful lady with curly auburn hair. She exhibited enthusiasm—none of the nervousness sometimes evident in interviews of this type—when she visited our home in July 1992. Carol and I greeted her and the interview commenced.

Eloise informed us that she was born in Evanston, Wyoming on August 14, 1942. She was raised as a first child in Wyoming where her father was a barber, and where her grandfather had also been a barber and a mayor. Her parents moved to Davis County, Utah, when she was a senior in high school. There she met her future husband, David, whom she married at age 17. They subsequently had six children, four girls and two boys.

Eloise began telling of her experiences: "The first unusual experience I remember was when I was nine or ten years old. I was in bed with rheumatic fever, which I'd had for about three months, and I was very sick. We lived on a corner where there were no lights and no other houses around us. My parents had just taken my brother to the doctor because of something he swallowed, and I was alone and frightened.

"My parents told me to keep the door locked and to stay in bed. I was scared and crying, and I remember praying for help. All of a sudden a great light filled the room. Standing there by me in the light was Jesus. He put His hands on my head and I felt this enormous outpouring of love.

"Jesus was all dressed in white, and he was very handsome. His eyes were the most wonderful blue, and there was the most warm, wonderful feeling emanating from him. I don't remember Him saying anything—just His hands on my head. It seemed that He was there for a long time, and the room was very bright. Then He left, and the room was dark again.

"When my folks came home, I told them what had happened. And they . . . you know how parents are, they just sort of patted me on the head and told me to go to sleep. They took me in for a test later that week, though, and all of my tests were absolutely wonderful. The doctor said I was almost completely well."

Eloise paused as though in thought, and I interjected: "You said that when the room got bright you saw Jesus standing there. How do you know it was Jesus?"

"Oh, I knew it was Jesus. His beautiful face, His countenance, His hair, it was . . . it was a beautiful brownish-golden color. And those wonderful big blue eyes. He had a little beard—and when He put His hands on my head I felt His strength. It was a strength that I felt through my whole body. I'll never forget the feelings that I had in His presence."

"What were His clothes like?" I asked.

"They were white; they covered His arms down to his wrists, and they were open at His neck a little way. They were flowing, and white; and the room was gold and blue and pink. It was radiant—it was just wonderful."

"Did He glow too?"

"Oh yes, there was just a . . . it was like an aurora coming off of Him. And the feeling. I'll never forget the feeling of His hands on my head.

"I never had any other experiences of that nature as a child."

A Premonition

"In May 1990, my husband and my children and I were living in Layton, Utah. My husband and I decided to take a trip to Missoula, Montana where we could go biking. We were both bikers, and we felt that it would be a short second honeymoon. Four of our six children were still living at home and we felt that we needed a break by ourselves. We were busy getting ready, and Dave had the car all packed, and . . .

"Did you ever feel that things weren't what they should be—sort of a premonition of something wrong? We were supposed to leave at 10:00

a.m. with a group of people we would be traveling with. The car was all packed from the previous evening, and Dave said, 'I'm ready to go.'

"It was 8:00 a.m. and I mentioned that there was still time before ten o'clock when we were to meet the others. Dave repeated that he felt we should go, then.

"When we went to the car, the bikes weren't on the bike racks of his car where we had loaded them the previous night. Instead, he had unloaded them from his car and put them on mine. I asked him why he did that and he said that he felt that we should take my car.

"As we got ready to leave, my seventeen-year-old daughter came up and pleaded to go with us. She said that she really wanted to go. Dave explained that we needed to get away for a separate vacation. She continued to beg her dad. He smiled and said: 'Okay, if you want to go, climb in just as you are—no clothes or other packing.'

"I'm sure that my husband felt my daughter would not go with us when he told her to climb in without packing, but she did. She got in and we took off. Dave drove for a time, and then I drove.

"When we reached Dillon, Montana, we stopped for lunch. Dave seemed compelled to keep going. Normally we would have relaxed for a time during lunch, but he insisted on eating in the car while we were traveling. He said that he felt we should get there and then relax. He also took the driver's seat though it was my turn to drive. He argued that we would get there quicker with him driving."

A Terrible Accident—Strange Visitors

"About twenty minutes after we left Dillon, and while I was laying my head down on the passenger side, I heard Dave holler: 'They're going to hit us.' And that's when the car hit us—in the front-side of our car.

"It was two o'clock in the afternoon; we were on a highway without another car around, and this older couple, coming from the opposite direction, apparently fell asleep. They hit a guard rail and it redirected their car back onto the highway but toward us. Their car was airborne when it plowed into my husband's side of the car.

"Our car rolled over many times. We were all wearing seat belts so we stayed in the car. When the car quit bouncing I looked over at Dave, and he was slumped over. I thought he had left me, and I took a deep breath. I was totally awake, and as I attempted to take the breath I found that I couldn't breathe. Immediately, I knew that my neck was broken.

"Looking into the window I saw two personages. Who they were, I don't know. I could see them from their shoulders up. One of them said to me: 'Pull your legs up to your chest, hold them tight and breathe shallow, and you will live.' Then they were gone.

"I think they were two men, from the tone of voice of the one, and they were dressed in white. The white was as bright as . . . it was as bright as the snow when the sun hits it. And there was a warm, calm, sweet feeling in that light.

"I did as he told me; I pulled my legs up, and I held on tight. That action probably saved my life. Later I found that the first two vertebras in my neck were broken, my spleen was ruptured, all my ribs were broken, my lungs were collapsed, and my diaphragm was in fifteen pieces. When I pulled my legs up, though, it's a mystery why my spinal column didn't rupture. The medics said that I couldn't have pulled up my legs because I was wearing the engine of the other car underneath my arm and my chest.

"Nevertheless, I know those people were there, and I know what they told me and what I did. Someday when I meet them again I'll know who they were."

An Embrace Out-of-Body

"After the people in white left it was a while before anyone saw us. There was very little traffic on the highway. Three kids were on a hill, though, and they had binoculars. They were watching for a white fox which they had seen the previous day. As they were watching for the fox they saw our dust. It took them about ten minutes to get to us.

"The kids came and began talking to us. My daughter was screaming from the back seat. My husband was conscious by this time and he was telling them his name and address. Finally, after what seemed a long time, other help came and they began the process of trying to get us out. There were the police and the paramedics. They were frantic because it appeared that we were in danger of dying.

"The paramedics got my daughter out first. Then they began to pry on the door where my husband was. Dave kept saying how badly he hurt, and they were afraid he was dying. He turned toward me, and that's when everything in the car got really bright, very warm, and very quiet. I didn't hear my daughter screaming anymore, and I didn't hear any voices coming from outside the car.

"I felt Dave's presence very close to me, and suddenly we were above our bodies. He held me really tight, and he said: 'Hang in there babe; I love you.' That's what he always called me. Then he said: 'I'm being called home, and you need to go back and raise our girls.'

"I remember telling Dave that I really didn't want to go back without him, but he told me I had to return. Then the warm feeling left, and I was hit with pain—immense pain. The pain was more horrible than when the car first hit us.

"I could hear the people again, and I saw Dave as they were pulling him out of the car. He winked at me. Then they began doing CPR on him; I knew he was gone. I could feel his presence near me. He had a habit of brushing my hair off my forehead—I could feel him doing that, and I felt very calm.

"Dave lived as long as he did, I think, (three hours before they got him out) so that he could encourage me to live. I wouldn't have struggled to live as much as I did without him there to help me."

Further Questions About the Experience

"Eloise, can you describe the light you saw?" I asked.

"It was just radiant and brilliant; it was soft and warm. The experience was almost as if I were sitting by a mountain stream and hearing the creek babbling, and the little birds. It was the most peaceful feeling I have ever felt—just absolutely wonderful."

"Why did you use the word peaceful?"

"I felt so great. I didn't feel any pain."

"When you went out of your body could you see your physical body in the car?"

"Yes. I could see myself with my knees pulled up, and I could see Dave slumped over."

"As you were embraced by Dave how did your spirit body feel?"

"It felt just like me; I was exhilarated from the embrace."

"When you were out of your body did you see anything or anyone else?"

"No, I've read about other experiences, but I didn't see a tunnel, or flowers or trees, or . . . . There were just Dave and I and the soft, beautiful brightness. It was soft, just so soft."

"Why did you use the word *soft*?"

"It was kind of a pastel color—just soft. When I saw the two personages, they were radiant and breathtaking. But with Dave in the light, it was just a soft . . . it reminded me of a cloud that puffed around us in a soft, cuddly, warm way."

"Could you tell us a little more about the two personages? What did they look like?"

"I could see them from the waist up. When I first saw them I couldn't tell whether they were men or women, but after I heard the tone of voice of the one I assumed they were men. They were dressed in white—very, very white. Everything was white."

"After seeing Dave, when you were out of your body, do you remember going back into your body?"

"I just remember him kissing me and hugging me, and then the noise came back. The pain—it was so terrible."

"You said that you looked at Dave as they were removing him from the car, and he winked at you. He must have been back in his body . . .?"

"Yes, he must have been back too. They were just starting to take him out when he gave me that little wink that he always gave me. They pronounced him dead at the hospital, but I think he was dead right after they took him out. I felt him brushing my hair with his hand shortly after they got him out."

"After you reached the hospital what was your recuperation like?"

"We were in Butte, Montana, in the intensive care unit of the hospital. My daughter and I both had life-support systems on us. We were in that hospital for two-and-one-half weeks. Then they flew us to Utah, and my daughter went home. I went to the McKay Hospital in Ogden and stayed there for another two weeks."

"How did they treat your broken neck?"

"First they had to treat my internal injuries. Then they put a *Halo* on my head with screws to hold it in place. It was very painful, and I wore it for five months."

"Did you have any permanent damage?"

"I was paralyzed on my left side for a while. I have a stiff neck, still, and I often get headaches, but my recovery truly was miraculous."

"Did you have a feeling at the time that you had a choice to stay or to come back?"

"No. I felt I had to come back."

"After that experience did you tell many people?"

"Yes. I told my brother, my parents, my children, and some of my religious leaders."

"Did those people believe you?"

"Oh, yes."

"Had you read anything up to that time on the near-death experience?"

"No, but I sure have since the experience."

Final Thoughts on the Experiences

"The experiences I have had have made me a much stronger person. I understand, now, that life is really short. We need to make the best of each day, to love our children, to have humility, and to have charity toward others. We also need to know that Heavenly Father loves us, and no matter how hard our difficulties are everything will be okay.

"My perspective on death has changed. I used to be a real coward about death. I think the fear that was in me—and that which is shared by many people—is, in part, because our body has a survival instinct; it doesn't want to give up. I now feel that death is a piece of cake. It doesn't scare me anymore."

Chapter 2

HUNTERS—A MAN AND A BOY

Derald Evans

Hunting for Bighorn Sheep

I first met Derald Evans in early December, 1990. He was a tall man dressed in running clothes. He had an easy smile and soft-spoken manner which quickly put me at ease. His graceful movements, typical of one who spent much of his time outdoors, belied his sixty years. Derald said that he had run a race that morning and was, therefore, still in his running clothes.

As background to his story Derald explained that he was a hunter. In mid-September of 1968 he had drawn a Desert Bighorn Sheep tag for the San Juan area of Utah. Only eight or nine tags a year are given out, and Derald was excited to get it, because if successful in his hunt he would have a "grand slam," to represent the four types of bighorn sheep—he already had the others.

He drove into the remote area of Utah where the sheep were, near Blanding, in his four-wheel drive truck. It was a hot time of the year, 98 degrees Fahrenheit, and he had to carry a lot of water with him because there was none available where he was going. He put food supplies, bedding, tent, and ammunition in his pack and set out to climb the Mancos Mesa, one of the largest mesas in the world. Upon reaching the top, he pitched his tent and settled in for the night. Having seen some rams before he began his climb, he intended to track them the next morning.

Derald woke early, had a quick breakfast and put on his day pack with about a gallon of water. He got his rifle and started tracking the rams. By late afternoon he had covered fifteen miles on the top of the mesa, when he spotted one of the rams. He started jogging, and after about two miles, suddenly, the ram appeared fifty yards ahead of him. He raised his rifle, almost automatically, and got the ram with one shot.

As he went to cape the ram—skin it and remove the horns—he noticed large clouds gathering in the south. They appeared ominous and black, so he worked rapidly, caping the ram and packing the meat in his pack. By the time he finished it had begun to snow. The temperature dropped from the 90s to the 30s within about fifteen minutes—and Derald was dressed in a T-shirt and light trousers. There was no shelter and no firewood.

Derald began to run towards his camp, which was seventeen miles away. By this time it was snowing heavily, thunder and lightning were crashing all around him, and the wind was gusting to eighty miles an hour. He could see where he was going only by the lightning flashes.

It was about eight o'clock at night and he began to shiver uncontrollably from hypothermia. In one of the lightning flashes he saw a place where the ground dropped off near a ledge. Upon examining it close-up he found a crevice that he crawled into, and he covered himself with sand, which was still warm. It saved his life, and he spent the night under the sand.

Struggling to the Truck

The next day it had stopped snowing and Derald started for his camp, which was still about eight miles away. His food and water were gone, and he was extremely weak. He ate snow to quench his thirst as he traveled. It took him all day to reach the camp, which, when he arrived, had blown over the cliff from the previous night's storm. He despairingly spent another night, without food, buried in the sand.

Derald tells his own story from this point. I asked him how he made it down the cliff in his weakened condition.

"With great difficulty. It took all the energy I had to get down, and I still had five or six miles ahead of me. Also, by now it was dark again. It had taken most of the day to climb down the cliff. There was a partial moon so I could see, and it had warmed up so there was no longer the danger of freezing, but my energy was almost gone.

"I rested for a short while; then I started towards the truck. I could picture a jar of peaches in the cooler, and the thought of that peach juice kept me going. I staggered along for a time until my energy level got so low that I could only walk for ten steps, then lie down—then stagger for another ten steps and lie down again. Each time I could barely make the ten steps. Finally, I could see the white truck ahead of me. By now, though, my energy level was so low I could only crawl.

"I crawled up to the truck and let the tail gate down. I lay on the tail gate for awhile. Then I got the jar of peaches from the cooler. I was so weak I couldn't open the jar. I got a jug of water and tried to drink it, but my throat wouldn't swallow. I massaged my throat and washed my face until I felt a little better. Then I took off my boots and was astonished to see that my socks were completely gone on the bottom; I had worn them out.

"I stood in my bare feet on the sand beside the truck and many little sand burrs, which were all around, hurt my feet; I had to climb back into the truck. My energy was still gone, though. I felt that if I could lie down on my bed in the back of the truck for a short period I would be all right. I managed to get into the bed with my clothes on—I was completely exhausted."

Life or Death—An Argument

"The next thing I knew I was standing beside the truck and wondering how I got there. I thought to myself: *How did I get here? That's foolish to come out here again. Why don't my feet hurt from the burrs?*

"The moon was up and I could see in the back of the truck, and I saw myself lying there. As I looked in the truck I said to myself: *I look like I'm dead. I've never seen anyone look so bad. What in the world is going on? This must be a bad dream from which I will soon wake up. How can I be standing here in the sand and see myself lying in the truck? This doesn't make sense.*

"I kept looking in the truck and wondering about the strangeness of the scene. Suddenly everything started getting bright."

"It was still dark outside, wasn't it?" I asked Derald.

"Yes, except for the moon, it was dark. But the back of the truck and the surrounding area started to get bright. My first thought was: *Terrific. Someone is coming with their car and they will be able to help me.*

"I turned around to look at the source of the light. It was a white light. As it came closer I put my arm up to shield my eyes. It was bright . . . no, it was white—so white. I had never seen anything like it. It was brilliant.

"I was absorbed in watching the light—the beautiful bright white light. It gave me a feeling like . . . almost like soft music, or something that was one-hundred percent pure. It's hard to describe in words. I had never seen nor heard anything like it before. It was not frightening, though. More softening. And it kept coming closer . . . getting brighter and brighter. I had to keep my arm over my eyes to shield them, I couldn't look directly into the light. I will never forget the feeling I got from the light.

"Next I became conscious that there was a male individual standing in the light. I was aware that I knew him but have subsequently been unable to remember who he was. I am sure, though, that I knew him from somewhere."

"Did he communicate with you?"

"Yes, he said, 'You know why I'm here—we've got to go.'"

"What was your reaction?"

"I told him that I couldn't go. He responded that I didn't have anything to say about it. He said I had to go with him and it would be all right."

"You disagreed with him?"

"I argued as strongly as I had about anything in my life. I told him that there were children that I had to care for. I mentioned my two daughters and I told him that there were other children that I couldn't explain to him right then, those other children also would need my care.

"For some reason I seemed to know that there would be more children in the future that would be dependent upon me. It puzzled me, that I would know about some, as yet, unknown children, but I did. I continued to argue for some time and the individual in the light listened."

"When the individual talked to you, was it as if you were speaking, or was it more a transference of thought?"

"It was as if I were talking to you."

"Why did you argue so hard to come back? Didn't you like it where you were?"

"Yes, I liked it. In fact, there was no pain, I wasn't hungry and thirsty anymore, and I wasn't exhausted from the ordeal I had been through. I wanted to come back, though, because I felt I hadn't lived my life through yet. For some reason I knew that I would be needed. I wanted to do more hunting, and I knew I had more children that I would be responsible for. I was disturbed over the thought of not being able to complete living my life to its fullest, as I saw it. I knew I was arguing for my life."

"And you explained this to the individual?"

"I sure did—and he was sympathetic and seemed to understand. He was calm during the entire discussion."

"So the decision to come back was yours?"

"Most certainly."

"What happened next?"

"As suddenly as it had come the light began to diminish. It disappeared towards the east."

"Did the individual go with it?"

"Yes, he had been standing in the light; when the light disappeared, he disappeared. I was left alone in the night standing outside the truck wondering about the whole experience.

"When he left I knew that I had to get back into my body so I tried to enter it. I found that I had to go in through the head. It was a strange feeling—like trying to get into a tight-fitting shoe, trying to squeeze into it. I struggled as if I couldn't easily fit into my body. Suddenly I was back."

"How did you know that you should enter your body through your head?"

"I have no idea, but that's where I went. It was from the head down, and I can remember how difficult it was. I struggled and struggled to get in. Once I started entering it went fairly easy."

"When you first left your body were you aware of passing through a dark hole or seeing darkness before you saw the light?"

"There was no special darkness that I remember, other than the night."

"Okay, so you were back in your body, then?"

"Yes, I was in my body lying on the bed. As I lay there I could see my heart beating in my chest. It was palpitating and I was sweating. I was almost afraid to breathe. I thought: *I'm not going to move. If I move I'll die again.*"

Returning Home—Aftereffects

"I stayed in my bed, afraid to move, until morning. With the morning light I got enough courage to sit up. Still being extremely weak, I drank some water, and I managed to get the peach jar open and drink some of the peach juice.

"Carefully getting up, I stood in the sand; the burrs hurt my feet again. I put on my boots and walked around the truck looking for tracks in the sand. I couldn't get over the marvel of the experience I had had and I wanted to see if some human had brought the light and left tracks in the sand. I circled the truck several times but I found nothing."

"Did you realize what had happened to you?"

"I wasn't sure. I was still weak, though, so I rested for the remainder of the day and took nourishment. Gradually my strength returned and I felt well enough to drive.

"When I got back home and my wife saw me she remarked: 'You are the walking dead—you look like you died.' I was astonished. What a strange statement for her to make. Still, for some time I didn't tell her or anyone else what had happened. Ultimately, I told her and she was shocked.

"My life continued normally from that point until one year later at my daughter's wedding my wife died. She had an aneurysm and died on the spot. Prior to the wedding my wife and I had expressed concern that the man my daughter was marrying was unsuitable. My wife felt some distress because of this disagreement but we had no warning of her impending death.

"My daughter had three little boys from the marriage, and then her husband left her. She returned home and I helped raise the boys—in fact, they think of me as their father. They are now ten, nine, and eight years old, and my daughter has never remarried.

"I married again, and my second wife had two children whom I have also helped to raise. As you can see my life has been involved in caring for children. How I knew that during the time when I saw the light, I don't know."

"Has your experience changed you?"

"It has made me softer—more patient in dealing with others. My frustrations used to be expressed with outbursts of anger; that is no longer true."

"Did your religious beliefs change before and after the experience?"

Derald looked thoughtful and was silent for a moment. Tears came to his eyes. Finally, he said: "Not really. I have always loved nature. Sometimes when I am out with nature I get a spiritual feeling. Once when I was lying looking at the stars with one of my hunting buddies he asked me who my hero was. Without hesitation I told him it was . . ." Derald choked back some tears, ". . . it was Jesus Christ."

Mike

He had just finished a busy day at work when I visited him at his home in Salt Lake City on an early spring evening in 1993. Although obviously tired from his work, Mike extended a cheerful hand, and he seemed anxious to tell his story.

Mike was born in Salt Lake City, Utah, in 1962, and he had two older brothers and two older sisters. His intermediate education was at Granger High School, and he worked for a while after graduation. Then he attended Salt Lake Trade Tech for three years. In 1985 Mike married his sister's best friend; at the time of my visit he and his wife had three children.

Prayer, a Hunting Trip, and a Fall

Mike began to tell his story: "The first experience that brought me closer to God was when I was about six years old. A little kitten that I had got its neck broken through my accidental closing of a door. It really hurt my feelings, and I prayed, and prayed. . . . I prayed that it would wake up, but it didn't.

"Feeling terrible, I put it in a box and gave it a burial with a little cross over its grave. My prayer, then, was that Heavenly Father would take it into heaven. I had a spiritual experience that helped me to understand my prayer was answered. From then on, I knew that there was a God.

"The next experience I had with the Lord happened when I was about nine years old. A seventeen-year-old neighbor boy, who was friendly to me, invited me to go on a hunting trip with him to Price, Utah. It was just to be a weekend trip, and my parents gave permission for me to go. Two adults were to go with the two boys.

"On Saturday morning we hiked up to a ridge in the mountains above Price. There was a cliff, and we climbed the back side of it until we reached the summit. Sitting on the top, we rested and had lunch. After lunch the two adults went exploring and told us to stay. In an hour we got impatient, and the other boy left.

"It was a cold fall day, and the afternoon was getting late. I shouted to see if anyone would answer. There was no response, so I decided to go back the way I came. Our vehicles were just below the ridge.

"Leaving the ridge in the direction I thought would take me down, I soon found myself on the edge of the cliff. A small draw appeared to offer a way to get down, so I started to climb down it. Jumping off a large rock, I landed on a crevice that became a dead end. I couldn't go forward, and the rock I had jumped off was too high for me to climb back up.

"Stretching to reach the top of the rock, I grabbed something and lifted—it gave way and I fell. My fall down the cliff was about 250 feet. There was no feel when I landed; I don't remember the fall or when I landed."

Out-of-Body and a Visit to the Stars

"The next thing I knew I was standing looking at myself on the ground. It was dark outside and starting to snow, when I fell, and it was a strange scene as I tried to contemplate what had happened to me. The really peculiar thing was that while I could see my body lying on the ground, I . . . the real *I*, was standing with my feet about six inches off the ground.

"There was a sense of floating, and the realization came that I must be dead. As part of my discovery that I was dead, I leaned close to my body and reached out to touch it. My hand, and it was a hand, went right through my body lying on the ground. It was a shock.

"Suddenly I felt myself being drawn into the sky. The stars went by until there were no more; then I entered a tunnel of light and my speed seemed to accelerate. Eventually I came to a black void—there was no light at all. Wondering what was happening, I put my hand in front of my face, but I could see nothing.

"While I was in this black void, there was a noise in the background. The noise was from the whispering of many others in the void, and I could feel their presence. I kept asking: 'Who is there? Who is there?' but I got no response. Whispering noises continued, so I put my hand out to see what was there, and I touched something. Whatever it was that I touched let out an awful noise. It sounded as if it were a snarl or roar from some wild cat. I was very frightened by the noise.

"At the same time that I was in the black void, I could hear the people that I had gone hunting with calling me. It was very strange. I knew I had left the earth, yet I could hear them calling my name."

A Place of Light and a View of the Future

"Coming out of nowhere, while I was puzzling the whole situation, a giant cone of light appeared. It was off in the distance, and I started going toward it. During this whole period I continued to hear my friends calling me, but since I didn't know where they were I kept moving to the light.

"Something in the light seemed more important to me than anything else. The light was more important than my friends calling me. I was drawn to it.

"When I reached the edge of the light, I could see the shape of a human in it. A man in the light reached out his hand, and I reached to touch him. Upon touching him, I knew immediately who He was. The confusion that I had felt, and every fear, left me.

"This wonderful Being called me by a name, not my earthly name, but some other name. I knew He was addressing me, but it was not a name that I had been called while on earth. I have since forgotten it.

"The Being urged me to enter the light, and He said: 'Come, I want to show you something.' He took me up, and we went to another place, a different world bathed in light. Located in a large field was an enormous and beautiful gate. It had jewels on it and it was of a shining golden color. My guide pointed at it and said: 'That is the gate to heaven.'

"Next, the Being said: 'It is not your time, yet, to be here. You must go back.'

"I knew it was the Lord I was with, and I begged to stay with Him. He again told me that I had to return. So I asked Him why. His startling declaration was: 'I'll show you why.'

"Five figures appeared before me in a bright light. The Lord let me know that one of the figures was I, as an adult; a second adult figure was my wife, and three smaller figures were my children. I was told by the Lord that one of my future children would perform significant service for Him, and I had to go back so that His purposes could be fulfilled.

"That was the end of the experience. The Lord took me by the hand and brought me back."

Rescue and Recovery

"When I regained consciousness, it was morning. It was hard to walk, but I scooted down the hill. While I was resting before trying to get to where the car had been, I heard people calling for me. Yelling as loud as I could, I listened for them. They heard me and told me to stay where I was.

"The Search and Rescue team had been looking for me, and they were above me on the mountain. They had to go around from up above and come at me from below. When they got to me they put me on a stretcher and took me to the hospital in Price.

"After the initial examination in Price, they flew me to the University of Utah Medical Center in Salt Lake City. At the Medical Center, they found that my arm was broken in several places, my nose was broken, and worst of all, I had a head fracture. They had to operate on my head and arm.

"All together I was in the hospital for three months. I don't remember everything about it, but I got better."

Questions About Mike's Experience

Mike agreed that I could ask him some questions. I began: "How did you feel when you first found yourself looking at your physical body?"

"At first, before I went into the black void, I wasn't afraid or anything. Mostly, I was interested in finding out what had happened. That's when I reached down to touch my body and my hand went right through it."

"How did you feel when you were in the black void?"

"I was scared. There was this multitude of whispering beings around me, and they confused and frightened me. Then when I reached out and touched that thing . . . or whatever it was, the snarl was scary."

"The cone of light that you saw, can you describe it more fully?"

"That's the thing . . . it wasn't there, and then it was. It was sort of in the middle of my vision. Above the cone it was black, and below the cone it was black. It just appeared and I felt drawn to it."

"Can you describe the figure that was in the light?"

"The figure was a man; he was in a white robe, he was transparent, and he was very bright. Instantly, upon His touching my hand, I knew it was the Lord. I was filled with peace, I felt calm, and there was an assurance that the peace would stay with me. There was an overpowering love coming from Him to me—I could feel it. The warmth I felt. . . There is no experience in life that can duplicate what I experienced there in His presence."

"How did you know it was the Lord?"

"There were the love and the comfort that He gave. He was radiantly beautiful, dressed in a white robe, and He had long brown hair. His dress and appearance were that of the Lord—He showed me the nail prints in his hands."

"Where were the nail prints?"

"They were on his wrists."

"Was there anything else about the Lord that was unusual?"

"There was the music, and there were angels. When I was in His presence, I heard this wonderful music. It was beautiful."

"Describe it."

"I can't."

"What kind of music do you listen to here?"

"Country-western."

"Was it like country-western?"

"No. There were a multitude singing something like hymns, or humming. The sound was unbelievable . . . it is hard to explain."

"What do you mean, a multitude?"

"There were angels, thousands of angels, dressed in white robes and singing. They were kneeling down with their arms outstretched, and they were singing."

"When you were told to go back, why didn't you want to go?"

"I'm not sure. As far as me missing my mom, or my friends, or my dad, that didn't seem to matter. Nothing could replace the feeling that I had when I was with Him, and I didn't want to leave."

"When you went with Him to another place, what was it like?"

"We first went up, then down to the ground where the beautiful gate was. There was a large wall that the gate was mounted on, and He let me know that heaven was beyond the gate. I was then shown myself and my family."

"How did it feel to be looking at yourself, as a child, but seeing yourself as an adult?"

"It excited me. That vision, or whatever it was, convinced me that I should go back. I was enthralled with the idea that one of my children would provide a special service to Him."

"Could you recognize the features on your children or your wife?"

"No. The faces weren't that clear. They were shapes that seemed to be about twenty feet away. It was bright where they were, and they were shadowy figures."

"Could you see anything that looked like landscape?"

"Yes. Rocks and other things were there. All around the gate there was a large field."

"Were there colors?"

"Mostly the colors were associated with the gate. It sparkled with many jewels and with the golden material that it was made of."

"After the scene with your future family, then you returned?"

"Yes. Taking me by the hand, He told me that He would take me back. We returned and I could see my body lying there. He had me lie down, and I sort of floated into my body."

"Could the whole experience have been a dream or a hallucination?"

"I know it was not a dream or a hallucination."

"How do you know?"

"When I first came out of my body, the first thing I thought of was that it must be a dream. That was when I reached down with my hand and it went through my body; then I noticed that my spirit body was standing above the ground. I looked around and could see the forest, the trees, and it was starting to snow. It was too real to be a dream. I can still picture it as a vivid experience."

"Have you told this story to many people?"

"No. Just my wife."

"Have you read much about stories like this?"

"I've never read any stories, but I have seen some things like this on TV. The television stories that I saw were a year or two ago."

"Are you associated with any organized religion?"

"I'm just a believer. When I do go to church it's to the Christian Fellowship Church."

"Are there any messages you would like to leave for others?"

"My message to others is that when they see the Lord they will know who He is. There will be no question about whom it is when they see Him—if there is the slightest doubt then it is not the Lord. Doubt will flee when He appears; He will know you and you will know Him."

Chapter 3

UNUSUAL HEALINGS

Ruth

Some Near-Fatal Medication

Ruth was waiting for us as my wife and I drove up the snowy street on a gray day in January. She motioned us into the warmth of her lovely home. She explained that her husband was a nuclear engineer, with a PhD in that field, and she had traveled to various places with her husband. They had moved from California to Utah because of a job opportunity for her husband.

I asked Ruth to tell us a little of the background leading up to her experience, and she began: "I had a lukewarm Catholic background. My mother was not Catholic, and my father was a Catholic who never went to church. We lived in a small town in New Hampshire, and the church there was extremely small; it was a reconverted restaurant. So we went to church weekly, but there wasn't much real spirituality.

"In 1963, when I was in my middle thirties, I had a thyroidectomy. Then, a couple of years later, it seemed that my left lung was deteriorating. I used to smoke, not very much, but apparently it was too much for me.

"I didn't have a church—I wasn't a spiritually organized person. But I was always kind of interested, on the edges. My husband was not. He's an engineer and he is not interested in religion at all."

"Where did you meet your husband?"

"I met him in Boston at an intercollegiate club. He was doing his graduate work at M.I.T.

39

"In 1964 my health was bad. I had started having these, sort of, nervous tizzies. They were not too bad; I'm normally a stable sort of person. But I figured it was the result of the medication that was responsible for my out-of-body experience."

"Was the medication for the problem in your lung?" I asked.

"No, the lung problem was later. This medication was . . . we were going to go to Europe and the doctor gave me birth control pills. I would take the medication in the morning, and ten minutes after I had taken the pills it would seem that my breath had stopped. I would, by instinct, breathe in and out and the breath would start again, like a motor. It would just catch, and then I would be okay—until the next time I took the medication.

"I normally took the medication in the morning but one day I took it at night. And that was a mistake because I was always a sound sleeper."

A Tunnel and Beings of Light

"I had taken the medication, and as soon as my head hit the pillow I was out. The next thing I knew . . . I knew it was too late. I knew that I was dying. I felt a little bit curious but very apprehensive. And I knew it was too late.

"It was as if I were proceeding down a tunnel. Then I came to the end, and there were three beings of light. They were waiting to greet me, and they were so filled with love. It was the most pure, unself-conscious, beautiful experience of my life. . . ." Ruth began to cry.

"They didn't look like anybody. They were composed of, let's say, tissues of light. I recognized them, I knew them, yet they didn't have faces, or names that I know now, but I knew them, and they knew me. We knew each other very well and it was like . . . like a reunion.

"They didn't say a word, and then . . . then I thought of my young ones. My children were still young, very young, and . . . and I snapped right back into my body. And I was wide awake and I knew that something important had happened.

"I later told my doctor about my experience. He told me to never take that medication again. He knew that there was a connection between the medication and the experience. I didn't take it again, but I read in the newspaper a couple of weeks later that some woman had taken that same medication and she had died. She was not as lucky as I was."

"Where were you living at the time?"

"That was in 1964 and we were living in San Diego. The experience was so . . . so real, it's just as though it happened last week."

"As you were with the three beings of light do you remember if they communicated any special messages?"

"Nothing specific—it was just love."

"Why did you leave that wonderful place?"

"Because of my loved ones—I had two small children."

"You were aware that that was the case?"

"Oh yes. I knew it . . . I knew it, that was the answer."

"What did your body feel like when you were in the spiritual world?"

"Peaceful, very peaceful. Yes, as soon as I reached the three beings I felt fine. The fear had gone, totally; there was no apprehension. I was where I was supposed to be. That was the feeling I had."

"Did you notice whether you had any form? Could you feel gravity?"

"I felt exactly like *myself*. I had not lost my identity—I was still me."

"Did it feel like a dream?"

"I would say it was like a dream, only more so. It was an intense experience but very natural. It was vivid, unforgettable . . . so it must have been in my highest consciousness."

"When you first were aware that you were dying did you have any cognizance of seeing your body lying there?"

"No. I've read about that type of thing but I didn't experience it."

"You mentioned seeing a tunnel. What sort of a tunnel was it—can you describe it?"

"It was large, not cramping at all. But I've thought about it later. Maybe . . . maybe actually it was movement, you know, spinning out, whirling out. I'm sure my soul had left . . . on a journey. And maybe that's why it looked like a tunnel.

"Every time I drive through a tunnel, now, that experience comes back. We went to Italy a few years ago, where there are many tunnels, and they reminded me of my experience."

"What was the light like which you saw at the end of the tunnel?"

"It was an opalescent blue. And each being had a somewhat different color. One was golden, one was kind of pinkish, and the other was a blue-blue."

Lung Problems and a Healing

"About a year after this experience my left lung started giving me trouble again. I mentioned that I smoked—not much, maybe ten or twelve cigarettes a day, but it was too much. I went to a doctor and he did a number of tests including an x-ray. I had had flu, pneumonia, pleurisy, and other related problems. His x-ray showed that I had a spot on my lung.

"I went to another doctor and he told me that eventually the lung would have to come out. He asked me if I smoked, and when I told him I did he told me to quit. The doctors had scared me enough that I stopped instantly.

"Anyway, during this period I went to a church in San Diego that someone had recommended. It was the Self Realization Church, and it was based on spiritual precepts. I was sitting in the back of the church and I felt this tremendous peace, and . . . and I had a spontaneous healing. I didn't know it was a spontaneous healing—it felt like electricity, and it came from my neck and spread down over my back. It was so powerful that inside I was thinking that I wasn't ready for this, whatever it was. In fact, I hoped it would stop." Ruth laughed as she thought back.

"I went in for a chest x-ray, a month later, and I didn't expect anything different. The doctor came out; he was just beaming, and he said, 'This is perfect, your lung is completely healed.'

Lois Clark—A Car Crash

Lois Clark was living with her, as she characterized it, best friend and mother when Carol and I visited her in her home in West Valley, Utah during the winter of 1991. She had been married but was presently single. She proudly described her five children and one stepdaughter who lived in disparate places around the country. She was born in El

Paso, Texas, in 1934, but her parents had moved around considerably, in the summer each year, due to her father's occupation as a railroader for the Southern Pacific.

Lois began her story: "In 1965 my husband and I had been Christmas shopping and we ran out of gas. He parked the car alongside the road and went for gas. I stayed with the car with the children in the back seat, including my baby girl. As we sat there a drunken driver hit us and knocked us into the median; I was thrown out of the car. Then the car rolled backwards over me. The children were relatively unhurt in the back seat.

"I was unconscious for a period. When I came to my oldest son was standing over me and he said, 'I'm going to lay over you, Mommy, in case the car blows up.' Shortly after that I became aware of the pain. When they got me to the hospital they found that I had massive injuries. One kidney was messed up, I had a broken jaw, and my teeth were all knocked loose.

"I kept going in and out of consciousness, so they didn't have to use as much anesthetic as they otherwise would have. They were using a syringe to try and extract a sample from my kidney—they wanted to determine the damage to it before they operated, or to see if they needed to operate. I had so many broken bones they weren't sure I could stand the operation. I heard them say, 'You'd better do something, she's flattening out.'

A Bright Light, Forms, and Beautiful Music

"I didn't hear anything else for awhile—and I'm floating up here—and I'm looking down at this woman on a table, and . . . and I realize it's me. There were all these people working around the table, and there was this form lying there.

"I thought, *What's going on?* and all of a sudden I saw this bright light. I've never seen anything like it as long as I've lived, since. It was just beautiful. So I started walking towards this light to see what was beyond it, but . . . but every time I started to take a step towards it I was told, 'No, go back.'

"I didn't want to go back to all that pain. But finally I went back, I guess, because I kept hearing the doctors say, 'Okay, okay, she's starting to get stabled out.'

"When I woke up the next time I was in my hospital bed with all this paraphernalia around and on me. And I felt a little bit at peace, but I was angry."

"Why were you angry?"

"Because they wouldn't let me just die, I guess, 'cause I kept praying to die. I hurt so badly . . . well my whole body was just a torment of pain."

"What happened next?"

"I talked to some people who helped me to realize that I should pray to be relieved of the pain, and to get better, rather than to die. I did this and things started to get better."

"While you had this experience did you see anybody or anything?"

"I saw forms. I didn't see recognizable faces or anything, just forms . . . and the one was brighter than the others. But they just all kept telling me to go back, and I didn't want to. I wanted to stay."

"Okay, so you saw some forms that you didn't recognize. And one seemed brighter than the others, you say?"

"Yes. One seemed to just shine with brightness. The others seemed at peace—sort of idyllic. It was really strange, because I thought, *Well they should know the pain I'm going to have. Why are they making me go back into something I don't want to? Afterwards I talked to a friend of mine in the church, and she suggested that perhaps they knew I had something more to do.*"

"Did you have a feeling yourself of why they wanted you to come back?"

"Not until ten or fifteen years ago when my mother and I started living together, and we realized that we were here to take care of each other. That brought it home more than anything else. I knew that I had the children to raise, but that didn't bother me so much as to be . . . as to be in a place so beautiful."

"How many children did you have then?"

"The four—my baby girl was not quite two."

"Have you felt since, that one of the reasons you had to come back was because of the children?"

"Yes, in fact there have been incidents since then when I have been close to death—not as bad as with the automobile accident—but each time it has been the children who drew me back. The children have always been my life."

"When you saw this light, did you see anything dark ahead of time?"

"The only dark I saw was to the side. I saw that light and wanted to go towards it, that's all my mind would hold."

"What did the light look like?"

"It was kind of a . . . a yellow, mellow, bright, white light."

"Was it hard to look at?"

"Yes. It was so bright to begin with that I had to, sort of, look down, then up, and then blink my eyes down again."

"Did you feel as if it was real, or a dream?"

"At the time that I was in the place to see the light I thought it was real. The whole thing . . . oh, there was the light, and there seemed to be soft, soft, soft . . . you couldn't really hear it, you more felt this music. It . . . it was soft, and immaculately beautiful. There was, I guess there's no way to really describe it, there was a feeling of peace, beauty, love, and . . . it just felt like this is what I want. This is the ultimate. You're so at peace within your whole being that you just seem to float, like . . . ."

"Could you see the doctors working on you?"

"Yes, when I wanted I could look down and see, there I are." Lois laughed as she described the situation. "I thought, *Okay, I've left that there, now, and I can go on—it's marvelous.* And then to be told that I had to go back, I fought the thought."

Breast Cancer and a Remarkable Healing

"I had another experience about three years ago that helped me a great deal."

"What was that?"

"I had cancer of the breast, and they told me that if they couldn't get it all when they did surgery they wouldn't give me very long. It was that bad already. My husband was retired military and we had been using K.I. Sawyer, a small military hospital. They transferred me to the better equipped military hospital at Wright-Patterson for the surgery.

"I asked for a blessing from a friend I had previously known in Texas, and who now lived in Cincinnati. I called him. He came to the hospital and gave me a blessing in which he asked Heavenly Father to please let me be rid of the cancer so that I might continue to be able to raise my children and grandchildren. After he left I told my daughter, Trisa, who had been with me in the hospital that something was wrong."

"What was wrong?"

"I didn't feel the same way as I had before—the pain had been terrible, almost unbearable at times. Now I felt different and I couldn't explain why."

"My daughter said that maybe I was just excited and tired. She suggested that I go to bed and rest some before the operation. So I went to bed, although I still felt different, and I went to sleep with the help of a sleeping pill.

"The next morning I woke up, and I . . . I had no pain. The nurse had me take a shower and use medication to prepare for surgery. As I walked back to my room I understood, all of a sudden, why there was no pain. The cancer . . . ." Lois had difficulty continuing. "The cancer had been taken away. I was overjoyed.

"The Doctors came in and told me to go get the final x-ray for the surgery. My daughter joined us and we went downstairs where the x-ray machine was. They took a mammogram and then they came in and said: 'There's something wrong with this machine. We're going to have to take you to another machine because this one doesn't show us what we know is there.'

"I just smiled because I already knew what was going on. I told my daughter, she was kind of teary too, and we went to the other machine where they took a second mammogram. The doctors came in and the surgeon said: 'I don't know what's wrong. I'm sure with two machines we should have gotten a true reading, but there is no cancer showing. Yet we know there was cancer, because we have the original set of x-rays right here. We won't cut into someone, though, where there's no reason to cut.'"

"How did you feel about it?"

"I was happy but I didn't understand it. As lowly a person as I am, I still don't understand. Why me?" Lois began to cry.

"When you got your blessing you said that you knew something had happened to you. What did it feel like?"

"During the blessing, and when he was saying let me be rid of the cancer, I felt, from the tip of my head to the end of my toes, I felt . . . it felt like a washing through process. Like little waves going through my body. Afterwards, it felt kind of like, you know, when your hands are asleep and they come awake again. It felt like that down through my chest. It was mostly my chest but also the rest of my body. Like I'd been asleep for a long time, and I was waking up."

"Has there been any recurrence of the cancer?"

"None."

Chapter 4

A VIETNAM EXPERIENCE

David Herard

Background and Initial Combat

I first talked to David Herard on the telephone in Bangor Maine, where he was remodeling an old farm house, in late March, 1991. Later I met him at my home in Bountiful, Utah, where he and his former wife, Peggy Cassidy, came to meet Carol and me.

David was relatively small in stature (5'-6" tall) but large in spirit. He was dark-complexioned, of French Canadian heritage, with a mustache and a large smile. He explained that he was born in 1946 and grew up in Waterville, Maine. He said that he grew up on the tough side of town, but that he had fun with his two older brothers and an older sister. He began by telling of his military experience:

"In 1965, three months before I graduated from High School, I enlisted in the Marine Corps. I enlisted specifically to go to Vietnam."

"Oh you did? Good for you," I commented, "not many people would say that, I guess."

David continued: "I grew up in an environment where I heard that wars and rumors of wars were things that should not be taken lightly. That economic and religious freedoms, if not protected, would be lost."

"Do you still feel that way?"

"Yes, but I'm more isolationist than I was."

"So you went into the Marine Corps. Where did they send you for training?"

48

"The day after I graduated from high school I was sent to Parris Island. I stayed there for three months, after which I was sent to North Carolina for training in field telephone and radio communications. Then I went to my parent unit, Eighth Communications Battalion, for three months, and at that time, in December, 1965, I volunteered to go to Vietnam. In January, 1966 I had one-and-one-half weeks free leave, then I reported to Camp Pendleton, California for advanced infantry and jungle warfare training, after which I was shipped out."

"When did you arrive in Vietnam?"

"In May of 1966. I landed at Chu Lai Airbase—which was taking mortars. It was a quick step from a commercial airline to a large quonset hut for processing. I was assigned to the First Battalion, Eleventh Marines—it was a 105mm artillery battery—as a wireman. I was part of a team that kept the land-lines functioning in the field.

"To get me used to the climate, for the first three weeks, I filled sand bags. After that I was assigned to a four-man wire team. We had a three-quarter ton truck. Three of the men worked on wires and the fourth stood guard—as shotgun. The shotgun man carried an automatic weapon. It was a week on duty and a week off; there were three teams."

"How long were you on that duty?"

"I was there for two months. Then they shipped me out on an operation to guard an ammo dump with twelve other men. The ammo dump was about the size of a football field, or a little larger. We only had grenades and our personal weapons to guard it, and we were in 'Indian territory.' It was one-hundred percent alert every night, and work all day. When the trucks came, we were the labor to load them."

"How long were you there?"

"It was three weeks. Then I was shipped back to my parent unit and to a wire team. We were sent to the First Marine Division near DaNang, which was on combat operations off and on. I was assigned as a radioman to an infantry unit where I didn't know anyone."

"Were you a replacement?"

"Yes, the life expectancy in the field for officers, machine gunners, and radio operators was very short. The reason was that the NVA was trying to destroy the command structure of our units."

"How long were you in Vietnam before you got hit?"

"It was September 7, 1966. I had been shipped back to my regular wire team and we were repairing communications. We were standing in a group, four of us—something that we had, up to that time, never done. The NVA had downed miles of communication lines. We had started at 5:30 in the morning to repair them and we were getting tired.

"At the particular place where we had stopped to repair the lines, we were standing in a group about three feet apart. The NVA command detonated a booby trap which blew up right in the middle of us. There were three hand-grenades which went off all at once.

"Two men were killed instantly, including the team leader. One man had multiple shrapnel wounds and was unconscious. I was the only one standing at the edge of the hole where the explosion took place. Everybody else was blown all over the place. I had shrapnel in my legs, and the explosion had ruptured both of my ear drums—I couldn't hear anything."

"Did you return to the States for recuperation?"

"I was sent to Okinawa to recoup, and I finished my thirteen months overseas there. I had put in papers to go back to Vietnam but the Commanding Officer told me, 'no way'; I was going back to the States. I spent thirty days free leave and then was assigned to various units in the States."

Second Tour in Vietnam

"I volunteered to go back again. I had to waive my rights for a one-year tour of duty in the States. I arrived back in Vietnam in February, 1968, just in time for the Tet offensive."

"That was good timing."

"I thought so too when I got off the plane. I landed in DaNang and wound up in Hue assigned to the First Battalion, First Marines."

"What was your duty?"

"I was just a grunt."

"You were a replacement, I presume."

"Yes, the units were suffering anywhere from fifty to sixty percent casualties at the time, and they just needed warm bodies that knew how to shoot to kill."

"What was your rank, then?"

"I was a Corporal, E-4."

"Why don't you tell me the circumstances leading up to your out-of-body experience?"

"In the last week of June, 1968, I was up in the hills, Hill 881-North, near Khe Sanh. While we were on the hill we were running daily search and destroy missions in the bush. I was holding three jobs at the time: a wireman, a radio operator, and a grunt. We were suffering a lot of casualties so we had to do extra duty.

"We went up on the hill as a fully manned infantry company, over 250 men with 81 mortars, and within thirty days we had lost between 20 and 30 percent. The last half of June we got word that we were going to evacuate the hill, just turn it over to the NVA—we were just going to pull out and leave it to them.

"We were told that because of the lack of helicopters 82nd Airborne was going to evacuate us off the hill. This was supposed to happen in the last day of June and the first day of July. To prepare for the evacuation we tore down all our bunkers and all our trench lines. Airborne never showed up."

"Good night, you were sort of exposed weren't you?"

"That's right. When the NVA saw us blowing up our bunkers they started dropping mortars and rockets on us daily. With our bacon hanging out like that our Commanding Officer, a Captain, was really angry and he called in helicopters. Some Chinooks came and took us off Hill 881-North and put us on Hill 681, five miles away.

"The night we landed on Hill 681, on July 6th, we ran into heavy fire-fighting. It lasted from midnight to about five A.M. We had NVA coming into the wire—it was face-to-face fighting. I usually carried fifteen magazines that hold twenty rounds apiece, six grenades, and full bandoleers for extra ammo. In the morning, after the fire-fight, I had one magazine left, with, maybe eight rounds, no grenades—everybody was in that same situation. We were all running around looking for ammo.

"Around seven o'clock, after everybody had relaxed for a while, we decided it was time to stock up on food, more ammo, and other necessities. Everybody was tired, they didn't want to do anything, so I got angry and said: 'The hell with you, I'll do it.' I started humping ammo for the people that were near me and ammo for the 81mm mortars."

"How far did you have to go to get the ammo?"

"Approximately one hundred yards. About nine o'clock I was on my ninth or tenth trip, and we started getting some 122mm rockets, 82mm mortars and small arms fire. I was tired, I was angry, and I was put out by the whole situation. When everything started coming in I said to myself: *the hell with it, all they can do is kill me.*

"On my last trip, I was told this later by one of the Corpsmen who attended me, when I came over the crest of the hill a 122mm rocket landed about twenty feet behind me. When it went off it picked me up and threw me twenty feet down the hill. I landed on both my knees with my head on the ground. My right arm was behind me. I was dazed—I wasn't unconscious, just dazed.

"When I looked down where my right arm was I didn't see anything. I swore, and thought: *They got me, they really got me this time.* I felt for my arm and pulled it out from behind me. It was all torn up. I didn't pay much attention to the rest of my body. I was looking for a Corpsman and I got up. One of the guys I knew told me to look at my legs. I did, and saw that they were in shreds and were bleeding profusely.

"I collapsed and lay there on the ground. They came over and took my flak jacket off, what was left of it, and attempted to stop the bleeding. While the Corpsman was working over me, I just . . . I had a feeling of: *I'm tired, I'm going to sleep, I've had enough of this.* I almost lost the will to live. I closed my eyes—the pain had just started catching up with me."

"Hadn't they given you any shots for the pain, yet?"

"While I had my eyes closed one of the men asked the Corpsman why he didn't give me a shot of morphine. He said that he couldn't, it would just leak back out. I had shrapnel wounds in both feet, both legs, both cheeks, both arms, both hands, the back of my neck and the small of my back.

"After hearing the Corpsmen talk about me, I felt that my time was up."

A Different World with People Dressed in White

"I first became aware that everything was black. Then I saw a light coming towards me, and I remember wondering why there was no pain.

It felt so good. The light, at first, was like a candle. But it kept getting closer and brighter until it was a blinding light."

"Could you look straight at it?"

"No I couldn't. I tried everything not to look at the light."

"Why was that?"

"I don't know. I wasn't afraid of it. It was extremely bright. The light finally caught up to me, and I opened my eyes, not literally, but I looked at it. And I saw a river.

"Across this river there were a lot of people waving at me. They were gesturing me to come across. They were people that I hadn't seen before, and they seemed really happy. I was getting a feeling of warmth, of happiness, of great tranquility.

"As I began to walk towards the river, and the people on the other side, I felt a hand on my shoulder. I tried to turn around to see who was putting a hand on me and I . . . I couldn't move. A voice that I heard said: 'No, it's not your time, go back.' Then I was back. I opened my eyes, and this Corpsman was pounding my chest. He was screaming at me: 'Don't you dare die on me.' An hour later I was choppered off the hill."

"When you saw the river, what was the terrain like on both sides of the river?"

"On my side it was fairly white, like a brand new coat of white paint. Closer to the river there were shades of green. The water was a shimmering blue, and I could tell it was moving. On the other side of the river it was white, but it had color also."

"Did you see shrubs and things of this sort?"

"I saw trees, bushes, flowers—vividly colored flowers."

"Were the bushes, shrubs and flowers similar to what you had seen on earth, or were they different?"

"Similar in that their growth patterns were similar, but their sizes were more robust, their colors were more vivid, and everything was very warm."

"Did you have a feeling that you knew any of the people on the other side?"

"I've often asked myself that. At the time I thought: *I know those guys*. But I couldn't see their faces. All I could see was their bodies. I knew they were gesturing to me but I just couldn't see their faces. I could see their hands fine, and I could see their physical makeup all right, but not their faces."

"But you had a feeling that you knew them?"

"Right. It seemed like there were people there that I knew. Maybe my team leader who was killed earlier, and maybe some of my other Vietnam buddies. But I couldn't swear to it. I knew a lot of men in Vietnam who had died, but I had no relatives who had died."

"Could you tell how they were dressed?"

"Everybody was in white. Some had robes, and some had shirts and trousers, but they were all white."

"Did it appear that there was light coming from them, or could you tell?"

"It was light behind them, but I couldn't see way beyond them. I knew that they were overjoyed to see me."

"Did you see a bridge?"

"No I didn't. As I walked towards the river and the people someone stopped me. I couldn't move, my eyes were locked straight ahead looking at these people. And the voice simply said: 'Don't be afraid about not going over there. It's not your time yet."

"Did you have the feeling that you could walk over the water if you had wanted?"

"I never had the feeling that I was walking. It was more like . . . I was just moving. And when the hand came on my shoulder I had such an overwhelming sense of love and tranquility; everything that we here are looking for and have such a hard time finding, I had completely, in abundance, and I didn't want to come back to the earth."

"Why didn't you want to come back?"

"Because it felt so good there."

"Did you have any feeling of what it was you were supposed to come back for?"

"No I didn't. After I was told that it was not my time, I would have to go back, I had things to do, that was the end."

"Was it quick when you came back into your body?"

"The blink of an eye."

No Pain, Just Knowledge and Love

"When I came back I had pain in abundance, and it was instantaneous. There was no pain on the other side. I knew . . . everything worked good while I was over there. My body worked good, my hands worked good, my legs worked good. I had the feeling that I knew why things are as they are—why all the problems on the earth were as they were. It was an overwhelming feeling of knowing, but I couldn't tell you now what I knew."

"Did that feeling come over you when you felt the hand, or was it before that?"

"It was when I was going towards the people and felt really good."

"When the hand touched your shoulder, you didn't get a chance to turn around and see who it was did you?"

"No. All I can tell you is that, as I see it, it was God's hand."

"That's what you felt?"

"Right."

"And it was just a single contact where the hand touched your shoulder?"

"Actually, after it touched my shoulder, I felt an embrace—as if I were being embraced from the back by someone. And I could see a bright light from the side."

"How did that feel?"

"When I was embraced, I felt a warmth all through me. And there was the feeling of . . . of love. As if it were all the love there is."

"Do you mean you felt that all the love in the world was there?"

"No, it was like that was all the love there was, everywhere. It was like . . . I can't explain the feeling. It's beyond words."

Life After the Experience

"After the experience, when I thought about it, it scared me. When I was, quote, back here, it scared me to death—and it still does. What really scares me is death."

"Why do you feel that way?"

"I've been pondering that for years. I don't know if it's because of the thought of the loss of going through the routine humdrum of life, or the thought of not being around to physically touch my children. I have this feeling that I want to live forever."

"Well, David, you probably will in one form or another. Let me ask you, as you came back into this life, or subsequent to coming back, did you get a feeling for why you came back?"

"In a way—over the years people have sought me out with their problems. I've advised them to be more patient, and I've given them other advice. In ninety percent of the cases they've done what I suggested, and it has worked out well for them."

"One of your feelings, then, is that you've been able to help other people?"

"Yes, and unfortunately I've not always been able to help myself."

"What about children, have you had any feelings about a necessity to come back for them?"

"Yes, I love children to death. They give me a sense of immortality. I have three children, aged thirteen, eight and six."

"Have you told others of this experience?"

"Only Peggy, I think."

"Have your religious feelings changed as a result of this experience?"

"I was never a person for organized religion. I'm a Catholic. I'd like to clarify; all religions in some way or other feel they are the true religion. One is no better than the other, in my opinion. We all believe in one very important thing—no matter what we call him it still comes out, God. I don't care what peoples' religions are. It doesn't really matter. What I try to impart is that we are all here on this little planet, so let's try to cooperate. Why do we have to beat our heads against a wall and kill each other?"

"Do you feel, then, that there is a God?"

"Oh yes, I believe in God, I believe in an afterlife, and I believe in old man Satan."

"When you had your experience did it seem real or not?"

"It was vividly real. The other thing that gets me is that about four days before I was hit I knew I was going to be hit. And I knew I was going to die."

"That's interesting. Others I have talked to have had similar premonitions about death."

"Yes, you know, out there in the bush we didn't talk about death very often. Death was an accepted thing. On my second tour in Vietnam I kept myself quite friendless. I became a loner because I didn't want to associate death with people I knew."

"How long did it take you to recover from your wounds?"

"A little over a year. It took six months to learn how to walk again, and I had to learn to write left-handed instead of right-handed."

"Did they have difficulty saving your right arm?"

"When I was in Japan, where they first brought me, they were going to take my right arm and left leg off; the arm at the elbow and the leg at the knee. I became quite animated. I told those doctors that I was born with those suckers, and I was going to die with them. They said there was no way I would ever have the use of them again. I told them not to bet on it.

"When I was in Chelsea Naval Hospital in Boston I went through a lot of physical therapy and many operations on my arm—and physical therapy to learn how to walk again. I still have problems with my hand and my knee, and the pain in my arm is constant, but I do get function from them. It gets harder each year to remember when I wasn't in pain, or when I was physically whole."

"Do you have any messages you would like to leave?"

"The most important message I would like people to understand is that we are not who we think we are. We have that side of us that is extremely good, but we keep pushing it aside and concentrating on self. We keep thinking: 'I want money, I want things, I want fame.' It doesn't work that way. We have to take more time thinking of and helping others."

Chapter 5

CHASED BY AN EVIL SPIRIT

Dee

A Bad Marriage

Dee was waiting for Carol and me as we parked in front of her house in Salt Lake City. Her living room was light and cheery, and Dee matched it with her cheery disposition. One beautiful but shy cat sat on a small rocking chair; another, a ragged-looking waif of a cat, poked its head around the corner and looked timidly at us. Dee told us that she had rescued both cats from the animal shelter where she worked.

Dee said that she was born in Indianapolis, Indiana in 1949. She was raised in the Catholic church by an Irish-Catholic mother, and by a father who was a convert to that church. She had a happy youth and went to high school in Indianapolis. She went to nursing school for two years but did not graduate. She began to tell her story.

"In 1969, when my first husband was stationed in Virginia, and we were living there, I had become close friends with another girl, Janey, whose husband was a Corporal. My husband was a Sergeant. Both of our marriages were bad, and we tried to help each other; we spent every waking minute together.

"Janey got pregnant and she was very unhappy about it. She said: 'Look what I've done now. I've got a really rotten marriage, and now this. What am I going to do?'

"Janey was about seven-and-one-half months pregnant when we left Virginia; my husband got an early-out discharge. We came back to Indiana and we stayed with my mom and dad.

"My parents could tell that I was unhappy, but I'm not the type of person who tells my problems to everybody. I just wanted, somehow, to get out of the marriage before I got pregnant. The possibility of getting pregnant was the scariest thing, because I did not want to bring a child into the marriage.

"It was summer time and it was hot. My mother and dad lived in an old farm house. I can remember thinking: *Gee, some months have past—Janey is going to have that baby. I'm not going to be there.*

"We had planned so much for me to be there. As I thought about it, I was tired, and my mom told me to go upstairs and lie down for awhile so I would feel better.

"I went upstairs and lay on the bed. I looked at the ceiling and was thinking: *Look what I've got myself into. I'm 21 years old and I'm miserable. Janey will have that baby and I won't be there to help. What will she do?*"

An Out-of-Body Trip to a Friend

"As I thought about Janey, the very next second, I was floating—like I was walking down a staircase, and I came right down onto the base in Virginia. While I looked at the base from above I thought: *Oh my gosh, look at this! This is great. There's the house I used to live in.*

"I walked down the street, going south, toward Jane's house. I was going fast, it was like a floating walk. I walked right up to Janey's house, and I walked through the closed screen door.

"I could see Janey sitting there with a cigarette, drinking coffee, and rubbing her temple. When she rubbed her head I always knew she was depressed. I knew, looking at her, that she had had the baby. She had shorts on, and she never wore shorts. I gave her a pair but she would never wear them, no matter how hot it got, because her husband made fun of her legs.

"She seemed super-depressed and I decided I didn't want to bother her. I wanted to see the baby, though. That was the most important thing in my mind. So I went upstairs, floating up the stairs, right into the baby's room. I looked around and it seemed so sweet. When I looked at the baby I knew it was a boy. I just knew. I remember thinking that it looked more like her husband than her.

"The next thing I knew I was back in Indiana. Smack—boom! I was back in Indiana. I was upstairs on the bed and I could feel the fan blowing on me. I ran downstairs and told my mom what had happened. She told me to get on the phone and call Janey.

"I called Janey and told her I had just been at her house. She started laughing. I told her that she had on a pair of blue shorts that I gave her. She agreed that she did, and she asked me how I knew. I told her, again, that I was just at her house.

"Janey said I was just dreaming. I explained that it was no dream, and that I saw her fat little baby boy. I remember when I first saw her, when I was out of my body, that she had a piece of paper, and she was writing. She told me that she had just been writing me a letter to tell me that they had the baby, and that they had named him John. We talked a little longer and she promised to send a picture."

"Did she believe you?" I asked.

"No. Janey's a real skeptical person. I couldn't talk religion to her, she just laughed it off. She said something about the power of the mind, and she mentioned that I knew she had blue shorts because I gave them to her, and she said I was just guessing she would have them on.

"My mom believed me though. I thought the whole experience was great, and I tried to repeat it for weeks. But it never happened again until later. I thought: *What a great way to travel.*" Dee laughed as she thought about it.

"We moved out of my parents' house, but the marriage continued to deteriorate. I finally left him and got a divorce."

A Second Bad Marriage

"The next incident took place in the winter of 1983. I had married again, and this marriage was worse than the first one, but I didn't want to end it. My husband used to tell me that if I ended it I would be a two-time loser. That preyed on my mind, because I had a little girl and she loved her daddy. I didn't want to break it up.

"It was a bad marriage early on, but I kept thinking I could change him. At first he was gentle and nice—then that changed. After the birth of our daughter we moved to Salt Lake City. Both my husband and I had good jobs.

He worked for the Union Pacific, and I worked at the airport in the control center.

"One day, out of the blue, he said let's move back to Indiana. I was sick about it, because I loved Utah. We both had good jobs and I liked the climate."

"Why did he want to go back?" I asked.

"He was homesick; he was the oldest of ten kids. He missed his brothers and sisters. He was a country boy and I was a city girl.

"The minute we got to Indiana we went from living a good life to being desperately poor. I hated it, because I kept thinking that there was no reason we had to be so poor. All he had to do was get himself together and get a job, but he wouldn't do it.

"Things got worse and worse. Finally, we were living on unemployment, and we saw an ad in the paper where there was a house for rent for one-hundred dollars a month, with fifty-two acres of land. He said that we could farm it.

"I hated the house from the very beginning. It sat way out in the woods; the nearest neighbor was three-and-a-half miles away. I didn't like that much solitude; it scared me. The climate was sticky; we were in an old farm house, and the only noises we heard were the crickets and locusts and other bugs. To a country person those are great sounds, but to a city person it was disgusting. The noise, to me, was deafening.

"We had started chopping wood to get ready for the winter. My husband was gone most of the time, I was alone with our little daughter, and as it began to get cold I had a terrible time with the stove. My mother-in-law kept calling me and telling me how to stoke it, remove the ashes, and so forth. I knew diddly about wood stoves.

"I felt abandoned, in a house that I hated, miles from the nearest neighbor, and in a miserable environment. We didn't even have running water—I had to haul it.

"Finally, it reached the point that when my husband was home, which was seldom, he would sleep near the wood stove on the far side of the bed. It was a big, old-fashioned bedroom. I slept, separately, on a couch in the bedroom; my little girl slept in the bed with her dad. We all bundled up with covers in an attempt to stay warm."

Emotional Trauma—Then Out-of-Body

"One night, just before dawn, I was lying on the couch and shivering because of the cold. I had on a pair of blue-jeans, heavy socks, a wool sweater, a bathrobe, my coat, and blankets—and I was freezing. I could hear my husband snoring, and I was miserable. I remember thinking: *Come spring I'm getting out of here. I don't know where I'll go, but I'm taking Sara and I'm getting out. I won't spend another winter in this lousy house. I hate it here. I hate winter here, and I hate summer here. I'm going to get out.*

"The next thing I knew I was out of my body; I was over the bed looking down and I was thinking: *Here we go again.* It seemed like the first incident had happened only yesterday.

"I remember floating above the bed looking down at my husband, looking at Sara, and looking at myself on the couch. I thought the scene was peculiar, because I saw this . . . it was like a spider's thread coming from my chest on my body up to me—where I was floating. It seemed to be fastened to me. I remember wondering how far the thread would let me go."

"Could you feel this thread fastened to you?" I asked.

"I couldn't feel it, actually, but I could sense it, and I could see it. And I wondered how far I could go."

"What did it look like?"

"It was like a string off a spider's web, like it had dew on it, or something. As I wondered how far I could go, the next thing I knew I was floating right up through the roof, and I was outside. It was just starting to get dawn, way out in the country, and I thought how wonderful it was. I started moving above the treetops and down the road to the bridge.

"I wondered if I could make it to the bridge, which was way down at the end of the road, and I saw, off to my left, cows in a field. The cows were lying down, and I could see the steam coming from their noses where it hit the cold air.

"I kept thinking how great and how wonderful it was as I continued to head for the bridge. I looked up and saw the stars twinkle—it's like there were a zillion stars."

An Evil Spirit

"The next thing I knew was . . . there was something behind me, and I was afraid. I felt this awful presence—and I knew that it was after me. I looked back and I saw that my string, which I was hooked to, was getting tight. I was afraid, and I was thinking: *What is this thing behind me?* I started to circle, because I knew I had to get back to the house.

"The thing was coming after me fast, and I had the feeling it could kill me. I was moving through the tops of the trees, and I was thinking that I couldn't break my string, and I had to get back quick. Then . . ." Dee's hands were visibly shaking as she tried to continue with the story.

"This . . . this thing, this awful, this terrifying thing—I could feel it on me. It was pushing me away from the house, and I could see the string getting tighter. I was sure I was going to die. I was frantic for Sara, frantic over the idea that if I died she would be stuck with my husband. I felt I had to get back, but the thing kept trying to push me away from the house.

"Every time I would circle and try to get back to the house the thing would come up behind and push me. I knew I was going to die. I could feel the tug at my string. I was being chased by something that was the personification of evil. And it wanted *me*. It wanted to destroy me. I was terrified and I was crying, and I remember thinking: *Oh God, help me, help me God.* I got all my strength to go as fast as I could—I could actually feel this thing on the back of my neck."

Return to Her Body

"The next thing I can remember was: SLAM! I was in my body and I was screaming. My husband and my daughter woke up, and I was screaming and shaking. My husband said: 'What's the matter with you? You were only having a dream.' I told him: 'That was no dream. Something was trying to kill me.'

"My husband just . . . we were total opposites. I couldn't explain this to him. My little girl was terribly frightened because she had never seen her mother scream. She was only four years old.

"I got up, paced the floor, and put fire in the stove. My husband kept insisting it was a dream, and I kept telling him it wasn't. I told him

I hated the house and that we had to get out of it. I also said that if he didn't get me out of the house I would leave.

"The next day I drove in the Van to my mother's house, fifty miles away, and told her about it. She said that I had to get away from my husband. She told me to look at myself, how distraught I was.

"After that, things got progressively worse in our marriage. We moved out of the farm house, bought a house closer to town, but it only lasted a year. He physically abused me, and I couldn't stay. I came to Utah with my daughter."

Other Thoughts About Experiences

"The evil spirit experience was horribly real. Look, I'm shaking just thinking about it. I know that if that thing had been able to push me away so that my string broke it would have killed me. I believe that these two incidents happened, maybe as a warning, a signal, or something, so that I would get out. I stayed in the second marriage because of my daughter.

"Before I left Indiana I was very suicidal. I wouldn't have committed suicide, there is no way, but I felt like it. I was depressed and I was filled with hate. I was ripe for the experience I had with that thing.

"I've had to repair my life since then. Little by little I've gotten things back together. That incident pretty well scared the hell out of me."

"Let me ask you a few questions Dee. On the first incident, do you remember a string being attached to you?"

"No, not on the first one."

"In both experiences, how did your body feel when you were out?"

"I don't know what you call the other thing, my soul, my spirit, or what, but there was no feeling. The first time, when I glided down from the air, there was no feeling. Just a lot of thought."

"Did you feel as though you had a body?"

"I didn't think about it. I knew where I was—in Virginia."

"You felt like you were walking?"

"Yes. It felt like walking. My body didn't feel heavy. You know how your body feels . . . I remember when I walked through the closed screen door, and I thought that this was great. Then I walk-glided up to the bedroom and thought how terrific it was.

"As soon as I got my wish I was back. The important thing was to see the baby. I loved Jane dearly, and I wanted to see the baby."

"So that was a good experience?"

"That was a wonderful experience. And I remember—I don't know how to express it, how I was zapped back into my body, or what made me go back . . . . I believe when I started thinking about Indiana and wondering where my body was, as soon as I started thinking about my body, zap, I was back. And I knew I wasn't asleep. I knew that for sure."

"So it wasn't a dream?"

"It was no dream. As soon as I was back I could feel the heat again—it was so hot."

"And you didn't feel the heat when you were out?"

"No, there was no heat. It was a nothing sensation, a floating feeling."

"You didn't see any lights or anything of that sort?"

"No. No flashing lights; should I have?"

"We can talk about what others have seen in a minute."

"It was bright if that's what you mean. It wasn't a fog. It was, like, brilliant-bright. There wasn't a distinct light. It was just very bright."

"Around you, or where?"

"It was everywhere, everything was bright. Brighter than it normally would have been."

"Was that true in both experiences?"

"No, because the second experience was at night. It was just before dawn and I could see the frost on the ground and the steam from the cow's nose. I could see a mist on my string. My string had a glimmer to it."

Feelings of Terror in Second Experience

"When I first became aware of the presence of the thing, in the second experience, it was the most terrible feeling that I've ever had in my life. It was like I was going to die, or worse."

"What did you feel that the presence was?"

"I thought that it was the Devil, or a spirit that was trying to get my body. That's what I thought. I've always had a healthy fear of evil spirits. As soon as I felt this presence behind me I knew that this was ugly, this was terror, this was the worst . . . it was the most ugly, the most horrible thing that I had ever encountered. It was going to get me—it was going to destroy me—it was after my body.

"I knew that if it broke my string I would be dead. It kept pushing me away from the house; it was trying to get me as far as it could from my body. It wanted my string to break. The most important thing in my mind was to get back to my body, so I wouldn't leave my daughter.

"The terror was awful. I could feel myself wanting to scream. I was flailing my arms, grasping for something to pull me back, but there was nothing to hold onto. I was fighting to go back, and I flailed my arms to try and get the thing away from me. It was the most horrible experience I had ever had. Even today, when I think about it I am terror-striken. Look at my hands!" Dee's hands continued to shake as she remembered the experience.

"When I got back into my body I was screaming, because I couldn't . . . maybe that's it. I guess I couldn't make vocal noise out of my body. Maybe I was screaming, and as soon as I got back to my body I could vocalize it. It was a blood curdling scream—because that was the most terrifying thing that had ever happened to me."

Chapter 6

A MAJESTIC BEING

Ann

A Child with Leukemia

Ann was a lovely lady, forty-two years of age but looking much younger, who came to our home in Bountiful on a clear January day in 1991. She told us that she had been raised as a child in Southern California. She had been trained as a medical technician, and although previously married, she was presently single. She had four children who were dependent upon her.

She began: "My first experience happened when I was four years old. My parents moved to a new home in Glendale, California, and I had my own room. I had been ill several times and my parents knew that I wasn't feeling well but apparently were unaware of how very sick I was. I had been hospitalized several times as they attempted to find out what was wrong with me. The Doctors knew it was some type of blood disease—later identified as leukemia. The hospital had sent me home to be with my parents; my mother couldn't be with me in the hospital all the time.

"I was tired, listless, and generally sad of heart. My parents loved and cared for me, but I couldn't seem to communicate to them how badly I felt on this particular occasion. My father was having severe back problems and this may have accounted for their seeming indifference.

"Anyway, on this one night my mother put me to bed and tucked me in. She was worried about my Dad and didn't seem to notice that I had a hard time climbing into bed. I felt so tired that . . . that I simply wanted to get to sleep. I lay there for a moment waiting to go to sleep when I noticed a light coming into the room. It was a beautiful golden-white light which seemed to appear in the wall to the left of my bed."

"Did you notice anything besides the light?"

"Not at first. And I wasn't afraid, just curious about the light. It was about three feet up from the floor and mid-length of the bed, which was located near the wall. As the ball of light grew the pain and feeling of illness suddenly left me. I had no idea what was happening, but I felt at peace."

A Beautiful Lady of Light and a New World

"I sat up and watched the light grow. It grew rapidly in both size and brightness. In fact the light got so bright that it seemed to me that the whole world was lit by it. I could see someone inside the light. There was this beautiful woman, and she was part of the light; in fact she glowed."

"Did the light hurt your eyes?"

"No, even though it was bright by mortal standards."

"Tell me more about the lady in the light."

"Her body was lit from inside in a way . . . it's very hard to explain what she looked like. It seemed as if she were a pure crystal filled with light. Even her robe glowed with light as if by itself. The robe was white, long-sleeved, and full length. She had a golden belt around her waist and her feet were bare. Not that she needed anything on her feet since she stood a couple of feet off the floor."

"Were you frightened by her?"

"No, just the opposite. I had never seen such kindness and gentle love on anyone's face such as I saw in this person. She called me by name and held out her hand to me. She told me to come with her—her voice was soft and gentle but . . . but it was more in my mind. Communication was easier than when you verbalize thoughts. At the time I thought of it as 'mind talk.'

"I asked her who she was and she explained that she was my guardian and had been sent to take me to a place where I could rest in peace. The love emanating from her washed over me so that I didn't hesitate to put my hand in hers.

"As soon as I was standing beside her we moved through a short darkness to a beautiful, even brighter, light. And then I saw . . . there was this astonishingly beautiful world before me. It was like nothing else I have since seen on earth. Somehow I knew, inside of me, that the earth had been left behind. I had no idea where I was, and I didn't care. I felt a deep, profound peace . . . no, it was more than that. It was a world of peace and love.

"The new world looked sort of like the world I had left behind, but it was also very different. Everything glowed from the inside with its own light. The colors were beyond anything on earth—they were more vibrant, brilliant, and intense. And there were colors I had never seen before—don't ask me what they were. There were shrubs, trees and flowers, some of which I had seen on earth, like evergreens, and others which I hadn't seen before, and I haven't seen since. They were beautiful, beautiful.

"I asked my guardian why she took me to this place. She said that I needed the rest because life had become too hard for me to live.

"There was also grass all around, and a little hill with sand at the base in a sort of play area where several other children were playing. My guardian took me to the area and left without my knowing it. I immediately joined the children in play. There were toys in the sand and we built castles and roads and played with the toys. I was totally immersed in this new world of love, peace and play."

"Did you stay with the children very long?"

"It seemed long in one sense; in another, it seemed timeless. I felt thoroughly refreshed, enlivened and spiritually rejuvenated. I was filled with a zest for life. It is impossible to explain what it felt like to be lighter than air, with no pain, and totally at peace with everyone and everything around. I simply accepted my existence in the new world and lived.

"When my guardian returned I thought we were going to another part of this fascinating and wonderful world. Calling to me, she gently took me by the hand and said that I had to leave. When we started back the way we came I realized that we were returning to the earth, and I asked her why I had to go back. She told me it was time to return, and it would be easier for me to live on the earth now.

"We came back through the darkness, as before, with the surrounding light making a sort of tunnel through it. The peace followed me and

I was content. We emerged back in my bedroom. My guardian smiled
at me, and suddenly I was back in bed without the slightest idea of how
I got there."

"Could you still see your guardian?"

"Yes, but the light was diminishing. I waved at her, and she smiled
and waved back. Then the light sort of gathered around her and she was
gone. I went into a peaceful sleep content in the knowledge that
someone loved and watched over me."

"Did you tell your parents?"

"Not until years later when I told my mother. I didn't think they
would believe me. The next time they took me to the hospital for a
checkup my blood tests showed that I was normal."

"So you must have been healed during or after your experience?"

"I think it was during the experience."

"During your experience did you feel like you had a body like the
one on this earth?"

"No, it was lighter."

"But you had arms and legs?"

"Sure, I could touch the other children, and I could feel and smell.
I played in the sand and made sand castles with my hands. As we were
playing, sometimes I would walk, and other times, when we went as a
group, we just floated."

"It's amazing that you remember all those details after so many
years."

"It's because it was so real. I still remember it as one of the more
realistic events in my life. I was able to do things that I never did in any
dream. It was real."

Spinal Meningitis and a Wonderful Experience

"I was approximately twenty-eight when I had my next experience,
and I was living in a trailer in Southern Utah in the Skull Valley area.
My husband was a physician, and I was working to help in a construction project in the area, as well as caring for my two children.

"One day I felt quite ill, but I was cleaning up the trailer, because
I knew I had to or I would be in trouble."

"In trouble with whom?"

"My husband—he was having emotional problems, and he took some of his problems out on me."

"Okay, so you were feeling ill. What seemed to be the trouble?"

"Well, when I first got up I felt just fine. Just a little while later, though, I suddenly got this fever and a really weird headache. I didn't know what it was but I thought it might be the flu so I kept going. In about three hours my head felt awful and my back hurt; my whole spine ached. I also noticed that I had these spasms going up and down my spine, and they would pull me backwards. The spasms got stronger and stronger as time passed, and I knew something was wrong. My temperature had climbed to over 105 degrees in less than three hours.

"I didn't realize how sick I was. I figured I could keep working and it would go away. At one point I fell down and couldn't get up, but I kept working on the floor. By this time I couldn't think properly. While I was on the floor one of the workers from the project came in and found me on the floor. He took one look at me and left—he rushed to a phone and called my husband. He told my husband that I appeared to be seriously ill. In fact, he said I looked like I might be dying.

"My husband came and looked in on me, but by then I had managed to get on my feet. I didn't want him to see me when I was sick because I was afraid of what he would do. He was abusive to me. He asked me how I was and I told him I was just a little tired. He said he had to see some other patients and would be back to check on me.

When my husband came back he made me lie down on the couch, and one of those terrible spasms bent me backward. He took my temperature and checked my other vital signs. Then he took me into the bedroom and put me in bed—he had to lift me onto the bed. He got his hypodermic needles and gave me a couple of shots to control the spasms. He also took some blood for a blood test.

"I drifted in and out of consciousness and sleep for the next several hours. I remember my husband coming in and going to bed, but it was mostly a haze for those hours, until I awoke and found that I could hardly breathe. I was just breathing these little gasps. I tried to lift my arm but it fell back. I knew I was in desperate trouble, and I was kind of afraid. All of a sudden I wasn't there, I was . . . I was floating. It was so fast I didn't realize what had happened. And the pain—it was gone. There was this tremendous relief. It was, I don't know, just suddenly—WOW!

"I was floating, I was floating, and there was no pain. I looked up and noticed that I was coming up to the ceiling. I remember wondering what was on the other side of the ceiling, and then I went right through. I found myself standing, and still moving up, and I went into this blackness. I traveled in the blackness—sort of like a tunnel—until I came to this person who blocked the way."

A Beautiful Man

"There was this person standing in the way, and I couldn't go around so I stopped. The person was in a brilliant, brilliant light. I was fascinated. Even the hair was lit up, it was beautiful. In fact the person was beautiful, it was a man, he had this . . . oh, I didn't know that men could be that beautiful.

"I wondered who he was and he identified himself as my Savior, Jesus Christ. And I thought, *WONDERFUL.* I had this joy, that was, you know, welling up inside of me. It was like an explosion going on in me.

"Then He said, almost immediately, that I had to go back." Ann covered her face and began to sob as the memory of that event flooded back. Carol and I waited for several minutes while she regained her composure. I asked her, gently, "You didn't want to come back, I take it?"

With great difficulty Ann continued, "No, I cried to Him: 'No, please. I don't . . . .'"

"You had children then, didn't you?"

"Yes, I had two."

"Did you know why you had to come back, was that explained?"

"At first I cried out, I . . . I pleaded with Him. I didn't want to go back. There was the pain I had just been in, the pain . . . it was far beyond anything I could handle."

"And that's why you didn't want to come back, right?"

"Yes, and the other reason was that life had become just plain hell for me."

"Because of your husband?"

"Yes."

"Did you get back all of a sudden, or was it . . . ?"

"No, I pled with Him and He held me for a while. I don't know how long I pleaded and begged, it was a little bit of time, then . . . then I knew that He was feeling my sorrow and pain.

"Suddenly I felt this tremendously powerful . . . it's beyond the words of powerful, it's . . . I was suddenly enveloped in this deep, deep peace. It surrounded me, enveloped me, and He said: 'If you will go back I will put you immediately to sleep and when you wake you will be completely healed. And the pain will be gone.'

"Well I stopped crying, and I thought for a few moments. I looked at Him and I knew that this was an absolute promise if I did what He said. I knew this was my Savior, and He was asking me . . . He was giving me the choice. I bowed my head and said that I would, and that very powerful peace stayed with me. It finally penetrated into my heart, I relaxed and turned around."

Return to This Life

"I went, again, into the darkness, and I came out under the ceiling of my room. I stopped and looked and I could see the whole room; it was almost as if the moonlight was in there. I could see my husband sleeping and my own body next to him. My husband was breathing but my body was motionless. I didn't look at my face because I was afraid that the agony of the pain would be on it. I instinctively knew that if I looked at the face I would not go back.

"I knew that was my body, yet the real me was up near the ceiling. That thing down on the bed, it . . . it repulsed me. But I could feel the presence of my Savior, so I went over to my body and turned around. Then I settled down into it, sitting up. I hesitated in this position because I really didn't want to complete it. I was afraid I would feel that awful pain again—yet I felt reassurance from Him. I could feel that it would be all right.

"I lay back and . . . and that terrible pain hit. I gasped because of the awful severity of the pain. Then instantly I was out; before I could take another breath I was unconscious. It was so fast that the next morning when I woke I realized I hadn't even had a chance to think.

"I awakened the next morning with a feeling of complete peace. The fever was broken, my body was covered with sweat, and there was no pain. I was kind of weak, but nothing like I had been, and I knew what had happened. I remembered back—and I prayed—and gave thanks to my Heavenly Father and to my Savior.

"In my prayer I promised to do what I had to in order to live on, because there had to be a purpose. He had told me, and I remembered, that my missions were not finished. I remember wondering about *missions*. Why not *mission*? And I remembered that when I had gone to the other side I was pregnant with another child. I had to return for that purpose as well as my other children."

"Did you find out what had made you ill?"

"Yes. Three days later the test results came back. It was a very deadly form of spinal meningitis—one that normally kills. My husband tried to make me think that it was his shots that made me well, but I knew better.

"My husband died about one-and-one-half years after this experience."

"What is your feeling now about your experience? Did it feel real also?"

"Very real, even more so than the other one; because in the other one I was so young. There was no way to deny what I had seen. That much pain, and then being released from it, there was no way—"

"You subsequently read some of the books such as 'Life After Life', and . . ."

"Yes, my mother brought me some last year. When I talked to her I explained that I didn't know what to call what had happened to me. She told me that she had read a book which told about others having similar experiences. She thought it would help me, and it did."

"But you hadn't read any books when you had . . ."

"I'd never heard of it. I thought I was the only one who had gone through something like this."

"What is your feeling about death, now?"

"Because of my experience when I was very young my feeling hasn't changed much. When people talked about death I thought it was something else. When I was an adult, and after I put two and two together, it was hard for me to go on living. I remembered this beautiful place without pain."

"So, again, what is death to you?"

"Death is totally irrelevant from the point of view of the individual experiencing it. There is no death, there is no such thing, at least as most people think of it. It's simply a change. That's all it is."

"Do you have any messages you'd like to leave others?"

"I'd tell them that this fear about death which people have is a falsehood; it's a lie. If we have loved ones, and it's their time to go, let them go. If it isn't their time to go, because they have more work to do, they should complete their mission."

Jennette

A Heart Operation

Jennette was at her home in Salt Lake City when Carol and I met her. We admired her beautiful art, ceramic and other pieces. She had a delightful sense of humor despite numerous health problems. She explained that she was forty-nine years old, and that she had lost her husband the previous spring. From her demeanor it was clear that she missed her husband sorely.

"Okay Jennette, why don't you tell us a little of your background so that we may understand you better?"

"Well, I come from a background of English and German hard-heads. I was born in Pasadena, California, and I came to Salt Lake City about twenty-two years ago."

"Where did you meet your husband?"

"I met my husband in Salt Lake City when I was working in a machine-shop during the day and in a tavern on weekends."

"Were your parents here in Salt Lake City?"

"My parents were divorced when I was quite young, and I was raised by the strong arm and hammer of my grandmother, who is now deceased."

"Do you have children?"

"I have four living children—two boys and two girls. My daughters are both in the Salt Lake valley, one son is in Las Vegas, and the other lives in Denver. I also have three grandsons."

"It sounds as if you have a fine family. Perhaps you can tell us, now, what happened to you and under what circumstances."

"Three years ago I was on disability for asthma and depression. That summer I was doing a lot of fishing and camping, and I found that I always got out of breath and couldn't get far from the camper. Thinking that it was the high altitude and my asthma, I ignored it. Then, while I was baking a birthday cake for my daughter, I had such an attack that I thought I would go get a shot and finish the cake later.

"I went to the hospital and instead of giving me a shot they said, 'Honey, this is your heart, and we're putting you in intensive care.' I was flabbergasted. After a week of various tests they put me in surgery."

"Which hospital was this?"

"Holy Cross in Salt Lake. . . . My Doctors decided I needed a mitral valve replacement and a double bypass. The mitral valve had gone sour, because as an infant I had had scarlet fever.

"The original surgery was scheduled for early in the morning of February 28, 1988. And I wasn't fearful at all. After the surgery I went into Intensive Care where they determined that bleeding was occurring. They rushed me back into surgery to find the source of the bleeding. That was at five p.m. on the same day."

"This was bleeding in the heart?"

"Yes—it turned out my heart was misshapen and in the wrong place. Instead of a normal heart's shape, my heart looks like a mushroom. So the bleeder was on the back side of the mushroom instead of where they expected to find it. There was a vein towards my back rib leading to the valve and that's where the bleeding was coming from.

"The original team of surgeons tried to correct the problem on the second, afternoon surgery. They thought they had it corrected and put me back in Intensive Care. Eight to ten hours later I was still hemorrhaging. So for the third time in twenty-two hours, on February 29th, I went back into surgery, this time with a new team of surgeons. And this time they found the problem, but it was during this third surgery that I had my experience.

"I was on the operating table and I could see the doctors' faces, and I could hear a few words of what they were saying. I could see inside myself where the problem was. I tried to tell them, 'Look under that lip edge.' Of course, being anesthetized I couldn't tell them anything, but mentally I was trying to tell them, 'That's where the bleeder is, that's where the bleeding is coming from.'"

"Could you see them as this was going on?"

"I could see them—it's like I came out of my body and was two feet above them. And I could see what they were doing, and I could see the heart, and I could . . . I just knew where the bleeder was before I even rose up from my body. It just came to my mind . . . I just knew where it was.

"I wanted to explain where the bleeder was, but I couldn't, and in my anxiety to express it I came out of my body. I tried to communicate to the doctors, but I couldn't communicate, and I could see what they were doing. There were three surgeons and four nurses all working together.

"I finally decided that there was no use, the doctors weren't hearing me. And I kind of floated up to the top of the room. Like I was looking down from a distance, and still more distance, at them."

A Bright Light and a Marvelous Being

"Then the scene changed and I was surrounded by a greatness of light. Like a beautiful summer day with warm sun on the beach. Then I saw what appeared to be a great pipeline, like . . . something like a pipeline you might find buried alongside the road for sewage or something, you know, a great pipe.

"I walked into that, and there was the brightest light at the end. It took a long time to get to the end where the brightness was greatest, and . . . and a figure stood there in a white robe with hands outstretched. In my heart I know it was my Christ. It was . . . it was the form of Jesus Christ. I felt a lightness of heart and easiness—it was as if in a dream state but more real. There was no pain, or anxiousness, just serenity and peace.

"There were no vocal words, but there was no need for them. It was like my words were through my mind into the spiritual mind of my Christ and back to me, without hearing. There was no need to hear. So, definitely no need to speak, and yet a communion was there.

"I was so happy to be in that place, so close to my Savior, and feeling such warmth and comfort, as . . . as I'd never known on earth. And my Christ spoke to me and told me that I must go back, my work was not yet done. I had more work yet to do. I felt sad, and I knew that I had to follow the direction."

"Why did you feel sad?"

"Because I really wanted to enter . . . I truly wanted to enter. I didn't want to leave that glorious peace. The serenity . . . there are no words that can explain . . . ." Jennette began to cry but managed to continue, "the peace, the calm . . . ." she struggled for words.

"Love, I guess?" I added.

"Oh my, well you hear talk of angels. But it's like you *are* an angel. It's like you can perceive and know all, and all is so unnecessary. It's like a free spirit, a knowing being, I mean . . . I can see why they use sheep as an image of the Savior's pasture, because . . . things are so sublime—like sheep, so unobtrusive, so sublime. And I really think there's a connection.

"Well, then I closed my eyes on my Savior, and my youngest daughter was standing over my face weeping. When she saw me open my eyes she said, 'Mamma, mamma you're with us, you're going to be all right, I know you are.'"

"How old was your daughter at the time?"

"She was twenty-five, or thereabouts. So then it was in and out for three to five days. I believe I was five days in Intensive Care. Then they moved me to another hospital room and I was there for another ten or twelve days before I came home."

"When you were undergoing this experience, did your body feel like it was a body, or what was it like?"

"No, it was just something laying there, like another patient I was looking at."

"No, I mean your spirit body . . . ."

"Myself?"

"Yes, yourself. What was it like?"

"It was an amazing thing, it was . . . there was no weight of a body. It was like floating on water, only there was no water around."

"Did you have arms and legs?"

"Oh, as far as I know I did. I really didn't look at myself. I was getting places somehow; now whether I was floating, or walking, I'm not sure. I don't understand how I did it, and I didn't question it before now. It's not in my nature to question things like that."

A New Direction

"After I came home I took my rest, of course, and took it easy, and . . . and I didn't mention this to anyone right away."

"You didn't mention this to your family?"

"No . . . no, it was something I wanted to hold inside myself. About seven months after the surgery, though, I had such a pressure inside myself, that . . . that things weren't right, things were incomplete. And I knew that I had to go to church, because I hadn't gone to church since that time.

"So I went to a Four Square Gospel Assembly in Salt Lake, and I stood up before the congregation and gave my testimony of the beautiful light, and the wonderment of being that close to my God. And the true knowledge and glory of what it would be like to walk hand-in-hand with him . . . and how he had given me that wonderful opportunity, and then how he told me that my work was not done."

"Did you understand from that what your work was?"

"No sir, I still didn't know what my work was. Now I believe I do."

"Okay, what do you believe it is?"

"Well, He has pointed it out in funny ways, or . . . rather in ways you wouldn't think of. A family, in Salt Lake City with nine children . . . and somebody calls me. 'Where will we go? We need food, we need clothing, we need a house. What will we do? One child has no arms.' And I go, whoa. And I jump in my car, and I spend four days running to get things like welfare assistance, social security changeovers, Shriner's Hospital appointments for the girl with no arms, housing, food stamps, food banks, clothing, and all those other things."

"So you sort of felt you were to help people, and perform . . . ."

"Yes, those things kept happening. And then a job opened up, through Valley Mental Health, where I began to get paid for helping people. In that position I was doing the paper work: of social security, to apply for needs that the State pays for, food stamps, Medicaid program, to help them with clothing, with financial help, knowing where to go to get their needs filled—and I was being paid for that. And I loved the work. I finally had to give it up, though, because my health deteriorated."

"So as a result of your experience you feel compelled to help people?"

"Yes. My daughter has remarked how I am more giving than I was before, to everybody."

"Is there any final message you'd like to leave?"

"For those who haven't had the experience I have, I'd like to tell them to fear not death. Fear not death!"

Chapter 7

TWO WHO TRIED SUICIDE

Karen

She was a shy, blonde, lady with a graceful, feminine manner. Her appearance illustrated the fact that she had been a model at one time. She spoke in gentle tones as she visited with Carol and me in late March 1993.

Karen told us that she was born in the state of Washington, in April 1956. She was raised in Washington until the age of nine. Her parents were divorced, so Karen spent part of her youth traveling between her mother and father. When she was nearly eleven, she moved on a semi-permanent basis to be with her mother in a southern state, where she spent the remainder of her youth and early adulthood.

There were eight siblings, including Karen, in the two families of her mother and father. Both of her parents were loved and enjoyed by Karen. She graduated from high school and finished two years of college.

Travel and illness were frequent companions of Karen during her adult life. She moved to Salt Lake City about five years ago.

Karen's Suicide Attempt

The story, as told by Karen, begins: "In 1976, I was going through a divorce, and my best friend and I went to Los Angeles, California. My friend and I shared an apartment in Burbank.

"A therapist I was seeing, because of depression, had prescribed some tranquilizers to get me through this trying time. Everything that had happened to me was overwhelming, and I was unable to cope. The divorce, the move, the work, the depression—they were too much.

"One night as I was lying in bed, asleep, I was awakened by a male voice saying: 'I'm going to get you. Sooner or later, I'm going to get you.' The event frightened me and I sat up, wide awake. I told my roommate, and she said it was just a dream, and not to worry about it.

"About a week later, everything seemed so hopeless that I took the bottle of tranquilizers. My full intention was to kill me. It seemed the best way to handle my problems, just go to sleep.

"It didn't work out the way I wanted, though, because I fell out of bed and woke my roommate. She called the ambulance at about one o'clock in the morning. At the hospital, I found out later, they pumped my stomach and put charcoal in it. They didn't think I was going to make it. My heart had stopped, and they used defibrillator paddles to restart it.

"During this period I became aware that I was conscious, but I was enveloped in total darkness. It was pitch-black all around, yet there was a feeling of movement. My conscious self assured me that I was in the form of a spiritual body.

"A male voice spoke to me, a different voice than the one I heard a week before. This voice said: 'You have a choice. You can stay here, or you can go back. If you stay here, your punishment will be just as it is, right now. You will not have a body, you will not be able to see, touch, or have other sensations. You will only have this darkness and your thoughts, for eternity.'

"Terrified because of the experience, and because of what I had heard, I understood that this would be my private hell. There would be no contact with other life or with the sensations of life, for eternity. Yet I would remain conscious with my thoughts in total blackness.

"Frantically scared, I knew immediately that I had made a terrible mistake. Telling the voice that I had made a mistake, I asked to go back, to return to life. The voice said, 'All right, you may return.'

"Suddenly I felt myself being pulled back. It's hard to explain. There was total darkness, yet I had the feeling of movement as I was pulled back.

"Next, I found myself in the hospital room, in an elevated position, looking down. I could see the doctor, I could see my roommate, I could see my body in the bed. My roommate was crying, and the doctor was explaining something to her. It was clear that they thought I was gone.

"While I was watching this scene, I felt myself slowly descending. Then, suddenly, I was sucked into my body. It was fast.

"My next conscious act was to open my eyes and see my doctor looking down on me. Surprise and a relieved smile showed on his face. He asked me if I could squeeze his hand. With great effort I was able to do a feeble squeeze, and I knew that I was back by the grace of God."

Questions About the Suicide Experience

Karen agreed that I could ask some questions. I began: "You said, Karen, that there was total darkness where you were. Did you have any physical sensations while you were there?"

"None at all except for the feeling of motion when I left and when I arrived at the dark place. The sensations that I felt were in thought form only. I was so frightened of the concept of being stuck in total darkness. It was horrifying to me, and it still is today."

"You said that this would have been your hell. Is that what the voice told you?"

"No. He didn't tell me that, it was an inner knowledge."

"What is your feeling, now, about suicide?"

"I know beyond a shadow of a doubt that if you do commit suicide, there is a hell for that. There might be different types of hell for other people, but for me that darkness—with just my thoughts to keep me company—would have been absolute agony."

"Under the same circumstances, would you try it again?"

"Absolutely not. It's kind of ironic now, because I am a cancer survivor, and I've had to fight very hard to stay here on earth. Life is now very precious to me."

"Why is life so precious to you?"

"Because I am here for a reason, and we all have lessons to learn. Life is a gift from God."

"How do you know that?"

"From the suicide attempt, and from past experiences that I have gone through."

A Devastating Experience

"In 1988, after marrying again, I had a heart-breaking experience. My husband, whom I loved dearly, left me for another woman. I was pregnant, which we had planned, and I was at a loss with regard to what I should do next. My life seemed over. Abortion is against my belief, and I had a moral dilemma, yet I could see no alternatives. So I decided to terminate the pregnancy.

"After the procedure, my sister and I were sitting in the waiting room, and I started to hemorrhage. They took me back into the room where they had done the procedure. I just kept bleeding. The physician was unable to stop the bleeding, and it was excruciating.

"It became very scary, and I began to pray. I prayed: *God, forgive me for what I have done. Please take the soul of the child that I destroyed to heaven—please forgive me. And please don't let the child feel the pain that I am feeling.* Through all this, I knew that I was going to die. Then a strange thing happened. In the corner of the room, up near the ceiling, I saw a black dot. The dot sort of opened up, slowly, until it was about two feet in diameter. It remained for perhaps one minute after I prayed, then it slowly diminished in size and disappeared. I was astonished, and I couldn't explain it, but I knew, somehow, that the black dot or hole was a passageway.

"Finally, a nurse said: 'Doctor, I think we are losing her. She is going into shock.' They called for an ambulance which took me to a hospital where my lost blood was replaced, and I recovered."

Further Questions About Karen's Experiences

"Based upon your experiences to date, including your first out-of-body experience, have they changed your outlook on life?"

"Most definitely."

"How?"

"I know that God and Jesus are always with me—they are with all of us. To have contact with God and Jesus we must pray and meditate daily, and have faith.

"There is no question in my mind that there is life after death. I am certain that there are heavens and hells. For us to be with Him, all he asks is that we do the best that we can and follow Christ's teachings."

"Did you always feel that there was a life after death, and that there were heavens and hells?"

"No. But after my experiences there was no question in my mind. It's a certainty within me that can't be taken away."

"Could your first experience have been a dream, or a hallucination?"

"No. It was real."

"Why are you telling me this story?"

"I'm not proud of what I did. But I feel that by telling my story I will be able to help other people. Also, I work with a cancer survivor's group, for example, and I try to help where I am needed."

"Are there any messages you would like to leave others?"

"Just that we have a purpose here, there is a life after death, and there is a God who loves all of us—a forgiving God. The love that God feels for us, we should try to replicate in our feelings for others. Our purpose in being here is to learn what life presents us with and to overcome obstacles. Life is a training ground. As situations present themselves we should try to do the best we can, that's all He asks of us."

Dallas

He was a short, but rugged looking man, with a neat beard and a sparkling sense of humor, when I visited him at his home in the spring of 1993. Dallas was born in Beacon, New York in 1939. He was one of the twin boys his mother had, and he had two stepsisters from a later marriage of his mother.

Dallas went to high school in Toledo, New York, and he joined the navy from 1958 to 1962. From the navy, he moved to Houston, Texas where he spent most of his life. In Texas, Dallas found employment in the oil fields, and this led to an extensive career in construction.

After moving to Texas, Dallas married a lady he described as a beautiful redhead. With three children and three grandchildren, Dallas was a vibrant looking grandfather when I visited him.

Taking a job as an oil field supervisor in Wyoming, Dallas moved to that area during the oil boom of the '80s. This area of the country attracted him, so he moved to Utah when the oil boom ended.

Dallas finished telling me of his youth and early adult life, and I asked him to tell the circumstance that led to his out-of-body experience. He began.

Despair and a Suicide Attempt

"In 1973, after ten years of marriage, my wife and I broke up. The breakup was in part due to conflict with her mother, but I was devastated. In addition, I had serious health problems. I struggled along for five years or so, but life was not good. Just before Valentine's day, and after my fortieth birthday in 1979, I decided that life was not worth living.

"To commit suicide I decided to use a rifle. Carefully disconnecting the phone so that it would not interrupt my concentration, I got my twenty-two rifle and loaded it with a hollow-point bullet.

"Gathering my courage, I braced the butt of the rifle against some furniture, put the point on my chest just opposite my heart, and pushed the trigger with my thumb. Penetrating my chest, the bullet broke two ribs, tore into my heart as it disintegrated, passed through my diaphragm, and penetrated my kidneys and my liver.

"It was about 6:00 p.m., and I was in my home in the master bedroom. As soon as the gun fired, I was overcome with enormous pain in my chest. The pain was so bad that . . . I would never do that again, no matter what the reason."

Out-of-Body to a Marvelous Place

"Suddenly I felt myself slipping out of my body. Everything went black; then I felt myself traveling through a tunnel of light. When I was nearly to the end of the tunnel, it became very bright and beautiful. There was a garden, and the beauty was indescribable. I've been to many art museums around the world, and it was more beautiful than anything displayed in any museum.

"Standing in the garden was the Lord Jesus Christ. The feeling I had was beyond description. As wonderful as the garden had been, it was no longer my center of attention. My whole being focused on this magnificent personage standing before me."

Interrupting Dallas's narration, I asked him to describe Christ. He struggled as he attempted to put into words what he had seen.

"The robe He was clothed in was white beyond any description, with a beautiful sash in the middle—it was gorgeous. His hair was long and it was a golden-brown color, and He had a beard. Actually, in terms of describing Christ himself, the closest I can come to it is the print of a painting I saw in a book store some years later.

"The painting is entitled *The Second Coming*, and the original painting was done by the artist Harry Anderson. I purchased a print that I hang in my bedroom, because it is the best representation of what I remember seeing when I stood at Christ's feet. When I first saw the picture it brought back the memory of my experience, and I stood in front of the picture crying. As good as that painting is, though, it is a poor representation of the magnificent being I saw before me."

A Conversation with the Lord

"The Lord called me by name and told me that I had done a foolish thing, and it was not my time to be there. He said that there was a lot of work on the earth that I must do for Him. There were certain things I must accomplish with my family before I would be allowed to return to the Lord. If I did what He asked, He said that my life would be great—not great in an earthly sense, but great in a spiritual sense, and I would be richly rewarded on the other side."

"The feelings I had when in His presence were overwhelming. It was an experience that . . ." Dallas paused in his description.

"How did you know it was Christ?" I asked.

Dallas chuckled, and then said with emphasis: "Because you can *feel* it. When He said: 'I have work for you to do,' and when He was talking to me, I just knew who it was. There was no doubt. I knew it was He as well as I knew who I was.

"The Lord then said that I had to go back, but I told Him I didn't want to go back. He made it clear that it wasn't up to me; there was this work that I had to do, so I must return."

"When you spoke with the Lord, Dallas, how did you converse?"

"Actually, I don't think I ever spoke. It was more mind-to-mind conversation than it was vocal words. He was able to read my mind and know what I was saying, and I knew what He was saying . . . I could hear His voice, but it was more in my mind than my ears. We had telepathic communication going between us; it was so neat!"

"What were some of the things the Lord asked you to do?"

"Some of what He said I have forgotten, but I remember Him telling me that I had to do things with my family."

"What else did the Lord tell you?"

"That my health would be restored. At the time of my suicide attempt, in addition to the massive physical injuries from the gunshot wound, I had previously been diagnosed as having asbestosis and lung cancer. The asbestosis was from work I had done as an insulator on construction projects. The Lord said that all of these health problems would be cured."

"Are there other things you remember about being in the presence of the Lord?"

"I will never forget the feeling of being totally enveloped in warmth, it was . . . it was sort of like walking into a heavy fog, so heavy you couldn't see through it, that was everywhere. Only instead of fog, it was a feeling of warmth, of love, of compassion—it was a tangible feeling, almost physical in nature. This wonderful feeling enveloped me.

"When I first saw the Lord and that feeling encompassed me I cried uncontrollably. The feeling took over my whole body, every part of my body was affected. It completely shrouded me with an unbelievable joy. The scriptures speak of the love of the disciples for Christ, and I now know how they felt."

"So the Lord then told you that you had to go back?"

"Yes."

"How much time elapsed between the time you left your body and when you returned?"

"I have no idea. I cannot comprehend how time worked there."

"Did you, by any chance, have a review of your life while you were in His presence?"

"No. Only those things happened that I told you about."

Physical Recovery

"Finding myself on the floor of the bedroom, I felt this tremendous pain and burning sensation in my chest. Because I had lost so much blood and was so weak, I couldn't sit up, even though I tried. So I lay there all night bleeding onto the carpet (they later had to replace the carpet).

"In the morning I found enough strength to struggle into the kitchen and get a glass of milk from the refrigerator. In the process of struggling to get there I ruined all the carpet in the house by leaking blood all over.

"After drinking the milk I blacked out and collapsed again. Lying on the floor I kept drifting in and out of consciousness. Late in the afternoon, twenty-seven hours after I shot myself, I awakened and watched the room get light. It just lit up. There was no one present that I could see, but I felt a presence and heard a voice. The voice told me to reconnect the phone and call my neighbor.

"The voice kept urging that I fix the phone, but I felt so weak I could hardly move. The voice said: 'I told you that you would not die. There is work for you to do.' In my weakened condition I said: 'But Lord, I've lost so much blood that I can't stand up without passing out.' The voice then said: 'You can, now. I command you to do it.'

"Instantly, I was able to stand, reconnect the phone and call my neighbor. Upon arriving, the neighbor looked at me and commented: 'You stupid idiot, what have you done?' While he called the ambulance, I went in and took a shower to remove all the blood from me. Dressing myself, I went to the hospital in clean clothes.

"We got to the Veteran's Hospital in Houston about ten o'clock at night, and they operated on me an hour or so later. They later told me that I spent seven-and-one-half hours on the operating table. One-third of my blood had been lost before I got help, and they replaced it with thirty-six pints.

"Later, when some of the operating team members visited me during my recovery, I asked them what they thought when my heart stopped twice on the operating table. They asked how I knew that, and they wanted to know who told me.

"No one told me. Twice, during the surgery, I felt my heart stop, just as it did when I had my experience. During the surgery, when it stopped, I felt a hand on my shoulder, and the greatest feeling of warmth came over me. Then the voice said: 'I told you I wouldn't let you die. Everything will be okay.' That happened twice.

"The chief surgeon visited me sometime later, and I told him what had happened during the surgery. He said: 'I believe that you did have an unusual experience. Your heart was so badly damaged when we sewed it up we figured you only had about thirty minutes to live. There had to be a higher power—using better medicine than we had—otherwise you would be dead.

"In addition to sewing up the heart with about fourteen stitches, they had to repair the diaphragm, and they removed bullet fragments from throughout my body. Four small fragments are still lodged in the heart muscle, and they show up whenever I have an X-ray.

"A few years after my suicide attempt I had chest X-rays specifically to look at the state of my lungs. They found that the cancer signs had all disappeared. Previously my left lung was seriously affected. The later X-rays showed it to be clear, and the doctors thought the two sets of X-rays (before and after) were from different patients."

Another Medical Emergency

"Ten years ago when I was working in the oil fields I had several heart attacks, one in Evanston, Wyoming, and two in Utah. This time I didn't have the extensive out-of-body experience as I did previously, but I was again told that I would not die.

"At first it just seemed that I had the flu. Then, while I was at my place of business, an oil-field construction company that I owned in Wyoming, a fellow took my blood pressure. He couldn't believe what he read. They rushed me to the VA Hospital in Salt Lake City. The Salt Lake facility did not have the proper equipment, so they took me to the Denver Hospital. There, they performed an angioplasty procedure, through the arteries in my crotch, up through my heart.

"The doctors in Denver decided that the heart attack was unrelated to the previous gunshot wound. They were fascinated, though, by the fact that there were metal fragments in my heart which showed up on the X-ray.

"Damage to the heart from the heart attack was sufficient that they told me, without a heart transplant, I would only live for two or three years. They said that I was a candidate for transplanting, but I told them there was no point in a heart transplant. I assured them that I would continue living without it—until my time was up. Then the Lord would take me. I have outlived their prognostication by seven years, so far."

Final Thoughts by Dallas

"Those experiences have changed, forever, the way I look at life. People who knew me before and know me now cannot believe the difference. Work used to be a way of life with me. Fourteen and sixteen hour workdays were common. I made tons of money; I had a big house in Houston with a Lincoln, a Cadillac, and a large boat. My boots were handmade from alligator skin, and I had a hundred-dollar belt-buckle that was especially made for me.

"Last year, I made as much money in a year as I previously made in a few days, and I was happier than I had been for years. Money simply does not matter any more—I don't care about it. When I was on the other side talking with the Lord I took none of my worldly goods with me.

"My experience helped me to understand that the important accomplishments in this life are not related to material things. They are related to how we help others, to how we interact with family and friends, and to the love we extend to others.

"The Lord told me that I had work to do on this side. He didn't tell me to get busy and earn more money—He said I should work with my family."

After Dallas finished expressing these final thoughts, I asked him if there were any messages he would like to leave others. He said: "The first message is that suicide is not the answer to anything. The Lord gave me a second chance, but everyone might not be so lucky. He told me that I had made a terrible mistake, and I understood what He was saying when I was in His presence.

"The second message I might give would be to set your goals on service. There is no need to worship the dollar since you won't take it with you."

Before saying goodbye to Dallas, I asked him to show me the scars from his suicide attempt. Taking off his shirt, he showed me where the bullet entered his heart. In addition to the scar from the gunshot wound, there was a continuous scar running down the center of his chest from a point just under his collarbone to his lower abdomen. It was obvious that he had undergone significant physical trauma from the wound and subsequent operation.

Chapter 8

TWO YOUNG WOMEN

Margaret Amodt

Bob and Margaret Amodt visited Carol and me at our home in March 1991. They were a couple, in their late twenties to early thirties, who appeared to have a close-knit relationship. They explained that they had been together about ten years and had four children.

Bob was born in Salt Lake City where he graduated from high school. He currently was attending Salt Lake Community College, studying auto collision repair, in anticipation of opening his own shop.

Margaret was born in Salt Lake City and was raised in West Bountiful, Utah. As a girl, Margaret had a horse and was interested in rodeos.

Her Children Ran Through Her

Margaret began: "In 1983, I didn't know I was pregnant, I had an ectopic pregnancy."

"What is that?"

"It means the baby was in the tube. The fetus exploded the end of my tube. I was bleeding internally."

"Were you in the hospital?"

"I spent the whole weekend, and I thought . . . you know, I thought it was just stomach cramps. Monday it was getting worse so I called my grandmother to come and take me to the doctor."

"Did you know you were pregnant?"

92

"No. She took me to the doctor and he sent me to Emergency at Holy Cross Hospital. The pain kept getting worse . . . in my shoulder; I couldn't lift my arm. And I hurt all over, there was a lot of pain."

"Did your husband know what had happened?"

"Yes. He was called, and he came to the hospital. He was with me when I had to go to the bathroom. He helped me, and when I stood up the blood must have gone to my legs. He said I took two steps, and then I was gone. I don't remember passing out but he told me about it later."

Bob interjected, "When she fell down I caught her, and she was pale and cold; she was really limp. I yelled for the nurses to come, and they brought the thing to start her heart. Margaret was out for, I'd say, seven or eight minutes."

"What do you remember next, Margaret?"

"I knew I was . . . I felt so good. And I thought: *Wow, this is beautiful*. I really liked it, the feeling I had."

"The pain was gone?"

"Yes, the pain was gone."

"Did you see yourself—your body?"

"No, the first thing I saw was my kids. They had been taken to my parents' house. They were running around, laughing."

"How many children did you have?"

"Two little girls. They were playing and I was in my parents' house. I remember, I wasn't standing, I was, like, floating. And then my oldest daughter ran right through me."

"Did that surprise you?"

"Yes. I tried to hold her and I couldn't. And she started screaming . . . I could hear her scream, 'Mamma.' Shortly after that I was back in the hospital and I felt pain. It was awful."

"When your daughter was screaming your name, was that just a normal reaction of your daughter, or . . .?"

"No, I think that she knew I was there. That's how I felt, and later we talked about it."

"How old was she?"

"She was almost three years old."

"Was your mother present?"

"No I didn't see my mother, or my father. I saw my brother playing with the kids, but I was more focused on them. And then I knew that . . . that I had to come back."

"How did you know that you had to come back?"

"I don't remember anyone saying anything to me, but I just . . . I just knew it."

"Did you have any consciousness of how you got back?"

"I was just, all of a sudden, back, and I was yelling and . . . I don't remember yelling. I remember the pain, and I wanted to go back where I was before the pain."

"When you came to, and the pain hit, were you in bed or were you on the floor?"

"I was with my husband on the floor. The nurse was there sticking some stuff up my nose. I think that's what brought me back, because I didn't want to face the pain again."

"Did you see a bright light or anything of that sort?"

"There was, I would say, a bright glow around me. Not my body, it was around me when I was gone."

"You could see a glow?"

"Yes, it was bright, and it was around me. Kind of like a bubble. It was peaceful."

"When you were in your parents' home did your body feel like a body?"

"No."

"What did it feel like?"

Margaret thought for a moment. "It didn't feel like air either—energy!"

"Did this energy have arms and legs?"

"Just like me."

"As far as you can tell it was just like your present body?"

"Well, okay, I didn't look down. It was as if I were hovering, and I could see my children."

"And you actually tried to embrace your child?"

"Yes, my daughter. She was running and I reached out to hold her, and she ran through me. I saw her just run through me."

"Did the experience change the way you felt about religion?"

"I am not active in an organized religion, but I've heard a lot of things said—that there's no such thing as life after death. After my experience I *knew* that there was something else. And it's a lot more beautiful than here."

"Why do you say it's more beautiful than here?"

"I just felt good."

"How do you feel about death?"

"I can hardly wait," Margaret laughed, and continued, "when it's my time."

Stephanie LaRue

Early Memories

Stephanie LaRue was waiting for Carol and me as we drove up to her home in West Valley City, Utah, in late March 1991. She was a svelte, self-assured young woman with auburn hair worn in a short stylish cut. Her blue eyes were striking as they smiled at us. She informed us that she was forty years of age, but she could have passed for thirty.

Stephanie was born in Sacramento, California, but her folks moved to Utah when she was two years old. She grew up in Utah, went to school at a Catholic parochial school, and later attended the University of Utah where she become a Registered Nurse. During the Vietnam war she served on Oahu as a nurse, then in Arizona for a period. She moved back to Utah, updated her studies in cardiology, moved to Montana for eleven years, and then returned to Utah. Stephanie said she was married to a good man, and they were seeking to adopt children.

I asked Stephanie to tell us of the background leading up to her experience. She began: "Let me start by saying the first thing I remember in my life, this life, was looking in a mirror when I was about five or six years old. As I looked at myself I remember saying out loud to myself, 'You are not the person in the mirror who you appear to be,' or words to that effect.

"I recall that as I looked at the little girl in the mirror with short, curly red hair and missing teeth, I didn't look that pretty. Yet, inside, I felt this marvelous spirituality. My parents weren't that religious so they didn't teach me to feel that way, but at the time I felt that the reflection in the mirror was not the real me.

"As I grew older I would sometimes get flashes of thoughts, scenes, or events that would later come to pass. On one occasion, for instance, I called up my mother and asked her if she felt it. She asked, 'Felt what?' 'Why the earthquake, of course, I responded.' She told me that she hadn't felt any earthquake—an hour later we had an earthquake. Also, if there is going to be a death in the family I usually know it is going to happen.

"As a consequence of these intuitive feelings I have found that as they come to me, in my everyday life, if I respond to them I feel good. Things work out well when I do what my gut feelings tell me; when I don't, I get in trouble."

Illness and an Operation

"I had female problems for several years; they called it endometriosis. It's non-fatal, little tumors spread throughout the female tract. I was trying to have children, and they cauterized the tumors, but, in time, the tumors spread badly and the physicians had to perform major surgery. So on July 26, 1980, they performed a complete hysterectomy.

"The operation took place at the University of Utah Medical Center, and after the operation I was in severe pain. I knew that pain was normal but, for some reason, the pain seemed more than I could handle. They gave me morphine, but I found out that my body did not use morphine, it didn't block pain for me.

"While they were trying to find a solution for the pain, I began to hemorrhage internally, and I developed a temperature of 106 degrees. I also eviscerated, the stitches ruptured and everything came back out from the first operation. Needless to say I was in great distress. I felt awful.

"I knew that if I shut my eyes and went to sleep I would die. I was fighting to live, it was just a feeling that I had. They took me back into surgery, but, because of my deteriorating condition, they didn't give me a general anesthetic. They gave me demerol and, I think, valium in the arm, and they performed the surgery as quickly as they could.

"I didn't know it at the time, but the doctors told my husband that I probably would not live longer than 45 minutes. He called my parents and they rushed back to the hospital.

"When I came out of surgery the second time I had lost massive amounts of blood, and my chemistry profile was terrible. Fighting pain was, for me, like running a marathon. I knew that if I stopped I would die. Finally, after I felt that I had gone beyond the end of the race, a sense of calmness came over me, and the pain went away. My husband was holding me in his arms in my hospital bed, and I felt contented because the pain had gone."

Out-of-Body—Complete Knowledge

"All of a sudden, within the blink of an eye, I left my body. It was so fast and so natural. I wasn't afraid—of course I didn't know that this was death."

"How did you know that you had left your body?" I asked.

"I turned around and saw myself in the bed."

"What did you look like?"

"I remember saying: 'That's not the real me,' and I pointed at the hospital bed. 'This is the real me; that's only a shell,' and I pointed back, again, at the hospital bed."

"Could you see your husband?"

"I could see my husband, and I could see myself. And I remember, while I was out of my body, going through the hospital drapes and thinking: *After all these years, why do they have to have these green drapes?* And I didn't have to part them, I just walked through them.

"About this time I had an experience that I'll never forget. It was an experience of complete tranquility, peacefulness, wholeness—whatever the word wholeness means; like mind, body, and soul. Also a feeling of total, total knowledge without asking.

"It's like you and me sitting here, now, and wondering how far the universe expands, or . . . just questions we have on earth about the geography of the earth, craters, or anything. This feeling I had of total knowledge was just that, I knew everything without asking. It was an incredible feeling.

"I turned around and looked at my body again, and I knew why I was there; I didn't have to ask. The only way I can relate to it is to observe that I was more alive in that realm than I am talking to you, here, now. Another way to relate to it is . . . like you and I are more awake now than when we are asleep at night. That's how much more aware I was in the other realm."

In and Out of Body

"I turned around and looked at my body. I guess it wasn't time for me to go, because I got back in. As soon as I got back in my body there was a fear in me. I wasn't exactly sure what was going on. I jumped up as weak as I was with all the tubes hanging from me, and with my husband wondering what I was doing, I went around the corner to look in the mirror. I used my fingers to touch my face, my arms, and my legs, to verify that I was really back in my body.

"This happened off and on for the next few days."

"What happened?"

"I would leave my body and come back—the pain was so bad, or I was so sick, that I was going in and out of death. So, each time I woke up I looked around to make sure where I was. During those times, I didn't have the knowledge or experience that I did the first time. After that first time, though, whenever it happened, maybe three or four times, I welcomed it. The pain became less intense, and I didn't fight it anymore."

"The first time when you went out, Stephanie, did you see any light or dark spaces?"

"No, I didn't see black or white, nor did I see a tunnel. But everything was complete, in perfect harmony."

"When you say that you walked through the hospital drapes, did you walk through a wall, or what?"

"I remember that I was coming back from somewhere. I know that I left the hospital, but I don't remember where I went. I remember going down the hallway to visit a sick friend that I had met before surgery."

"When you traveled to these various places, did you walk, or was it by some other mode of locomotion?"

"I felt as though I traveled more by thought than by anything else. It wasn't like I had a body."

Feelings of Love, Wholeness, and Power

"When I left my body I was encompassed with a higher power. It felt like complete wholeness, tranquility, peacefulness, . . ."

"Love?"

"Oh definitely love, definitely. It . . . there are no words in the English language to describe it. It's more than love; the word love is just the tip of the iceberg, so to speak."

"When you had that feeling, did you have any understanding about where the feeling was coming from, or what was driving it?"

"It was everything. It was an accumulation of everything that ever lived—like the trees, the flowers, every human being, animals, anything that lives or breathes, a blade of grass. It was a totality of everything. Also, when I came back into my body I knew that everything had its place, its purpose, and there was a reason for everything. Even poor children that die of cancer at a young age, somebody's life that is taken; everything has a reason. But you don't *know* that until you are on the other side."

Coming Back—Subsequent Experiences

"I came back because I felt that there were things that I still had to do on this earth."

"Like what?"

"I could be wrong, but I had the feeling that I'm supposed to have two children. I felt that there would be a special spiritual person coming into my life. And I knew that I had to be there for that person or persons."

"When you came back into your body, did you feel that it was hard to come back, and did you have any say in it?"

"I just knew I had to come back, and there was a lot of pain when I got back."

"Was it hard to get back into your body?"

"No."

"Do you know how you got back?"

"No, I wish I did."

"Do you feel that the experience was truly out-of-body, and that it was a real experience and not a dream or a hallucination?"

"I'd bet my life on it."

"Did you want to come back?"

"Now I wish I hadn't."

"Why is that?"

"It's just that . . . once you've had something so good, and so perfect, why settle for less?"

"You apparently felt, though, that you had to come back for a purpose. And I presume that became an overriding issue with you?"

"Yes, it did."

"Has your experience changed your feeling about religion?"

"In terms of formal religion, not particularly, but it has made me more spiritual. I consider myself deeply spiritual, but not necessarily religious."

"Do you have any evidence of this increased spirituality?"

"Yes, sometimes I have experiences where I will see a light, like an aura around somebody, and I know, somehow, that the person is important to me. One example is my present husband. I was walking in a bowling alley, and out of the corner of my eye I saw this bright light around a man, but his back was facing me. I thought to myself: *I wish I could meet him. I know he is a good person.* Shortly thereafter, in the bowling alley, somebody called my name. This person introduced me to the man I had seen with the aura, and now we are married."

Chapter 9

DIVERSE EXPERIENCES

Joanne Jones

A Bleeding Ulcer

Robert and Joanne Jones were waiting for me in their home in Salt Lake City when I drove up. They welcomed me and we traded news of our early life. It turned out that Robert and I had both spent part of our youth in a small town, Dunsmuir, in Northern California.

Joanne explained that she had been born in 1930 in Cleveland, Ohio. When she was six years old, her parents moved to California where she grew up. She and Robert were married in 1954, and they had three girls, two of whom were still living.

Joanne began telling of her experience: "About 25 years ago I started with an ulcer. Like a lot of people I kept on smoking. About seven years ago we decided to go to Jackson Hole, Wyoming for the weekend. I hadn't been feeling good—the ulcers were kicking up, but I just thought they'd do their thing and I'd be okay again. Well, when we got there the ulcers had other ideas. They perforated, and I ended up in the hospital."

"Where was the hospital?"

"It was in Jackson. They kept me there overnight, enough to stabilize me so they could bring me in the air-lift ambulance to Salt Lake. I ended up in the hospital for eighteen days. After I got in the hospital . . . Robert knows more about what happened there than I do—you tell him Robert."

101

Robert continued: "In Jackson, they put eight pints of blood in Joanne, and on the way down they put three more in her. The blood was pouring out through the ulcers as fast as they were putting it in. Later, in the hospital in Salt Lake City, they operated and took out the lower half of her stomach—they found three ulcers near the duodenum. They put a butterfly, a temporary bypass, in her intestine. They pumped a bunch of blood into her, and she was getting ready to go home, and the next day her spleen ruptured."

"She must have been near death," I remarked. "How much blood did she get throughout the ordeal?"

"She got seventy-six pints. People from our church donated much of the blood. Anyway, they went in again and removed her spleen, the rest of her stomach, and eight inches of her intestine. Okay, you tell what happened next, Joanne."

Out-of-Body in a Beautiful Place

"After the last surgery, I think it was in the morning, the weirdest thing happened. I was laying in the bed; my body, anyway. But *I'm* not there. And this is the strangest thing, I look at my . . . . that is, my spirit, soul, call it anything you want, the part of me that's spiritually connected, it's out of my body. My body is there—I look down and I see me. Just a tired, sick old woman lying there.

"And then, I was in this most beautiful place I've ever seen in my life. It was outside, with mountains, and animals, and children. There was a country road, and I was aware of myself being there, not my body, but *me*, Joanne Jones. And I was kind of walking—floating, if you will—down this country road."

A Wonderful Face

"There was an entity coming toward me. At first I didn't know whether it was a man or woman. The person was dressed as we've been led to believe men were dressed at the time of Jesus Christ, with a white robe. Anyway, soon we were face to face, and I've . . . I've never seen a more wonderful face in my life. It was the Lord Jesus Christ."

"What did he look like?"

"He was fairly young; I'd say around 35 or 40 years of age. He reached for me, embraced me, and said: 'I love you. Not yet my daughter.' That's all there was to it. I found myself back again in my bed in the hospital."

Other Impressions About the Experience

"When you were first out of your body, Joanne, and could see yourself, did you see any darkness, or lightness, or were you just suddenly in this other world?"

"No, it's like I was transported from where I was to this other world. There was no tunnel, no light; it was just my Spirit, or my Soul going from here to this other place. It all happened in a hurry—the whole thing—maybe sixty seconds."

"What did the surroundings look like in the other place?"

"Well, okay, there were mountains, beautiful mountains, trees."

"Were there flowers?"

"It was mostly foliage, more beautiful, all kinds of beautiful stuff. Not necessarily from any one region, just gorgeous . . . it was beautiful. That's all I can say. The water was . . ."

"There was water there, too?"

"It seems to me, I can't remember exactly, there was either a river, or a fall. . . ."

"What were the colors like?"

"They were vivid. Not like here; if you imagine the most beautiful place you can think of here."

"Yosemite?"

"It's . . . it's a hundred times more vivid, more wonderful than that. You can't believe it, the colors were magnificent—you can't describe it."

"When you saw the Savior, you say He was good-looking?"

"Yes, I found Him to be an extremely attractive person . . . beautiful, with a strong, gentle face. A man who . . . He *was* a man, you could feel it, yet He was something else. And the embrace . . . I could feel the strength, and the love, and the gentleness."

"Was there light; did you notice any brightness about Him?"

"You mean around Him, like a halo or something. No, I don't remember anything like that. He was dressed in a long robe. And He was this very gentle, beautiful, loving, male entity."

"Did you speak to Him?"

"I don't remember saying anything. Only what He said, and then I was back in the hospital with my doctors, John Bowers and Mark Muir. They were standing on either side of my bed holding my hands. There were tears in their eyes, and John said, 'You are one tough lady. I don't know what happened, but you've come back from someplace.'"

Jackie

A Stopped Heart

Jackie greeted Carol and me at the door of her apartment on a windy spring day in 1991. She was busy preparing for a barbecue later in the day. She interrupted her preparations to visit with us.

Jackie was born in Colorado in 1959 and was raised in various parts of the country. They traveled extensively because her mother was a successful entertainer. Jackie proudly displayed a recent record release by her mother.

Two areas where she spent considerable time were New York and California. She went to school at St. Michael's Academy in Manhattan. Ultimately the family moved to Utah. Jackie married the first time at fifteen, just after graduating from high school, and she was divorced at nineteen. She had a daughter from the first marriage. She married again, three years ago, to a good man from Brooklyn whom she characterized as a service brat.

She began her story: "I was 22 years old in 1979, and I was living here in Salt Lake. I had just returned from Japan, and I was having a terrible problem with jet lag, and with insomnia. To help me through the problem I went to this doctor. He didn't do a physical on me but he prescribed 900 mg Placidyl tablets, one of the strongest sleeping medicines they make.

"Normally my heart rate is very slow, but the doctor didn't know that since he didn't check me. On the evening that I got the medicine I went to a party at Len's, my best friend's house, and I had a glass of brandy. At bed time I couldn't sleep, so I took a sleeping pill; the combination of the brandy and the sleeping pill made my heart stop.

"Later Len found me; I had already turned blue. He couldn't feel a pulse, and he took me in his car to St. Mark's Hospital. He was very upset—he thought I had taken the whole bottle of sleeping pills.

"At the hospital they rushed me into the cardiac unit and did everything they could to try and revive me. By this time Len was frantic. The hospital people told him that he couldn't sign the papers, or anything, since he wasn't related. He got my sister to come to the hospital.

"My heart had been stopped at least ten minutes, and the doctors told my friend there wasn't much they could do for me. They had shocked me, twice, with electrical paddles, and they had given me a shot of adrenalin with no success. When they told Len he began crying, sobbing."

Watching the Doctor Explain Her Death

"Okay, my body was in the emergency room, but I was out in the waiting room with Len and my sister. I really didn't walk out there. I was just standing next to Len when the doctor was talking to him. Len was crying. I remember talking to him and asking him why he was crying, but he couldn't hear me. It was as if I weren't there, to Len, to my sister, and to the doctor.

"Then, it seemed as if I were somewhere else. But I could still hear the conversation they were having. Len was screaming that I couldn't leave him now. He had been having problems, and I had helped him. He kept screaming that I couldn't leave, I couldn't die. He was pulling on my sister and crying.

"I was in a place where I didn't feel . . . it wasn't like I was physical. I could still hear them, though. It wasn't like I was floating around, like in ghost stories. It's that I was still there, like a presence, and I was feeling relieved. There was no pain, but no . . . just not physical.

"I remember light, everything was very light. And very, very—like relief. But I kept hearing Len's voice, and he was crying for me to come back.

"Then I remember going and getting into my body, and I don't remember anything after that. I was in a coma for seven days. After they revived me I was unable to remember any of the period that I was in the coma. The doctors were extremely shocked when I came out of the coma and there was no brain damage. So that's what happened."

Further Examination of the Experience

"Okay Jackie, let me ask you a few questions. When you were out of your body, how did it feel?"

"It felt like I had no weight."

"Did it feel good or bad?"

"It felt good—I felt free."

"Can you describe the light?"

"It was everywhere. It was just light, it was . . ."

"What color was it?"

"Like a pale blue."

"Were you in it or was it off in the distance?"

"No, I was in it. It was all around me."

"Did the experience feel real, while you were there, or did it feel like a dream?"

"No, it was real. I remember feeling that Len and my sister were pulling me back. Like I couldn't leave. I had an opportunity to leave—"

"Oh, you felt as if you could leave?"

"Yes I did. I think I could have, I think I could have left. I think they pulled me back."

"Did you want to come back?"

"No. . . . I guess I did." Jackie laughed as she considered the question. "I guess I did. You know, I was really, really close to him, and I felt like I was abandoning him. So I felt like, . . . I guess I'd better come back. I was at a point, though, where I could have left. I felt that I had to make a decision."

"Did you have any feeling about where you might have gone if you had made the decision to go?"

"To a higher plain. I felt like . . . I didn't feel in danger at all, there was no peril. I felt that I was headed toward happiness—beyond happiness, euphoria.

"Did you ever tell anyone about your experience?"

"Yes, I told Len after it happened. At first he didn't believe me, he just said, 'oh, sure.' Then I told him of the detailed conversation he had with the hospital people about signing papers and the later conversation with the doctor and my sister. That convinced him. He said there was no way that I could have known what he said unless I had been there. He was the only person who ever believed me."

A Friend Commits Suicide

"Another strange thing happened recently. My friend, Len, died; he committed suicide. And I truly believe he came here right after he died. We were inseparable for years and years. He was my best friend from grade school. We had come from similar backgrounds, broken homes and things like that, and he had other problems. He never had a supportive family, and it was too much—he drank.

"It happened last Labor Day, in September, and the coroner later told me the estimated time of death. At that time I was working on my computer here at home, and . . . all of a sudden, at the exact time of his death, a door slammed in another room. None of the windows were open, or anything, and I had this really funny feeling that he was right here with me.

"I don't think that he could leave this . . . I think he was really troubled and couldn't leave. I've never been troubled by things. I've had a hard life, but I've had a happy life. I've never hated anybody, and I've always felt that I would have a good place to go after this life. But my friend hated everybody. I think his grief kept him here."

"It's too bad that he felt that way, Jackie. I'm sure you helped him all you could. On a separate issue, have you ever read anything on near-death experiences, such as what you experienced?"

"No. Most books are in text form and I don't like to read text."

"Has the experience changed your religious beliefs at all?"

"A little. But I've always been spiritual; I descended from the Irish. I've always been Christian."

"Do you belong to any formal religion?"

"Not now, but I was raised Unitarian Universalist. They teach theology from all perspectives and tell you to look inside yourself and make your choices."

"Has your feeling about death changed?"

"Before the experience I wasn't sure if there was something beyond death. Now I know that there is something beyond this life. This is not the end."

Doris

Problems in the Navy

Carol and I visited Doris and her brother at their mobile home in West Jordan, Utah in the spring of 1991. Doris explained that she was born in Utah in 1921, but her parents moved to Iowa shortly after she was born. She was raised in Iowa until she was fifteen, during the Great Depression, when she had to leave home.

When she was twenty years old, during World War II, Doris joined the Navy. She was stationed in Washington D.C.

Doris began telling of her experience: "During my early life I had been told by my Dad that I was stupid. When I got in the Navy and I took some tests I found out that wasn't true. The Navy tests showed that I had an IQ at the college level. That made me feel great.

"I got stationed in Washington, D.C., in 1943, in Communications. I was running a decoding machine, and it was boring—I wanted to be an aviation mechanic. I put in for the necessary military school but, it turned out, my tested mechanical aptitude was too low, so they didn't accept me.

"They had taken me out of the secret decoding work, and the only place they had available was the mess hall. After finding out that I really had a brain, to be put in the mess hall just did me in. I was so furious that I decided I was getting out of the service.

"Back in those days you didn't get out easily. I tried to think of ways to get out, and I finally came up with the idea of not eating. My not-eating campaign started on Christmas day. I went through the line and didn't pick up any food. Someone noticed, and they sent me to the Captain's office.

"He asked me what I was doing. I told him I was mad at the Navy and I wanted out. I informed him that I wouldn't eat. He sent me to the doctor, and she gave me a bottle of pink medicine—I later threw it out and continued my non-eating campaign."

Looking Down on Body Which Continues to Walk

"I didn't eat for fourteen days. On the eleventh day, after I finished my duty with the spuds, I was walking back to my bunk and as I passed a cinder-block wall, all of a sudden, within the snap of a finger, I found myself high above my body. My body continued to walk below me.

"Naturally, I went into shock. I never had expected anything like that. I had never even heard of it. It took me at least a minute to get hold of myself. In the meantime my body kept right on walking below me.

"When I got hold of myself I figured I had to do something about it. I thought: *I just can't stay up here in the air with my body below me.* I came down to my body, which was walking, and I hovered in front of it.

"As I hovered there, with my body walking toward me, I studied the head and shoulders to try and figure out a way to return to my body. I almost despaired because I couldn't see any way to get back in. Suddenly, like the snap of a finger, I was back. That's all there was to it."

"How did you feel when you were out?" I asked.

"Light, very light. I didn't look around or anything when I was out; I was in shock. I was stunned—I just couldn't believe that that was where I was. I wanted out of the Navy, not out of my body."

"Did you hear any voices, or anything of that sort?"

"No. Nobody was around. I could see the cinder-block wall below me, the sidewalk, and the landscape."

"Did you have a feeling of peace?"

"If I did I didn't notice."

"How long were you out?"

"Two minutes at the most, maybe three."

"And your body was walking along during this period?"

"I could see it, it didn't miss a step. I apparently had control of it, but I don't know how."

"When you got back in, did you have any ill effects?"

"No. Within three days I stopped my diet, when the Navy agreed to let me out with an honorable discharge."

"You got out of the Navy then?"

"No, I decided to stay in. I guess all I wanted was my own way. I stayed in and served my one-and-a-half years."

"Has that out-of-body experience affected your thinking?"

"Well, I know that it's no big deal to get out of your body. And I've read a lot of books on the subject since the experience happened. I also know that the person that is *you* is the spirit inside of your body."

"So you believe it was your spirit that was out?"

"Oh, yes."

"And you think your experience was real, not a dream or anything like that?"

"It was no dream. You don't dream while you're walking down the street."

"Do you think there is a life after death?"

"You bet I do. I don't even think—I know. And there is a God."

"Do you have any messages to leave for others?"

"I'm not one to advise other people, but I think what we do here is pretty important."

Maureen Daniels—Paroxysmal Hemicrania

Maureen Daniels and her husband Todd were waiting for Carol and me in their apartment in Murray, Utah on a lovely spring evening in 1991. They were a young couple, obviously very much in love, with enthusiasm for life and for each other. They had been married since the previous September, and they were expecting a baby in the next September. Maureen was a trim blonde with freckles.

Maureen indicated that she was born in 1960, in a suburb of Boston, to an Irish-Catholic family with six children. She was raised in a large, close-knit family, in a small town—she had 36 first cousins living near her. She moved to San Francisco when she was 21, by putting her finger on a map, to become more independent.

She began telling of her experience: "It was August, 1983, in Arlington, Massachusetts, and I was in a situation where I was running after a car that had hit my cousin's car, along Massachusetts Avenue.

All of a sudden I got a piercing pain in my head. It was so severe it pretty much put me out and they got an ambulance."

"You hadn't been hit, or anything, had you?" I asked.

"No. At first they thought it was an aneurism but it turned out to be chronic paroxysmal hemicrania. It's a nerve disorder of the brain which is in the pain center of the brain. It sends false pain signals. There actually is no pain, but the pain center tells you there is. The only methods they have for treating it are surgery, which I declined because of the risks, or morphine.

"While I was in the hospital, for two weeks, I got regular morphine injections. The nurses felt bad for me, with the pain which I had, and I think they got off schedule with the injections. I was being transferred to Mount Auburn Hospital in Cambridge, and they must have given me tons of morphine to make the drive. My parents and brother and sister were with me during the transfer.

"While I was in the elevator of Mount Auburn to go to my room, they code ninety-nined me. I could hear them announce the code ninety-nine, and I could feel them running with me. After that I don't remember what they did with me. My parents told me later—they were with me in the elevator."

Feelings of Love—A Visit by Deceased Grandparents

"The voices faded from my consciousness. Then there was . . . I wouldn't say there was music, but there was a knowing of . . . of a calm sound. Not unlike waves, or a seashore, which I frequently went to. It was as if there were a beach kind of sound. And there was a feeling of brightness, not necessarily a bright light, but a feeling of being surrounded by love.

"Approaching me from the front, and I recognized them immediately, were my grandparents. My grandfather had died in 1968, and my grandmother had died three months before the incident, in May, 1983. We grew up in a duplex with them, and I was very close to them. It really hurt when my grandmother died.

"They approached me. I knew that it was them, but they weren't old as my grandparents had been. They walked very upright, with no arthritis, and with no wrinkles—but I could tell that they were my grandparents. They came, and they didn't physically embrace me, but I felt embraced by them.

"They greeted me, and loved me, and then they started talking between themselves. They weren't arguing, but they were having a conversation. My grandfather was telling my grandmother, Mary, that I couldn't stay. She was very excited that I was there. She couldn't wait to have me with them, and to be with me again.

"My grandfather kept saying: 'No, Mary, she can't stay now. It's not her time to stay.'

"It felt like a long time that they talked back and forth with each other. Grandmother finally said: 'He's right. It's not your time, but we will see you again.'

"The next thing I remember was getting mouth-to-mouth resuscitation. That's about all I remember."

Final Thoughts About Maureen's Experience

"Well, Maureen, that was a choice experience. Let me ask you some questions about it. What did you feel like when you left your body?"

"A knowing. A calmness—it wasn't a fear at all."

"You used the word, music. Why did you use that word?"

"I guess because I like music and it calms me. I felt calm."

"You also used the word love, even before you saw your grandparents. Was that what you felt?"

"Yes, I felt it in the brightness. I didn't actually see a light source, but it was a brightness."

"What did your body feel like when you were out?"

"It felt very light. I don't really remember walking, I remember *being*. I don't remember floating. When I first saw them they were walking, and I saw them on a surface. I was on the same plane with them."

"What kind of clothes were your grandparents wearing?"

"They had on clothes that I remember them wearing in life. My grandmother was in a housecoat type of dress, and my grandfather was in his straight-legged pants with cuffs."

"Did you want to come back?"

"I felt very calm and happy there. I went along with what they said. I was happy to see my grandmother and, I think, I would have been happy to stay with her. I felt that happiness."

"Did you have a feeling for why it was you should come back?"

"Only that they told me it wasn't meant to be at that time. They told me it was all right to come back, and that they would see me later when this happened again."

"So was it their decision, or your decision to come back?"

"They told me, and then I agreed."

"You said there was a feeling of knowing. What did you mean by that?"

"I don't want to say all knowing, but . . . but it was a feeling of knowing what was going on. I really didn't question what was going on. I had a feeling that it was right, that this was a very normal happening."

"Were you glad to get back?"

"Yes, I felt this joy. I couldn't wait to talk to my mother, her sisters, and her brother."

"Did you feel pain when you got back?"

"Not immediately. But then later the pain came back to my head."

"Did you tell the story, immediately, to your parents and your family, and did they believe you?"

"Yes."

"Did it feel like a real experience, or was it more like a dream or a hallucination?"

"I questioned it, but it felt too real to be a dream or a hallucination. It was very real. It was more real than this life. I would say that it was something which there was no question about—there was no question that this took place and happened."

"Has the experience affected your religious, or other feelings?"

"There is no fear . . . I can't really say that I was ever fearful of death, and I won't say that I'm looking forward to it. I have a lot to do here. But when it does come, I know that my grandparents are there waiting for me."

"What is it that you think you have to do?"

"Have my baby. I would have thirteen of them if I could." Maureen laughed as she thought of the prospects for future children. Then she commented: "I feel I have a lot to accomplish here—with a family—and to leave behind."

"Do you believe in a life after death and in a God?"

"Both. I believe in God and that there is a life after death."

"Do you have any messages to leave for others?"

"That there is a lot of beauty out there. I think each of us have our own beauty, and I believe that we each experience our own beauty after death."

"You say there is a lot of beauty out there and after death. Did you see anything, in your experience, to lead you to believe that that was true?"

"I didn't see anything, but I felt it. I think it's that all knowing feeling that I had."

"When you saw your grandparents, did you see anything of the environment they were in?"

"It was just this bright . . . but I felt as though they had come from an environment . . . I wouldn't say that this was a way station, or whatever, but I felt it was something so that I wasn't put into a situation immediately. It seemed that we were in a place which was somewhat of a way station."

Chapter 10

A LIFE'S REVIEW
MIDST THE STARS

John Stirling—A Fascinating Man

I first met John Stirling on a beautiful spring day in 1991, up Emigration Canyon, northeast of Salt Lake City. Fresh greenery was evident throughout the canyon, and the sky was a cobalt blue with puffy white cumulus clouds drifting across the heavens. It was a good day to talk about eternity.

John's voice was cheerful, and full of the joy of life over the telephone, but I wasn't prepared for the great bear of a man who greeted me that day. I had pulled into his place, which had many automobiles in various stages of disrepair in front, and I walked to a shop area with the sounds of car repair machinery emanating from within. I knocked timidly on the door, and a voice responded.

A burly man with long hair, a beard, and dirt spread over him from the work he had been doing, greeted me. His smiling eyes repudiated his gruff appearance. As John's interview proceeded, and as John's emotions became evident, I concluded that he wasn't the gruff individual that he appeared to be—he was a marshmallow with a great love for people.

John invited me to sit on a chair, and he sat adjacent to me; we began our conversation sitting in the great outdoors of the Wasatch Mountains. John told me he was born in 1953 in Salt Lake City, where he was raised in a family consisting of his father, his mother, and three older sisters. He went to high school in Salt Lake City, and he went to college, for three terms, to study art. He had traveled extensively.

A Personal Crisis and a Motorcycle Accident

John began: "In September 1978 my wife left me and took my son. She wouldn't let me see him for quite a long time, many months, and I was pretty miserable. Through the whole thing I didn't want a divorce, I wanted to get back together with her, but she didn't want to get back with me. She was angry, inside, and couldn't pinpoint reasons for it. At the time my son was two years old.

"I was having a rough go of life in general. I was tired of it, pretty sick of living. I bought a motorcycle, a Yamaha 650, to have something to do at nights when I was bored or lonely; because I don't watch TV. I used to drive through the canyons for diversion, to think about things, and to relax.

"One Friday, during the day, I had a really strange feeling. I called everyone I knew that was close to me. I couldn't explain my conversations with them, but during each conversation I told them I was going somewhere. I didn't know where, and they would ask me where I was going. I said I didn't know—I told them I might go to Denver. I also told them that I might not talk to them again for a long time.

"I was really agitated and nervous all day. I called my mother and told her that I didn't know where I was going, but I thought I would be leaving on a trip somewhere. I said I would talk to her when I knew where I was going. As the day went on I had mood swings, and I was filled with a lot of confusion. I tried to figure out where I was going.

"A friend came over to visit and we talked for awhile. I thought, with him there, I would be able to determine where I was going—so I could call the airport and book a flight—if I was flying. We ended up getting on my motorcycle and going for a ride up to the cafe in Emigration Canyon.

"We spent an hour-and-a-half or so at the cafe; we had some beer, and we left and began coming down the canyon. I used to race motorcycles, so I knew pretty well what they would do under different circumstances. As we came down the canyon, we hit a washout in the road, where the water had washed out under the road, and there was a bump.

"With the combined weight of my friend and myself, and at the speed we were traveling, the bump bounced the motorcycle off the road and into the gravel. It was about eleven-thirty at night, and as I fought for control in the dark I considered heading the motorcycle up the mountain instead of staying in the gravel. I opted to do that, to go up the mountain, so that gravity would slow us down.

"We headed up the mountain a short distance, then I saw that the mountain had been discontinued where road work had been performed. I yelled at my friend, that he had to get off. We were still going fast—about fifty-five, and he wouldn't get off. I leaned back and knocked him off.

"I then hit the rock, where it had been blown away, and I thought to myself: *Well this is it*. The right side of my body crashed into the rock where it had been, kind of, curved. The bike rolled over on top of me and stuck the rear view mirror on the top of my head—I didn't have a helmet on. Then the bike continued to tumble and ended up about two-hundred-and-fifty feet away."

Out-of-Body in the Stars

"I remember the crash and the bike tumbling, then I remember lying there, for just a split second, and thinking: *Well this is it, I'm leaving*. I turned around and looked, and I saw a body that seemed familiar. It looked like me, but I had no emotional involvement with the body laying there.

"I then felt great relief and joy—that I was leaving, and that I didn't have to endure, any more, the pain of the divorce, or the pain of missing my child. So I immediately, without any further thinking about it, took off. Because it was what I had been wishing would happen.

"I could feel an ability in my spirit body to move at great speed, and I wanted to get where I was going as quickly as possible. I was going to a place that I *knew*. It was the place that I had *come* from. I wanted to get there as quickly as possible.

"I started traveling fairly slowly, in real time, when I first started. Then, as I got farther away from earth I traveled much faster. The stars started to look like the stars in 'Star Wars,' with a long trail, because of my speed.

"A voice came to me, as I was traveling at that high rate of speed, and . . . and I was so peaceful and comfortable. All the emotional pain that I had been feeling was gone. I looked at my hand, and I saw the shape of a hand, but . . . but it had an aura around it. It wasn't the same hand as an earthly hand. There was an energy field that defined it.

"And the voice . . . the voice asked me if I was done. And I knew the voice and it was . . ." John had difficulty continuing as he wiped away the tears. "It was a comfortable voice—a voice full of love.

"I said: 'Yes, I'm done. I don't want to go back there. I don't ever want to go back there.' The voice asked me a second time: 'Are you done?' And I said: 'Yes, I'm done. I don't want to go back.' The voice asked me a third time if I was done, and again I said that I was.

"Then the voice said: 'Well, let's look at your life.' And then I saw . . . I saw my life flashed before my eyes. Everything from when I was a child up to the present time. And every emotion that I had during my life, when I saw the scene, I felt the same emotion. I could feel the reasons that I did things as I saw the scenes unfold.

"I felt very comfortable with my life as I looked at it. It was all in color and three dimensional, and it flashed in a circle as if it were a deck of cards. I felt very comfortable that I would not have to come back to earth.

"The review continued until it came to the previous Friday, when I had had my son over, on Friday night. And it . . . the review traveled all the way up to that time.

"The scene, you can call it a card that came up for me to see, or, the vision that came to my view, it . . . my eyes locked onto that night. And the life review stopped. When that Friday scene first flashed up it looked as if it was going to go by, but when my eyes locked on it, then I knew I had to come back.

"So I . . . I said yes I would come back. Because I knew I had to raise my son as best I could. There was no further contact with the voice after I said I would return. I came back to my body so much faster than when I left. It was almost instantaneous. I can remember reversing in space and then waking up in my body."

Return

"The first thought that came to me when I was back in my body was that I had to find Richard, my friend who was on the motorcycle with me. So I stood up and started screaming for him. He answered and came down. When he saw me his face showed fear. I asked him to show me where he was hurt. He had scraped his elbow and his shin a little bit.

"I told him I would go get some help from one of the houses in the canyon. He told me to stay put and he would go get the help. I told him that he should stay, since he was hurt, and I raised my hand to brush away what I thought was sweat from my eyes. I saw that the sweat was actually blood—then I looked closer at my arm. My hand was at a right angle to it.

"At that point I told him: 'Well, okay, I guess I'm hurt worse than you. You go get some help.' As he left, and I waited, I looked a little closer at myself. I saw that both of my feet were folded underneath at the ankles—I was walking on my ankles. I didn't feel any pain at all. I had the same peace with me, that everything would be okay, as I'd had when I first left my body.

"A girl came up, dressed in white, in a Volkswagen. She said that she had just gotten off from work, and she was a nurse. She told me to sit on her car. So that's what I did while I waited for Richard to come back with help.

"The girl and I talked together. I don't remember what she said, very much, but suddenly my friend was there. He said that he had called the ambulance, and they were on the way. And . . . and I don't know what happened to the girl in white who came in the Volkswagen. I looked for her for a long time after that, and I asked people in the canyon if they had ever known her. No one knew anything about her. She told me that she lived in the canyon.

"That's pretty much what happened."

Further Analysis of John's Experience

"That was a remarkable experience, John. Let me ask you a few questions. When you went out of your body, did you see any light or anything of that sort?"

"Not that I can recall. At that point my main concern was getting out of here as quickly as possible. I was familiar with where I was, and I knew that . . ."

"So you had a feeling that you had been there before?"

"Oh, I knew. Yes, I knew—there was no doubt in my mind. And I wanted to get out of here as quickly as possible."

"You say you knew where you were. Did you have a feeling of knowing anything else?"

"I had an internal knowledge of where I was going."

"Did you have knowledge of other things?"

"Yes. I had an expanded consciousness. It wasn't like an earthly book-type knowledge. It was a consciousness that was larger, more spiritual."

"When you heard the voice, did you see anybody; or was it just a feeling of a presence?"

"I didn't see anyone."

"You felt, though, that you knew the individual?"

"Oh, yes."

"Do you know who it was, now?"

"Well, I would say it was Jesus Christ."

"You didn't have a feeling, then, that that was the case—or did you feel, then, that it was Christ?"

"Yes, I did."

"When you communicated with Him, was it vocal communication?"

"It was not a verbal type of communication. It was a communication within. There's something when you are there. . . . When you are on earth you may have all sorts of thoughts running through your mind, or all sorts of confusion in you mind, all at the same time. There, you don't feel that way. You are more at peace, and you are more sensory. Communication was within me and was given back the same way, without the spoken word."

The Life's Review

"The life's review came as a shock. When I heard the voice say: 'Well, let's see your life,' I didn't know how it would happen. It was totally unexpected, and it was right there in my view. It was as if both the voice and I were viewing it—and both of us could feel it as well as visually see it."

"Was there judgement in the voice?"

"Not at all. It was the same feeling you would get in a heart-to-heart conversation with a loving father about anything that concerned you. Not that judgement would be involved, but that you would both view the circumstances, see the way things were, and go on from there."

"So it was a teaching experience more than a judgmental experience?"

"It wasn't judgmental. I didn't know that I was coming back so I didn't realize, at the time, that it was a teaching experience."

"You mentioned that when you saw different events from your life you could also feel the emotions associated with those events. Did you understand that the voice also felt those emotions?"

"I felt, inside, that we both felt the emotions. As I recall, the life review started when I was two or three years old. The review, starting from that time, showed all the daily events, all the people involved, as I lived through the events. There were the funny times, the sad times, and my concerns at the time—for my age.

"So that when I was five, ten, or fifteen years old, for the wisdom I had at that age, I felt the same kind of emotions as I had when I was that age. I also knew where I was at, spiritually, for that given age. That's one of the reasons I felt comfortable with my life's review. Because I felt as if I really had tried as hard as I could, in accordance with what I knew at that age."

"Some people who have had this type of life's review indicated that they also felt, when they had done something good for someone, or when they had hurt someone, the emotions of that individual. Did you feel anything like that?"

"Yes. When I was younger I was a meek and timid kid, and I didn't do many things that would create a flash-back for me—adverse things that I would feel. My father died when I was a teen-ager, though, and I got kind of bitter and angry. Then I did do some things to hurt other people. I saw those events and felt the effect on the people. I also felt, at the time, my own bitterness."

"When you did something to help someone did you feel their response to that as well?"

"Yes. I could feel the joy and the happiness as well as the pain, depending upon the circumstances."

"When your father died, did you feel the pain again?"

"Yes. I felt the pain again, but it was a comfortable pain this time. It wasn't the hollow loss that it was the first time."

"Why was it more comfortable?"

"Because I was in eternity—and I knew it. And I knew that my father was there also."

"But you didn't see your father, did you?"

"No. After the experience, and I've thought much about it, I wondered why I was stopped midway to my destination. The conclusion that I came to is that if I had been allowed to go all the way, to be in the presence of the Savior, or to be greeted by my father, I would not have returned. I know that would have been true."

"As you saw the life's review unfold, did it seem as if it took a long time?"

"Not at all."

"But there were twenty-five years which you went through. That's a lot of years. How could you see that in such a short time?"

"Yes, it was a lot of years. But it just . . . it's hard to describe. It unfolded, it was large, it was three-dimensional, it was right in my view, I didn't have to turn my head or anything, and it just exploded right there. It was as if it were the ultimate movie—three dimensional, with feeling and color."

"All-in-all, though, you felt it was a comfortable experience?"

"Oh yes. I had worried much of my life about things that I did, that I might be doing things that would give me a failing grade in life. All the little things that I did wrong. In viewing my life, though, it was different than that viewpoint."

Other Thoughts

"You say that you saw an aura around your hand when you looked at it. Was that aura all over your body as far as you could tell?"

"Yes."

"How did your spirit body feel when you were out of your physical body?"

"Peaceful, calm, real, existing . . . ."

"Okay, so it didn't feel like a dream?"

"No."

"Did it feel as real as any experience in this life?"

"Yes, even more real."

"Has the experience changed your feelings about death?"

"It has changed my feelings about life more than it has about death."

"In what way?"

"It's the way I feel about people, now, and life in general—that we are all part of the same plan. We are all part of the same program; in that the greatest value, for any of us, is to try and help another person in their situation. We shouldn't interfere with others negatively, nor should we hurt another person. We should not, in any way, detract from a life. Rather we should add to other people's lives."

"When you were told that you had to come back, you really didn't want to, I take it?"

"I wasn't told to come back. I saw my son come up in the life's review and I knew, when my eyes locked on him, that I had to come back. And I said I would come back. I wasn't told to—I knew I had to."

"So it was your choice to come back, not somebody else's?"

"Oh yes. I saw him and knew I had to come back. I knew that I wasn't done with this life."

"As a result of the experience, have your religious feelings changed?"

"Yes."

"In what way?"

"I was raised thinking, maybe, that God loved certain individuals more than others. Or that he cared about certain individuals more than others depending upon how they lived. I didn't find that to be true.

"I found that his love was extended to everyone, all the time. And that he understood why we are what we are, and why we are going through what we are going through. I found that we are all the same in the volume of his love. His love is not judgmental. He wouldn't think, for example, because we don't have the great amount of knowledge that he does, or the great strength that he does, that we are bad. His love is extended to everyone."

Physical Recovery

"Regarding your story, you left us with yourself sitting on the Volkswagen when your friend came back. What happened then?"

"I was taken to the emergency room of St. Mark's Hospital, and I was in great spirits. The doctor who received me was gruff and angry. He made it plainly clear that he didn't like motorcycles, and the accidents from them, and he wasn't going to put up with my accident very easily, either.

"The nurses who came in had to cut all my clothes off, with scissors, because I had road rash almost everywhere. I teased the nurses, as I saw their concerned faces, and I smiled and laughed at them. At that point my spirits were still elevated, and I could feel no pain.

"They put me under an anesthetic, after awhile, to reset the broken bones, and to try and get the rest of the gravel out of my skin. When I woke the next morning, it kind of settled on me, the situation that my physical body was really in. I hadn't noticed up to that time.

"I sat up in bed, and it was difficult because the bandages from the broken bones rubbed on the skin which I didn't have. I looked in the mirror. That was the first awareness I had of how bad the accident had really been. The skin had been ground off the whole right side of my face, from the center of the face outward, where I had hit the sandstone rocks. My face was all yellow, and red, and puffy, with no eyebrow, and I thought: *Boy, I've really done it this time.*" John laughed as he thought about it.

"I still didn't really care, because the peace resided within me, and the comforting feeling that everything would be okay. It resided in my soul. For the amount of damage that my body had sustained the pain was very little. I was in intensive care for three-and-one-half weeks. One of my friends who came in to see me shortly after the accident nearly fainted. I tried to joke with him but he had to leave the room. A broken beer bottle had gouged a gash in my face from top to bottom, as well as the grinding from the rocks.

"After three-and-one-half weeks my skin had all grown back, and I looked normal. There were hardly any scars that could be seen. I had to use a wheelchair and a walker for awhile until my broken bones healed."

"How is your relationship with your son doing now?"

"Very good. I see him every other weekend. For years I saw him every weekend. He's fourteen now and a great kid. We have had good times together, and we are very close."

A Final Message

"After the experience I went through, I had to read everything I could find in the scriptures and elsewhere to determine if the teachings agreed with what I saw. I found that the scriptures were true, but too many times our priorities are mixed up. We forget the lessons from the New Testament—to love our neighbor, and to do all the other positive things written there.

"We get carried away with the temporal aspects of our own situations. We become involved in seeking money, or newer cars, or nicer clothes, or something, and we forget the things that, I believe, the Savior was trying to teach—concerning love and his way of love, his way of understanding. We should not judge our fellow beings, but we should love them, and serve them. Those were the teachings that He taught.

"There's another thing, too. Paul, in speaking to the Corinthians, and he was talking about our present place in eternity, and his comments were based on his extensive experiences, said: 'For now we see through a glass, darkly; but then face to face: now I know in part; but then shall I know even as also I am known.' It seems to me that this scripture sort of summarizes what happens in a near-death experience. I had expanded consciousness during the experience, I knew more than I did on earth, and I knew that I was known by the voice; by my Savior.

"But after the experience, when I came back, I still saw through a glass darkly—the experience itself was largely indescribable in terms of my earthly experience. How wonderful it will be when we can, as Paul says, see Him face to face, and know as we are known."

Chapter 11

LEARNING EXPERIENCES

Elizabeth Marie

She was waiting in the beautiful old home of her mother when Carol and I visited her in the spring of 1993. Elizabeth was a shy young blonde lady who agreed to be interviewed after we met her at a local meeting of the International Association for Near Death Studies (IANDS). Her mother joined us after we exchanged greetings, and she seemed quite interested in listening to her daughter's interview.

Elizabeth was born in December 1964 in American Fork, Utah. Her upbringing was in Pleasant Grove, Utah, and she had two brothers and four sisters. She graduated from high school in Pleasant Grove. On a rock-climbing activity with some friends, she met her future husband. At the time of our visit, she and her husband had four children.

A Youthful Mistake

Elizabeth began to tell her story: "When I was fourteen years old, I got involved with drugs. On one particular day I was smoking marijuana with a boy I knew, and I accidently took a drug overdose. Without my knowledge the marijuana had been dosed with opium. The boy and I were having a contest to see who could smoke the greater amount. He passed out, and when he did I went in the house and managed to get back to my room.

"Upon reaching my room I lay down on my bed—I was stoned. After a time I noticed that I was looking down on myself on the bed. My immediate thought was: *I'm in trouble!*"

126

An Astonishing Experience—Indescribable Love

"There was no sensation of still being under the influence of the drug; my mind was clear. I knew exactly what had happened. The perspective I had was that of a fourteen-year-old, knowing I was in trouble, and I was very upset. My next thought was: *How will I ever explain this one to my parents? Mom will really be upset.*

"While in this disturbed state I found myself drawn into a tunnel and through it at a rapid rate of speed. Upon reaching the end of the tunnel I entered a room with many people in it—people sitting on chairs, and laughing at me. They were laughing because I was trying to hide. The embarrassment I felt as a fourteen-year-old—for having done what I did—was severe. Since there was no place to hide I was doing the best I could by crouching down and putting my head on my knees.

"Someone called my name, and I looked to see who it was. Everyone that had been in the room was gone, and I could see a light in the distance coming toward me. It was a very bright light. When the light got close to me He put His arms around me. And He . . . " Elizabeth was unable to continue for a moment while her mother got some Kleenex. When she regained her composure, I asked: "He? . . ."

"Yes. He put his arms around me and asked me if I had known that what I did was wrong. I told Him that yes, I had known it was wrong.

"The amount of remorse I had, I'd never felt before. It was remorse over what I had done. I felt so sorry; there was a deep disappointment over my previous activities. The feelings of remorse and disappointment were pure feelings that permeated my body.

"I was asked if I had known what was right and wrong—and I had. My knowledge, in the presence of Him, was that I couldn't progress from the place I had positioned myself. Knowing that I was stopped in my progression, and feeling great remorse, I asked if I could return and help others to come back to Him. There was an intense desire within me to amend for the pain and suffering that I had caused others.

"The love I felt from Him during this period was extremely intense. Love traveled from my toes to my head, filling my entire body. There are no words that can adequately describe that love. It was a fatherly type of love, and I knew that He was pleased when I acknowledged my sins and asked if I could amend for them.

"He held me in His arms the whole time, and . . . and the feelings were so intense. The love I felt was beyond belief. And while I was embraced by Him and felt of His great love, He asked me if I would help others to come back to Him. I said I would.

"Since my experience, though, I haven't known who it was that I was supposed to help. I've wondered if it was one person, or many persons. I understood that it was to help someone, or several people, who had lost their way, to return to His presence, but I still don't know who they are.

"We had hugged each other for a while, when I knew that I was to return—I was put back in my body, although I don't remember that event. That was the end of the experience."

Questions of Elizabeth Marie

Elizabeth agreed that I could ask questions of her experience. I began: "When you first found yourself out of your body, how did you feel?"

"I felt okay, but I was concerned because of what I had done."

"Did it feel like a dream, a hallucination, or a drug induced experience?"

"Heavens, no. It was a real experience, not like the stupor I had previously been in from the drugs. The drugs depressed my system and caused me to die. My senses during the out-of-body experience were alert and awake."

"And you could see your physical body lying there?"

"Yes. The picture of my body lying there, and the position it was in, is still vivid in my mind."

"Why did you call the next part of your experience a tunnel?"

"It was round, and I was moved through it very rapidly. There was a sound . . . like wind rushing by me."

"Did you feel alone in the tunnel?"

"There was no fear, and there was a light at the end of the tunnel. The sides of the tunnel, though, had some light. I could see the walls. It was big enough that if I had put my arms out they wouldn't have touched the walls."

"Did you have arms?"

"Yes."

"Did you see them?"

"Yes. My feet and my hands were visible to me."

"What did your hands look like?"

"Just like my hands do now. There was a white robe that covered my arms down to my wrists. The robe started at my neck and went to my ankles—it was a pure white. There are no words to describe that kind of white."

"When you came out of the tunnel and entered the room, did you know the people that were there?"

"I'm not sure. I didn't really want to know them because of my feelings of embarrassment. They seemed to think it was funny that I was trying to hide."

"Why were you so embarrassed?"

"It was because of what I had done—and because of the marks on my robe."

"What marks?"

"The robe I was wearing was white, a pure white, but it had black spots on it."

"Where were the spots, and why did they bother you?"

"There were several of them on my left side, down to my ankle. They bothered me because I knew that they represented some of the things I had done wrong. When I bent down I was trying to hide them, and that's what the people were laughing about. There was no way I could hide them."

"How were the people dressed?"

"They were also in white."

"Could you see the people very well?"

"Yes. There was this one person in particular that I remember."

"Describe that person, if you can."

"It was a male, with dark hair, and he had pointed at me."

"How old were the people?"

"They all seemed to be . . . gosh, about . . . there didn't seem to be any age to them, except the people seemed young."

"Describe the light in the room."

"It was light like in the tunnel. It was bright, but not nearly as bright as the light that came after He called my name."

"Where did the bright light come from?"

"It was high up and distant when I first saw it. The room boundaries seemed to disappear."

"What did the light look like?"

"When it got close to me, it was brighter than the sun. The sun is yellow, but the light was white. Yet I could look at it with my eyes."

"What happened to the light?"

"It came down and stood a few inches in front of me. It was a man."

"There was a man in the light, then?"

"I didn't see a man, but I knew He was there."

"Who was He?"

"It was Jesus."

"How did you know it was Jesus?"

"I just did." Elizabeth paused for a period to control her emotions. She continued: "I don't have words for it, but I knew it was He."

"You felt Him embrace you?"

"Yes. He put His arms around me and hugged me, just as my father would. The feelings I had at that point were extremely intense. My children and my parents, for example, I love with all my heart. Yet in this life I couldn't produce a small portion of what I felt in His presence. The love was a mutual feeling between us, and it went through my whole body."

"Did you have a life's review?"

"When He asked me if I knew the things I did wrong, they were brought back to my memory with full emotion. There was a clear understanding of each wrong event, and I felt remorse. The memories were very painful."

"What was His reaction when you remembered each event?"

"There was just love coming from Him. The sorrowful feelings were coming from me."

"In a sense, then, you were your own worst judge?"

"That's true, and it was extremely painful. It was clear to me what I had done wrong, and I suffered emotional pain as the memories came to me."

"Did you ask to come back, or were you told to come back?"

"I knew that He wanted me to, and I asked if I could. It was my choice, though; I could have opted to stay."

"How did you know he wanted you to return to this life?"

"By the feeling I had."

"How did He and you communicate?"

"Through my mind. I didn't speak, and I know that He didn't speak with His mouth. It was completely through thought."

"Was it as clear as you and me talking?"

"It was clearer. There was no mistaking what either of us was saying—there was no possibility of misunderstanding."

"That was the end of your experience, then?"

"There was one other thing that happened, but I don't remember everything from it."

"Tell me what you remember."

"There was a tall window. It was made of a purple stone with marble marks in it. It was crystalline-clear, and it was beautiful. Light shone through it, but I couldn't see through it. While I was in this room with the window there was someone that I talked to."

"Do you remember what you talked about?"

"Part of what happened was taken from my memory. I remember that we were making hard, important decisions about my future life, but I can't remember what they were. I've tried, but it's as if I'm not supposed to remember everything."

"When you returned to your body, what was the next thing that you remember?"

"It was morning, and I was on my bed."

"How long do you think your experience took?"

"I don't know. I didn't really have a sense of time."

"How did you feel when you woke up?"

"I was fine, but the experience changed my life completely."

"How did it change your life?"

"My decision, at that point, was that I would not do the bad things I had previously done. There would be no drugs or other bad things. And I changed. Someone told me that I couldn't change overnight, but I did. Even my friends were from a different group."

"Did you tell anyone about the experience?"

"I tried telling one of the counselors in the bishopric, at the time, but he said it was a dream. I knew that wasn't true."

"Did you tell anyone else?"

"Not for a long time. The fear of ridicule prevented me from saying anything. Much later, I told my mom. About six years ago I told my husband."

"Did they believe you?"

Elizabeth looked at her mom and asked: "Did you believe me?" Her mother smiled and shook her head yes.

"Had you read anything about out-of-body experiences when you had your experience?"

"Not at that point. Not for several years. Even when I did hear about others having such experience, I was excited, but I didn't dare tell about my own experience."

"Why did you approach me for this interview?"

"I don't know. I just felt prompted to talk to you. It was difficult, though, because I remember the problems I had after my experience, and I didn't want to relive those feelings. Initially, for example, there was a period of depression—because I felt unloved. The love with Him was so great that every other form of love seemed weak in comparison. Nobody could come close to what He gave me. It took me a long time to overcome the longing for that type of love."

"Are there any other experiences of a similar nature that you have had?"

"I have had other out-of-body and spiritual experiences, but they were for different reasons."

"Tell me about them."

Other Spiritual and Out-of-body Experiences

"For the last ten years I have had a serious heart problem. My problem is the result of blood vessels that are too small to deliver the blood my heart needs. The doctors call it Syndrome-X, and there isn't much they can do for it except to treat me with pain killers. They put a pacemaker in me sometime ago to help my heart keep a normal rhythm.

"Whenever I exercise, or put my heart under any kind of stress, I feel pain. The pain is similar to what happens in a heart attack. In late 1991 and 1992 I was pregnant with my last child, and the pain with my heart became severe.

"One night, during my pregnancy, I became ill and the pain was really bad. Medication had been given to me by the doctor to ease the pain, but nothing seemed to help. At one point I despaired, not knowing what to do, and I prayed to our Heavenly Father for help. As I did, I looked up and there were three men in my room.

"The men stood there looking at me, and I had a feeling of peace. One of them whispered something in my ear and kissed me. It was a most comforting feeling, and my pain was gone. Then the men disappeared."

"Did you know who they were, Elizabeth?" I asked.

"I didn't know their names, but they seemed familiar to me."

"Do you know what the man whispered to you?"

"I don't remember, except that it made me feel good."

"Tell me about your other experiences."

"My baby was born in July 1992. The birth was difficult and I hemorrhaged badly—I lost about half of my blood. There were severe chest pains from my heart, and the doctors couldn't do much for me. Pain killers didn't work. It reached a point where I couldn't stand the pain.

"Suddenly a strange feeling came over me—and I knew what was going to happen. There was a floating feeling as I left my body and floated above it. All pain left me, and I had a wonderful, restful feeling of peace. It gave me sufficient respite that, when I returned to my body, I was able to cope. The experience lasted just a few moments, but the relief was marvelous."

"What were your other experiences?"

"There were a couple of times when I had brief out-of-body experiences—all related to my heart problem. On one occasion after I had my baby, when I was in severe pain, I felt myself leaving my body again. It kind of scared me, and I said to myself: *No!* That stopped it, and I haven't had any repeat experiences since then."

A Message for Others

"The initial experience I had was profound, and it changed my life forever. The love I felt there was beyond expression, and that love, or a portion of it, came back with me. Permeating every cell of my body was a feeling of love, a feeling of peace, and a relief from pain. Heavenly Father loved me with infinite love, despite the wrong things that I had done.

"An important message, therefore, is that we should be kind and help others. Since my experience I have found that it is easier for me to accept people for what they are. Even people whom others shun; to me, they are okay people. We can't know the circumstances that cause people to behave as they do, so we should accept and love them for the fact that all of them are children of God.

"And we should love Heavenly Father and keep His commandments. To the extent that we disobey Him we will feel intense emotional pain—as

I did. It is okay to make mistakes, though, if we learn from those mistakes and stop repeating them. He is a loving God, and He is willing to accept and forgive us if we reach out to Him."

Lori

It was a spring day in 1993 when Lori came to our home. She was a slight, dark-haired young lady with penetrating green eyes, and she had an intense manner of speaking. Her birthplace, in 1964, was Burley, Idaho, a small town in south-central Idaho. With two older sisters and a younger brother, Lori had a happy childhood with her family and with the horses that they kept.

Graduating from high school in 1983, Lori went two years to the College of Southern Idaho, in Twin Falls, where she took accounting. When she was young, she went to the Lutheran Church; in the sixth grade she converted to the Catholic Church, due to the influence of a friend. Lori had been married and had two boys, twelve and six years of age, at the time of our visit. She came to Salt Lake City in 1991 and was employed in the accounting department of a Salt Lake-based airline.

A Serious Illness

Lori began to tell her story: "At sixteen years of age, I had a child that was born with a partially cleft palate. Depression bothered me from the many pressures; school, work, and my child. Fortunately, I had a supportive family.

"Waking one morning I felt worse than usual, and I thought I had the flu. My back hurt badly, so I called in sick at work. Not wanting another doctor's bill, I didn't go to the doctor. By evening, when I went to the bathroom, I fell to the floor and couldn't get up.

"Someone, my mother or my girlfriend, found me and took me to the doctor. After a brief examination, he put me in the Cassia Memorial Hospital in Burley.

"During the period that I was in the hospital, I kept going in and out of consciousness. On several occasions I woke to find myself above my body, in the corner of the room, looking down on myself. There was a feeling of floating as I viewed myself. While I was in this elevated position

I remember thinking: *Why am I up in this corner?* Often, when I was up there, I saw a tall, handsome man sitting in a chair next to my bed, and I wondered who he was. Later I found that he was my sister's boyfriend.

"At times I would want to stay in my body, and I would feel vibrations. The entire bed seemed to move with me at one point. There was a part of me that wanted to stay, and there was another part that wanted to leave my body. I was kind of in and out. After the first time that I left my body, the intense pain I had felt in my back left me. There was no pain after that.

"One of the times when I was out of my body, I became conscious of another man in the room, not my sister's boyfriend, but another spirit-person. He had form, and I could feel his presence, but I couldn't recognize specific features. It was as if the being were in silhouette form; there was a feeling of peace associated with him.

"This spiritual being placed his hands on my chest—I could feel them—and there was a feeling of warmth. The emotional feeling associated with his presence was overwhelming. Every emotion I had was involved; every fear was released, every anger was removed, and every joy was magnified. There was an intense sense of peace. Then I felt my spirit returning to my body. The spirit-man seemed to be there for that purpose, and to give me a feeling of security and peace."

"Did you know who this spirit being was?" I asked Lori.

"At one point, I remember asking who he was, and he said that he was a spirit guide."

"Was that the main extent of your experience?"

"Yes."

"Did you feel yourself reentering your body?"

"There was this gigantic feeling of peace, and I felt myself going back. As I was returning, I had the exploding emotion feeling that I told you about."

"Were you out of your body for a long time?"

"A single event may not have been long, but I was in and out of my body over a period of days. Frequently, I found myself up near the corner of the room, looking down on me. This caused me to wonder what I was doing up there. And I wanted to come back."

"Did you have form and shape when you were out of your body?"

"Yes. That's the strange thing, I could see my body lying below, yet I could also see my hands and feet on my other body from my elevated position in the room."

"What did your spirit hands and feet look like?"

"Just like they do now. There was a bright beam of light around my spirit body. My spirit body was surrounded by . . . colors."

"What happened when you returned to your physical body?"

"After I returned, and after the emotional feeling, I remember waking up and feeling hungry."

"How long were you in the hospital?"

"Fourteen days."

"Did they tell you what your illness was?"

"There was a kidney infection, brought on by the flu, and I became dehydrated as I didn't replenish fluids. I got too sick to drink, and my kidneys failed to function properly."

"Were you okay when you left the hospital?"

"It took a couple of months to recover my strength—I had lost a lot of weight. Sleep helped me to recover during that period."

"Have you had other experiences of this nature?"

"During the two months that I was recovering my strength I had vivid dreams. One recurring dream was of a wise Indian man who came to help me.

"Several times during the recuperation time, it seemed that I started to leave my body again. There was vibration, and I could feel myself leaving. It was a frightening sensation—I consciously resisted it and pulled myself back into my body. For a time, even the coming of night frightened me.

"One series of out-of-body events was somewhat amusing. After my illness I stayed at my mother's house. Still recovering from my illness, I slept on the couch frequently. Almost every morning I would leave my body and go into the kitchen to see what time it was. Then, when I awoke I would say things such as: 'Mom, why did you let me sleep so late? It's eight o'clock already.'

"My mother, at first, insisted that I couldn't know the time. The clock was in a location in the kitchen where I couldn't possibly see it from my position on the couch. Later, my mother and sister would tease me if we were driving somewhere. They would ask me to send my eyes up the road and tell them how much farther we had to go. I couldn't, of course, do what they asked since these particular out-of-body events seemed to happen spontaneously while I was sleeping."

Other Out-of-Body Experiences

When we finished discussing Lori's near-death experience, I asked her if there were other occasions when she left her body. She said there were, and she began to explain what happened: "Sometime ago I was dating a young man, and I felt he was not being honest with me. When I went to sleep, one night, I was disturbed because I believed he had lied to me about where he was going.

"In the middle of the night I became aware that I was no longer in bed. To my surprise I found myself at a strange house. I could see the street signs, the address of the house, and the lights—and I saw my boyfriend in the house with another girl."

"Had you ever been to that address before?" I asked.

"Never."

"Did you accuse your boyfriend of being with the other girl?"

"The next day I confronted him with what I knew. I asked him who lived at that particular address."

"How did you explain your knowledge?"

"By a dream—I said it was a detailed dream."

"Was it a dream?"

"No."

"What was the reaction of your boyfriend?"

"He was very quiet, and he went white."

"Are there other similar experiences?"

"Yes. My mother and I have always been close, and after I moved here from Burley I was concerned about her. This one night I found myself by her bed, and she was crying. When I called her the next morning and asked her if she were all right, she said that she had cried all night. She said that she was sad because she missed me."

"Are there other experiences?"

"There were several smaller instances, and one that was about like these two, except that it was in a beautiful setting."

"Tell me about it."

"About six months ago, I had been angry and hateful toward a particular person. Knowing this was wrong, and that it was consuming me with hateful thoughts, I decided to get rid of the anger and hate and replace it with love. So I called the person and apologized.

"After I apologized, I felt much better. On a particular evening after going to sleep, a sense of peace filled me, and I felt myself leave my body. Awakening, I found myself soaring over a beautiful valley. It extended for miles, and it had long grass in it and extremely colorful flowers. The flowers were vivid reds, yellows, and golds."

"Was it daylight where you saw the field and the flowers?"

"Yes it was."

"Do you remember going back into your body?"

"Yes. When I returned to my room, the light was dim. It was just turning daylight. The thought that crossed my mind when I returned was that it would have been nice to stay in that beautiful place a little longer. Then, instantly, I was back in my body."

"Do you know where you were?"

"I have no idea, but it was gorgeous. The grass was longer than I had ever seen before."

"Were all of these out-of-body experiences after you had your near-death experience?"

"I think so. I'm not sure, but I believe they were after my experience. The more extensive ones certainly were."

"Have all of these out-of-body events been pleasant?"

"No. The one where I found my boyfriend with another girl wasn't pleasant. Also, when I was under stress, sometimes, I felt an evil presence. Pressure on my chest accompanied this evil feeling, and it was as if someone or something were trying to get me out of my body. These events were very frightening. During one of these episodes I remember that my mother couldn't wake me for a long time. On another one I heard a terrible growling noise."

"How did you combat these negative events?"

"By prayer. Prayer and peaceful, pleasant thoughts keep them from happening."

"Have all of these events had an impact on your life?"

"Yes they have."

"In what way?"

"I am very non-judgmental of others. Most important, though, I have a strong belief in the Lord Jesus Christ."

Patricia

She was waiting in her lovely apartment, decorated with several paintings that she had created, when Carol and I visited her in the spring of 1993. Her even features, blonde hair and cultured manner bespoke a previous career in modeling.

Patricia made us comfortable and began to tell us of her background. She was born in Brigham City, Utah, in 1956, and she was raised with her brother and sister in the Salt Lake City region. Because of the divorce of her parents, she was partially raised by her grandparents. Attending Weber State College after graduating from high school, she studied elementary education and art. At the time of our interview, Patricia had two teenage children, and she was unmarried.

Having worked in New York, Arizona, and Houston, and having traveled as an adult, Patricia had exposure to various cultures. She said that she had no strong commitment to any particular faith or religious belief.

A Dangerous Experiment—A Strange Outcome

Patricia began to tell her story. "When I was thirteen years old and attending Davis High School, a speaker came to our school to tell us about drug abuse. He told us that students in our school had experimented with drugs. Some students had sniffed glue, others had sniffed gasoline, and he explained some of the ill effects that could result from sniffing these materials.

"A group of popular girls that usually did not get in trouble—two of them were cheerleaders—decided to try sniffing drugs. Our curiosity, after we heard the lecture on drugs, about what happened when you sniffed them got the better of us. So, a group of us siphoned some gasoline out of a lawn-mower.

"Not being quite sure how to sniff gasoline, we put the gasoline in a plastic milk container. Taking the container with about an inch of gasoline in it, I shook it up to get a good mixture of gasoline vapor in the carton. Then I exhaled all the air from my lungs, put my mouth over the carton opening, and squeezed on the carton as I inhaled.

"Instantly, my lungs burned fiercely, my head ached enormously, and I couldn't catch my breath; unconsciousness followed. My girlfriends tried to hold me up on the picnic table where I was sitting when I went unconscious.

"Watching my girlfriends struggle to hold me on the table, from an elevated position, I became aware that I was out of my body. They failed to keep me on the table, and I saw my body tumble to the ground. As my body fell, it tipped over a jug of gasoline that was sitting on the lawn. Trying to warn the girls to be careful, I told them to pick up the jug and put it on the table. I was frustrated because they didn't listen to me. My concern was that we would get in trouble from a gasoline spot on the lawn.

"The girls started giving me mouth-to-mouth resuscitation, and I could tell that I didn't look good. My body had turned a bluish color.

"Floating around above the girls, and watching them, I felt really good. There was no pain, but it didn't make sense to me. For a moment or two I went fairly high above them. Then, for no apparent reason, I snapped back into my body.

"It was as if I slammed back inside my body. As I did, I took a large gasp of air. My lungs were burning, my head hurt, and my ears were ringing. It felt awful. We never sniffed gasoline after that."

"When you were out of your body, Patricia, did you see what your spirit-body looked like?" I asked.

"There was form to it. It was a whole body, and I had hands, for example."

"What did your spirit hands look like?"

"They were not like the hands on my physical body. They were more . . . they had shape, but it was like they were luminescent, not flesh and bones. It's hard to explain, but they seemed sort of lit up."

"Are you sure it wasn't a drug-induced type of hallucination that you had?"

"Everything was clear and real. The lawn and my girlfriends were clearly visible, and I could tell what the girls were doing. It was not a hallucination; it was real."

A Strange Force

"Up until I had that out-of-body experience, I didn't really believe there was a life after death. Even after my initial experience I didn't believe in concepts such as evil or good. My idea of a spiritual world was poorly formed, and I tended to accept only what I could see and feel in the physical world. Then I had another experience which, together with the first one, convinced me that there were spiritual forces.

"When I was twenty-five years old, I was going through a divorce. Depression was really bothering me; my husband had left me for a young model, and I had two children. My thoughts were almost suicidal.

"One night, as I sat in bed reading, a strange feeling came over me. It was as if someone, or something, had come into my room. And whatever it was felt evil.

"In my bed, while I was wide-awake, I was suddenly pinned down—I couldn't move. It felt as though some evil presence was trying to get into my mind. There was pressure so that I couldn't breathe, and my hands were immobile. I wanted to reach for the phone and call for help, but I couldn't.

"Something seemed determined to get into my mind or body. I was terrified. It felt like a see-through dark cloud that was overwhelming me. The only means I had of fighting the force was by thinking. My grandmother had earlier tried to teach me that if an evil presence ever came around I should command it to depart in the name of Jesus Christ.

"As I thought of my grandmother's words, the force pulled off of me. Released from the force, I sat up, and I cursed with relief. My uncle was a religious man, and I called him. He came over, and he suggested a blessing on the house, but I wanted to leave—and I did. The incident, whatever it was, fortunately never repeated."

Chapter 12

A COURAGEOUS MAN

Bill

It was a cold winter evening, in November 1992, when I drove up to Bill's house. He was waiting, in his wheelchair, with a cheerful greeting as I entered. Despite his obvious disability Bill had a muscular appearance, and he had remarkable mobility with his chair. He seated me in a large overstuffed chair, and he moved his chair so that I could easily use the recorder to tape his remarks.

Bill informed me that he was born on April 7, 1950, in Salt Lake City, Utah. He was the oldest of three brothers, and the family traveled extensively when the children were growing up—their father was an electrical engineer. Bill had a broad education; by the time he was sixteen years old the family had been around the world five times. They had lived in Australia, Saudi Arabia, Puerto Rico, Jamaica, and Venezuela.

As a young man Bill spent time in the Marine Corps, with two tours of duty in Vietnam, and then he finished his schooling at Westminster College in Salt Lake City. Fifteen years were spent working for the police department in Salt Lake City.

His immediate family was of a Protestant faith while he was growing up and Bill was exposed to a variety of religious beliefs. As an adult Bill had been married and had three children.

142

A Nasty Accident

Bill began to tell his story: "Over the 24th of July holiday in 1991, my brother Bob and I decided to go to Saint Anthony, Idaho, and ride our ATVs [All Terrain Vehicles] in the sand dunes near Saint Anthony. I had been an ATV enthusiast for a number of years, and we looked forward to a pleasant holiday of outdoor sport.

"We left Salt Lake early in the morning, and by early afternoon we had set up our camp in the sand dunes of Saint Anthony. We ate lunch—Bob's son was there with a friend, and we fed them—then Bob and I took our vehicles on a survey of the area. When we were about two or three miles from the camp site, I suggested that we return so as not to worry the kids."

"Were your vehicles three-wheeled or four-wheeled?" I asked.

"They were four-wheeled. We had started the machines up to return to camp, and we had ridden about two hundred yards—I'm not sure what happened, the speed was only about twenty miles-an-hour—and I remember being thrown over my machine. I hit on my head; I had a helmet on, but it was a tremendous blow when I landed. The pain was instantaneous and severe, and I blacked out.

"I was unconscious for less than a minute. When I came to I was face down in the sand, and I couldn't move any portion of my body. My brother, Bob, came running back, but all I could do was rotate my head. My arms and legs wouldn't move.

"When Bob came up I asked him what happened, and he said that he didn't know. I asked him where my machine was, and he said: 'It's on top of you.' I couldn't feel anything.

"Bob was able to remove the machine from me. I told him to go for help, but before he left I asked him to pile sand around my head to immobilize it. Because of the extent of my paralysis I was fairly sure that my neck was broken. I also told Bob that the paramedics should be informed that they would have to fly me out.

"Bob started for our campsite. About half way there he encountered a group of people, and he sent them for help so that he could return to me. The paramedics arrived within about forty-five minutes, and a helicopter arrived within about another forty-five minutes."

Medical Complications

"The helicopter transported me to the Eastern Idaho Medical Center in Idaho Falls. They gave me a CAT Scan, took x-rays, and performed other tests. The doctor came in and told me that my spinal cord was severed and I would be paralyzed for the rest of my life. My back was broken at T-4/T-5, about nipple level. I also had a closed head injury, and my neck was injured. My ribs were all broken in the left rib cage, and there were nine fractures on the right side. I had traumatic pancreatitis and many other problems.

"The accident happened about three in the afternoon. By one o'clock in the morning they had flown me to the University Medical Center in Salt Lake City. They had to get me to the medical center in Utah because both of my lungs were collapsing from the injuries, and they suspected that I might have torn the aorta of my heart.

"In Idaho, before they flew me to the University of Utah Medical Center, the doctor told me they might have to get a heart team together to operate on my heart. I asked him what would happen if they didn't operate, and he said that in that instance I would die. I wondered if death would come quickly or be drawn out, and he said it would be rather quick. A major concern I had was about my spinal cord injury, and, when I asked him about it, the doctor told me that I would never walk again. I was overwhelmed by the magnitude and suddenness of my injuries.

"Athletic and outdoor sports had always been an important part of my life. At the time of my accident I was training for a triathelon that was going to be held in Park City. I played football in high school and college, I skied from the time I was a small child, I enjoyed ATVs—in short, I was oriented toward sports and the outdoors—and the prospect of a life of paralysis was devastating. It seemed to me, at the time, to be a fate worse than death, so I told the doctor that I would not have the heart surgery that he thought I might need. I also told my brother, Bob, not to let them operate on me, just let me go.

"At the University Medical Center they did a number of other tests. By that time I had gotten Adult Respiratory Distress Syndrome (ARDS), which is usually fatal, and my heart was erratic. They put an external pacemaker on me to keep my heart beating regularly as well as other equipment to keep me alive. Then I developed pneumonia, and I got a staph infection in the blood. I was on a ventilator and I had tubes attached to various parts of my body; by this time I was comatose and the medical prediction was that I would not live."

Healing Hands

"Bob called a couple of my relatives who were active in their religion and asked if they would come and give me a blessing. My cousin, and Bob's brother-in-law, came to the University hospital and gave me a blessing. Medically, when they gave me the blessing, I was in a coma and could not hear what they were saying. The fact is, however, I could almost repeat verbatim what they said. I have, since, lost some memory of their words, but at the time I was totally aware of what they were saying.

"I still remember them laying their hands on my forehead and asking that I be given peace to accept whatever was the Lord's will. There was no specific request that I be allowed to live or that I be healed; rather it was that I would be granted peace and acceptance.

"As the blessing proceeded I felt hands on me—hands from those giving the blessing, but also other hands as well. The peculiar thing was that it was almost multi-dimensional—I could feel their hands, and I was looking at the scene as if from the perspective of a balcony. And . . . and there was this tremendous feeling of peace and well being that came into my body.

"From this elevated position I first saw my cousin and Bob's brother-in-law with their hands on my head. Then, as I looked at the scene, I saw other less distinguishable people around me; and I had the feeling that their hands on me were *healing* hands.

"Next, it was as if I shifted perspective from a balcony position to a position directly above my body. Looking down, I saw me, my body, with the people around it. Being somewhat quizzical, and trying to figure out what was happening, I looked, and . . . and I found that they were praying over me. It still wasn't clear why they were doing this, but I was filled with an awesome peace and calmness.

"It was strange, I could feel this warm peace in my body, yet I was looking at myself from above. The most fascinating aspect of the scene was that physically I only saw two people in the room besides me—my cousin and Bob's brother-in-law, who were giving the blessing.

Surrounding the bed, though, were all these other people with their hands on me; I could feel their hands on me. I couldn't distinguish them clearly, but I felt . . . I had a sense that they were relatives that had gone before me.

Through an Archway

"I can't tell you if my other experience was chronologically next, or how close it was to the experience with the blessing. I can pin the time down for the experience with the blessing because my cousin told me of the time—it was the afternoon of the day following the accident—but I can't do that with the next experience. All I know was that it was sometime during the four-and-one-half week period that I was comatose.

"The experience began when I found myself in a beautiful meadow; it was . . . I can't describe it. The meadow was incredibly beautiful, and I was walking along a path. The colors were vivid, and there was every color imaginable. It was just . . . I've tried to describe it to other people, and I couldn't—its beauty was beyond description.

"As I walked along the path in the meadow I came to a stone archway. It seemed almost as if I were called, or drawn, to the archway. I walked through it and entered a courtyard where I saw my father. He was dressed all in white, and he was bathed in sort of an iridescent white light.

"We approached each other, and I remember telling him that I was feeling lost and confused. I realized at that point that I was either in the process of dying, or I had already died. My confusion centered on my earthly life. I was feeling a great loss because of my children, and I was sharing that feeling with my father. Additionally, I wasn't sure that I wanted to live in the paralyzed state that the doctors said I would live in.

"My father said to me: 'You aren't going to be lost or confused any longer. Everything will be fine. It's not time for you to be here, now, but when it is I will be here.' Then he embraced me—there was an enormous outpouring of peace—and he took me back to the archway. As I entered the archway, I had the feeling that everything would be okay. That's the last thing I remember until I came out of the coma.

"When I came out of the coma, my youngest brother, Tom, was there, and my mother. They asked me if I knew where I was and what had happened. I remember telling them that I had been with Dad, in response to which they looked at me strangely."

Recovery

"When I regained consciousness, I became aware of the magnitude of physical problems that were still with me. During the little more than a month that I was comatose I lost 65 pounds. My paralysis was from the nipples down, and there were other complications. I had traumatic pancreatitis, pulmonary problems, and the head injury. These various problems kept me in the hospital for eight-and-one-half months, and for about half of that period I was totally immobile in a TLSO (a fibre-glass cast which immobilized my back and isolated it from my neck.) No food could be given to me by mouth for five months because of the damage to my pancreas. I was on the ventilator for the four-and-one-half months that I was in a coma, and I breathed oxygen for a short period after that.

"They transferred me to Seattle for my rehab., and I stayed there until March 1992, when I returned to Utah. They were unable to do any surgery on my back because of the location of the injury. I was in a back brace for about six months."

At this point in the interview, I commented to Bill that he looked remarkably well for the extent of his injuries, and for the relatively short time that had elapsed since his rehabilitation in Seattle. His comment was: "I've been doing really well. Actually, I had sort of a miraculous recovery. All of the doctors at the University Hospital referred to me as the miracle baby—there were at least seven different times when the doctors called my mother and told her that I wouldn't make it beyond the next few hours. They also told my family that because of the level of my injuries, if I did live, I would never be independent; I would always need help."

"And do you need help?" I asked Bill.

"No, I live alone and care for myself. I drive my own car, and I work every day at an industrial concern."

"You are kidding!" I responded. "What do you do at your work?"

"I am a salesman. I sell commercial laundry equipment," Bill said, and it was obvious that he was proud of that accomplishment—and legitimately so. In light of the relatively recent traumatic accident and rehabilitation ordeals he had borne, his recovery and achievements truly warranted feelings of pride. He also told me that he worked out three days a week in a special gymnasium. One of his goals, within the next couple of months, was to be fitted with leg braces. With the aid of the braces and crutches he hoped that he would be able to increase his mobility in a walking program.

Bill's house, as I saw it, was the picture of neatness. Certain areas had been modified to make them accessible by wheelchair. He did all of his own cooking, and he took care of his other needs. He performed his own dressing and personal hygiene, for example, and this he did despite being paralyzed from the chest level down. Medical personnel had continuously told him that he could do none of these things without significant help from others. Bill said that he had set for himself a goal to overcome obstacles that stood in the way of his independence.

Analysis of Bill's Experience

I began to ask Bill questions about what had happened to him: "Was there anything about your accident that you remember as particularly unusual?"

"There was the terrible surge of pain when I hit, then I remember thinking: *So this is what it's like to die. It is not so bad.* Everything happened so quickly that I didn't find it that unpleasant."

"When you had your first out-of-body experience and were looking down on yourself, and you saw these other people you thought were your relatives, can you tell me a little more about them?"

"I could definitely feel their hands on me. Later I talked to my cousin about them. I said: 'I could clearly hear your voice and that of Lance during the blessing, and I could see you guys, but who were all those other people holding their hands on me?' He responded: 'Bill, there was no one else there,' to which I said: 'Oh yes there was.'"

"Could you tell how they were dressed?" I asked.

"I could distinguish shapes, in, maybe, an off-white or gray color, but they were not as clear as those giving the blessing, or as my Dad was in the later experience. During the blessing I could feel a surge of warmth or energy going through me. It went from my head to my toes, and I had this enormous feeling of well-being. It's interesting that when the blessing was taking place I could feel things in my body, the warmth and the pressure of hands, despite the fact that I was paralyzed. Those were the only feelings I have been able to have in my body since the accident."

After I had interviewed Bill, in a separate meeting, I met Bill's cousin who had participated in the blessing. He had a written record of the incident, and he gave me a copy of the write-up. A significant difference from what Bill remembered was that the cousin said there were three individuals who helped with the blessing. Besides those individuals, Bill's mother, another lady, and another man were present in the room. However, Bill can only remember seeing the two individuals who gave voice to the blessing—plus the other spirit individuals who were his deceased relatives with the healing hands.

"Concerning the experience with your Dad, you mentioned that you went through the archway into a courtyard. What do you mean by a courtyard?"

"That was the impression that I had. I had gone from the meadow through the archway into this area that resembled a garden courtyard. My Dad was clearly visible, and . . .and I can remember seeing three other people who were in the background. They were not really clear, and I didn't have any contact with them. I sensed their presence, and then my Dad approached me and all my attention was focused on him."

"How old was your Dad when he died?"

"He was fifty-six years old."

"Did he look fifty-six years old when you saw him?"

"He really didn't have an age. He didn't look old, and he didn't look young—it was just my Dad."

"You said he was dressed in white . . ."

"It was more that he was bathed in white, an iridescent white."

"When you spoke to your father and he spoke to you, what kind of communication was it?"

"His lips may not have moved when we were communicating—but it was a clear message from him."

"You said that you felt him when he embraced you . . ."

"Perhaps it wasn't an embrace in the physical sense. I knew that I was embraced by him, though, and there was a tremendous amount of love and peace which flowed from him to me. I sensed that everything would be okay."

"Why do you keep using the word *peace*?"

"Because that, more than anything else, is the thing that I felt. And it continued after the experience. When visitors came to the hospital, for instance, many expressed the fact that there was an aura of peace about me. My cousin remarked that coming to see me was like recharging his batteries. Others made similar comments."

"Could the experiences have been dreams, or hallucinations?"

"I'm positive that they were not dreams or hallucinations. They were so different from anything I had ever experienced, and they were very real."

"How real is very real?"

"As real as you and me sitting here."

"How have the experiences changed you, if they have?"

"They have given me the ability to cope with what I previously thought was a fate worse than death. The other point is that when I was on my journey, if you will, I found that things I had previously valued highly, material things, really had no value. Feelings of love, on the other hand, persisted both there and here. The accident has also brought my family closer—in a more supportive way."

"Is there any message you would like to leave for others?"

"I think the message might be distilled from some of the things I learned. I was not prepared for what happened to me. When I think back on the time that I took to go on the trip to Idaho, for example, when I fussed with my jeep, the trailer, my camping equipment, and my ATV, as though they were the most important things in my life. The real issues in my life, on the other hand—the relationship with my children, the relationships with other people who were close to me—did not assume the importance that they should have. Material things no longer have the attraction for me that they once did. Love and relationships with my family and others close to me are now the most important things in my life."

I thanked Bill for telling me of his experience. As of the writing of this book, Bill, among his many other duties, is serving as the President of the local International Association for Near Death Experiences (IANDS of Utah). He also visits patients in local hospitals with serious illnesses or injuries to encourage them. He is an inspiration to the ill and the well alike.

Chapter 13

TWO WOMEN WHO SAW
THE LIGHT

Louise

The snow was stacked four feet deep in our front yard, in February 1993, when Louise drove up. She was a diminutive dark-haired young woman with a lovely smile. She greeted Carol and me with enthusiasm.

Louise was born in Logan, Utah, in February 1957, and she was one of five children. She was raised in Logan and attended school there. Attending college at Utah State and the University of Utah, she obtained a Bachelor's degree in Sociology. Louise had been married but was unmarried at the time of our interview. She was employed in the fields of sociology and law enforcement.

A Premonition and an Accident

Louise began her story: "At the time, in the late summer of 1981, I was married, and we were living in Rock Springs, Wyoming. We were moving back to Utah so that my husband could go to school. For about a month before we moved, we both had a feeling that something bad was going to happen to one of us. We did not talk about it to each other because it made us feel uncomfortable. We didn't know whom it would happen to or what it would be, we just knew it would be something bad.

"The day came to move, and we loaded a truck we had borrowed from my uncle. We drove to Logan and unloaded the truck without difficulty.

I was tired and wanted to wait until the next day before we returned the truck, but my husband insisted that we should return it to my uncle in Clarkston that night.

"My husband left ten or fifteen minutes before me in the truck, and I followed in the car. There is a little place called Amalga, and there is a house next to a bend in the road at Amalga. I came around the bend and saw a small dog alongside the road. He ran into the street and was barking. Another car was coming and I tried to keep going, but the dog did something that startled me, and I went off to the right side of the road. In trying to correct and get the car back on the road I hit the lip of the road. This flipped my car sideways into the path of the other car.

"The last thing that I consciously remember thinking was: *Oh my, they are going to hit the car.* Some time later I woke up on the road. In between when they hit and when I woke up I had my experience—when it started."

Two Men in White

"I found myself coming out of a dark tunnel toward a bright white light. There were two men, all in white, standing there. One, I could see clearly, and the other was standing behind a mist, an opaque mist.

"I wanted to keep going to where the second man was, but I couldn't move beyond the first man. Before this incident, I should explain, my husband and I had many questions about things, especially about children, and these questions came into my mind as I stood there with this being in white. I don't remember all the questions, but I do remember that we communicated without talking. It was as if words were exchanged through our minds, and many of the questions I had were being answered.

"While this was happening, the second man came out of the mist toward me, and I knew when he came forward that I couldn't go beyond the mist. I had to stay where I was.

"My happiness was extreme—it was the greatest peace and content-ment that I had ever felt. The experience was unique; I had never felt that way before, nor have I felt that way since. It was pure bliss.

"I knew I was going to have to go back, but before that happened there was a voice that came from the other side of the barrier. One of the main questions that my husband and I had was whether or not we could have children, and if so, when? The voice said: *Just be patient—your time will come to have children.*"

A Visitor from the Other Side

"Then I remember going back, and I woke up on the road with paramedics attending to me. When I first woke up, and for some time after that, my body and soul were separate. I heard somebody's voice talking to the paramedics say: 'Oh my back hurts,' and I remember thinking: *What on earth is going on—who is that whose voice is talking to the paramedics?*

"It took me about a day to figure out that it was I talking; and it was about three days before I stopped, off-and-on, being separate from my body. It was as though I could see a shell, my body, separate from *me*.

"During this period in the hospital I was visited by someone from the other side. I had a very dear friend who was killed, with her husband, in a plane wreck when she was nineteen. In the first forty-eight hours while I was in the hospital she came and stayed with me. I couldn't talk to her, but I could see her. She left a little bit before my body and spirit came back together."

Questions About Louise's Experience

Louise finished her story and sat quietly. I suggested that I ask her some questions about the experience, and she agreed. "Tell me about the bright light that you saw when you first left your body."

"It was just an extremely brilliant white light. It came, like from all over, and it focused on me. I've never seen anything like it."

"Were you in the light, or looking at it?"

"There was a sort of funnel toward me; I was looking into the light, but the light was coming to me. The farther out I looked, the more widespread the light was."

"Can you describe the mist that you saw?"

"It was a type of soft fog, and it was very definite along a wall-like line. The fog-wall came down to what I was standing on, and I couldn't see the end of it either up or sideways. I remember looking over my left shoulder and seeing stars behind me. It was as if I were in the clouds and the earth was below me. The second man was standing on the other side of the fog-wall, and I could see him less clearly than the first man—until he

came through the mist. I couldn't see anyone else, but I knew there were
other people behind the mist, and that's where I wanted to go."

"Could you describe the two men you saw?"

"It's been so long ago . . . there wasn't anything of particular note
about them, they . . ."

"How do you know they were men?"

"I just knew it; it was obvious. They were dressed in white and they
blended into the white light."

"Why did you use the word *peace* in describing how you felt?"

"I don't know how else to explain it. It was just an extremely calm,
happy feeling—something I had never felt before. There was an intense
peace, and I didn't want to leave it. I wanted to stay there very much, but
it was like my husband was pulling me back. It was for *him* that I came
back."

"When you first saw the two men, you said that *we* had questions.
What did you mean by *we*?"

"My husband and I. We had a few questions, but the main question
we had was about children, because we both wanted to have them. To that
point we had not been able to have any, and we did not have a medical
reason why not. Later we did get a medical reason why my husband could
not father children."

"Could your experience have been a dream or a hallucination?"

"Not to me."

"How did it seem?"

"Real. In a lot of ways it was more real to me than the rest of my
life."

"When you came back, you said that you heard yourself. Where was
the real you during this period?"

"I was inside my body, but it was as if I were standing in a shell—and
the shell was talking. I was separated, and yet I was inside my body. It
was as though I were in a space suit, my body, and it was talking while I
was in it. It's hard to explain . . . I was sort of in a facsimile of me, and it
was talking."

"You distinguished between what you called the spirit and the body.
Can you explain that distinction?"

"The body was the physical body, and the spiritual was the mind and
everything else. It was like . . . I don't know quite how to describe it. It
was as if the essence of *me* were a totally separate being from the physical

part of me. And the physical part of me was the shell. It was the essence of me that was functioning during much of the experience. When I was in the emergency room, for example, the essence of me was talking and joking, and I didn't feel any pain. The physical part of me was reacting differently, though.

"In talking to family members afterwards, it was amazing to me what they saw coming from the physical part of me as compared to what I remember coming from the essence of me. From their description, my physical person didn't move much or do anything. I just lay there and let the doctors work on me. Yet the essence of me was talking to all the people working on me, telling jokes—and I couldn't understand why they didn't laugh. I was in a good mood, and I could see the humor in my situation, but they didn't share in my humor. It was only later that I realized they didn't hear what the essence of me was saying."

"You mentioned that your friend visited you. How did you know it was your friend?"

"When she was alive we were so close we knew what each other's thoughts were. It was she; I just knew it. She moved like my friend, and she looked like my friend, with the same long blonde hair. She was always bubbly during life, and the spirit in my room had the same cheery, bright attitude. Her clothing was very light in color. When she first appeared, the hospital room was dark, but there was a brightness around her."

"Did she say anything?"

"No, she was there for comfort. She was just there."

"Has your experience changed your perspective at all?"

"Well, I definitely know that there is something on the other side, and I didn't know that before. Also, it is the place that I want to go back to when I die. When I have a hard time about things in life, this experience is the one thing that I hang onto as something that I know for sure."

"Are there any messages you would like to leave others?"

"Just that there is something on the other side, and I know that for sure. I'm looking forward to having that peace again."

Joyce

Carol and I drove up to Joyce's home on a cold winter afternoon in February 1993. She greeted us warmly, and she seated us near her as she arranged herself on a special chair designed to minimize problems associated with recent back surgery. Despite her obvious discomfort her eyes sparkled with anticipation and with the joy of life.

Joyce explained that she was born in Salt Lake City, Utah, in 1946. She was raised in a family of five children in the Salt Lake area. Joyce had previously been married, and she proudly showed us a picture of her son and his wife.

A Difficult Birth—A Strange Experience

Joyce began her story: "My son was born in December 1970, and he weighed nine-pounds-three-ounces; the birth was carried out as an emergency C-Section. My body was shocked from the operation, and my intestines stopped functioning properly. I had a bowel blockage a few days after the operation. All together I was in the hospital for thirty-two days.

"They took me off all oral food and water. I couldn't even suck on damp things. My tongue got so dry that they finally let me suck on lemon tasting cotton swabs.

"At one point they told my husband that I wouldn't make it through the night. My temperature was high, and they kept packing ice around me. I was asleep, and then—it seems so strange to talk about it—I found myself standing in a hallway. I think I had on my hospital gown, and I don't remember my feet touching the ground.

"It was dark all around me except for that light. There was a light that was the brightest thing I had ever seen in my life. Longing to go to that light, I didn't recognize anything else that might have been going on.

"There was a tunnel that went down and off to the right, and that's where the light was coming from. I felt that if I walked down the tunnel and around the corner I could . . . I had to go to that light.

"Momentarily standing still, I heard a voice to my left. I think it was a man's voice, but I'm not sure. The voice said: 'It's not your time, you have to go back. You have a husband to take care of and a baby to raise.'

"Then the thought came to me: *I've got a baby. I've got a son.*

"The next thing I knew I was awake, I was in the hospital bed, I was hungry, and I felt better. My doctor came to see me, and I told him that I had had a really weird dream. His response was: 'We lost you last night.' He let me know that he didn't think it was a dream.

"At the time I had never heard of near-death experiences. I thought it was some kind of realistic dream. After the experience I read about others having similar things happen, and I realized that I wasn't alone in what I saw. Now I know that there is another side, and I'm not afraid to die. I'm not anxious to go—I want to live, but I know that death is just another side of life.

"My experience made me appreciate something about every day—it doesn't matter if it's ugly weather, or if I'm not feeling well, or whatever—I find something beautiful about the day." As Joyce explained how she felt about each day, and even though she was obviously feeling the results of a recent surgery, her eyes reflected her joy of living and talking to us at that moment.

Analysis of Joyce's Experience

I began to ask Joyce some questions concerning her experience. "Can you explain what the light looked like?"

"It's hard to describe. How do you see a light that bright?"

"Was it similar to the sun?"

"If the sun were there . . . it would be like the sun was shining right into the room. Yet . . . it didn't seem that the light hurt my eyes. But I'll never forget it."

"Why will you never forget it?"

"It was drawing me. I *had* to go to that light—I wanted to go, but it was like I was stopped, and something wouldn't let me go on. Then the voice mentioned my son, and I thought: *I've got a baby.*

"My baby is the one that brought me back, I know he was."

"Tell me more about the voice."

"I'm pretty sure it was a man's voice, and it was off to the left behind me."

"Did you look to see?"

"No. I didn't turn; I don't think I was supposed to know who it was. There was a lot of love in the voice."

"What do you mean a lot of love?"

"It was a gentle voice, it was kind. And the love I felt was unconditional. It was wonderful. It was beyond any love I had ever felt in this life. The voice wasn't demanding when it told me to go back, but when it spoke I knew that was what I had to do."

"Did you hear it?"

"I don't know whether I heard it with my ears, or if I heard it in my mind."

"You mentioned that you first thought your experience was a dream. Did it seem as though it were a dream?"

"No, it seemed like it really happened, but at the time I figured that was the only thing it could be."

"What was your religious background?"

"I wasn't raised in a religious environment. I don't go to church all the time, but I do believe that God answers prayers. This experience changed my views on religion, and I now believe that God hears every prayer. I'm a big believer in prayer, and I worship God every day."

"Has the experience affected you in other ways?"

"Yes, it has made me appreciate life. Another thing . . . the voice said: 'You have a baby to raise.' I took that seriously, and I felt all those years that my primary goal was to raise my son. And, I assumed, when that was done I would be taken. My son is now my best friend. I've enjoyed every moment with him—he's a wonderful person."

"Do you have any messages you would like to leave others?"

"Yes; don't ever think that this life is all there is. I feel sorry for those who think that there is nothing else. There is so much more!"

"How do you know that?"

"It was the feeling I had while in the light—the peace that I felt."

"Why did you use the word *peace?*"

"That's how I felt; I felt serene, I felt loved. I know that death is only a word, and the spirit lives on. We are only a shell of our real selves."

Chapter 14

A PROFOUND EXPERIENCE

David Chevalier

It was his hair and beard, both a carrot red, that distinguished him when I visited him at his home in the spring of 1993. He smiled and explained that he had been taking a short nap to recover from an early session preparing for and teaching an English class. The morning had started for him at 4:30 a.m.

After exchanging greetings, David told me of his early life. He was born in Council Bluffs, Iowa, in 1953. His father was a railroader, and they lived on a small farm just outside the city limits. When David was two years old his father and mother were divorced, and David lived with his grandmother for three years. David's father remarried, and the Chevalier family ultimately consisted of the father and step-mother, one full-blooded sister of David, and twelve half and step-brothers and sisters. When David was fifteen years old, the family moved to Southern California where his father's job on the railroad took them.

Graduating from high school in Rialto, California, in 1971, David also attended junior college part time. His schooling was interrupted by three years in the army, until 1975, when he returned to junior college. He met his wife, Christine, in San Bernardino while they were working and attending junior college. They married and moved back to Iowa where David went to work for the Chicago and North Western Railroad until 1981. He completed his college education with a B.A. in business in 1985, and later, an M.A. from Northern Arizona University.

159

They lived in Flagstaff, Arizona, near Chris's parents, until 1991 when Chris's father had a heart attack and had to move from Flagstaff because of the altitude. Chris's sister had a house in Utah, and David and Chris liked the area, so they moved Chris's parents and themselves to Utah. David obtained a job teaching English at a local college, and Chris found employment as a conductor for AMTRAK.

During his youth, David was encouraged to decide for himself what kind of religious experience he wanted. As a consequence he attended the Lutheran, the Presbyterian, and the Baptist churches. At the time of our visit David and Chris had one small girl and two older boys.

A Terrible Wound

David began to tell of his experience: "It was Friday, November 13, 1981, and we were living in Iowa where I was working for the railroad. On that morning I had driven Christine to work, and I was dressed up to attend the funeral of a friend from work who had been killed in an auto accident. For some reason I felt it was necessary for me to attend the funeral, even though I normally didn't go to funerals.

"After taking Chris to work, I stopped by my grandmother's house in Council Bluffs to say hello. Offering me breakfast, she proceeded to cook it while I sat at her kitchen table. My uncle (on my father's side), who was living with my grandmother, came into the kitchen. He had a serious life-long drinking problem and apparently was in an alcoholic haze when he got up, because he immediately began to argue with me.

"Not wanting to get into a family argument with my uncle, I told him to leave me alone. Storming from the room, he left, returning shortly with a center-break single-shot twelve-gauge shotgun. Carrying the gun in his hands near his hip, haplessly, he pointed it at me and pulled the trigger as I sat at the table.

"The shotgun blast hit me in the lower right abdomen and blew me backward into the back door. Finding myself on my back looking out across the table at my angry uncle, I realized I had been shot. To my horror I saw him break open the shotgun and load it with another shell. My grandmother, who had just witnessed her son shoot her grandson, was in shock and unable to do anything.

"While lying on my back, I grabbed the nearest kitchen chair and used it as a device to fend off the shotgun—in much the same manner that a lion tamer would fend off a lion. With the end of the barrel caught in the rungs of the chair I was able, for a period, to keep the gun from pointing directly at me. Struggling to my feet, I managed to grasp the barrel with my free hand.

"Pleading with my uncle to stop what he was doing, I continued to wrestle with him over the gun for some moments. He finally seemed to understand what he had done, and he stopped fighting. Breaking open the gun and ejecting the shell, he convinced me that I could let go. The tone of his voice showed that he was again rational, so I released my hold on the gun. After dropping the shotgun, my uncle ran from the house.

"Having been in the military, my excellent training concerning the treatment of wounds was instantly called to mind—not looking at the wound; treating myself for shock; and making sure that I wasn't bleeding to death. These were all issues I was concerned with. Putting my hand on the wound, I withdrew it and saw that there wasn't much blood—just a circle, an outline, of blood where the shot had entered my abdomen. Because of the lack of surface blood I knew that I was bleeding internally.

"As the enormity of my situation became clear I fell on my knees, crying, and I began praying. I prayed for repentance of my sins. Upon completing a quick prayer, I recovered sufficiently to dial 911. Shortly thereafter the operator let me know that help was on its way.

"Knowing that help was coming, I lay on the couch in the front room, propped my feet up to treat myself for shock, loosened my tie and my shirt, and continued with my prayer. I'm not sure how long it was, but I next remember a detective from Council Bluffs coming through the door in a crouched position with a drawn .357 Magnum. When he saw me, he asked: 'Where is he?', and I pointed out the back door. He rushed out the door with his gun drawn.

"Following the detective were two paramedics. They treated me at the scene, putting balloon pants on me and inflating the pants to keep the blood in my upper body. When they got me into the ambulance and started the siren, I heard them radio to their dispatch and say that they were heading for Jennie Edmonson Hospital. There are two hospitals in Council Bluffs. I was born at Mercy Hospital, and I figured if I were going to die that's where I should be, so I redirected them to Mercy Hospital.

"At the emergency room of Mercy Hospital, I remember the nurses asking my name and other vital information. My thoughts were: *Here I've had the worst wound of my life, I may not live, and the nurses must still fill out the forms.* I carefully spelled my last name for them, because I wanted to make sure it was not misspelled if I didn't live. Upon getting all the information they needed, the nurses released the air in the pants—and I lost consciousness."

Medical Treatment, and Strange Happenings

"My next memory was of hearing a nurse read my blood pressure. Hearing her read it, I could see two nurses on the left-hand side of my bed, and the doctor on the right side. This view of the nurses and doctor working on me was despite the fact that I wasn't conscious. I was seeing this scene as if I were somewhat above a prone position in my bed. It was almost as if my ethereal body were holding and consoling my physical body's head in its lap.

"The nurse said that my blood pressure was sixty over zero; then she said it was fifty over zero. The doctor told them to alert the family and the clergy.

"As the doctor made his comment about the clergy, I heard another voice, my voice, but coming from outside me, saying: 'No. I'm not ready yet.' Instantly upon hearing that voice a feeling came over me that I could make it. It was a similar feeling as that obtained on getting a second wind when running a long race. I knew I could survive—and then I was in blackness again.

"During this unconscious period they operated on me. They told me later that I was initially in surgery for eight-and-one-half hours. There were two gurneys, one with me on it, and another at right angles. To repair my intestines the doctor removed and spread my entrails and laid them out upon the other gurney. In that manner they searched, cleaned and sealed those penetrations of my intestines by bird-shot that they could. Other portions of the intestines that they couldn't repair, they removed. They learned, during this process, that the shotgun pellets were size number 8 bird-shot. Some of that bird-shot is still in my body—even in my heart.

"Upon waking, later, I heard someone ask me if I wanted a respirator. Breathing was a problem for me, and I nodded, yes, I wanted one. It felt so good when they put the respirator on, and I drifted back into unconsciousness again.

"The next memory was of waking in Intensive Care with my father and my wife close by, and several nurses attending me. Seeing my father gave me a sense of relief. He had been in Arizona, and in order for him to be in Iowa it was clear that substantial time had passed—and I was still alive.

"Wanting to communicate, I motioned for something to write on. Because of the many tubes going down my nose and throat, and the respirator, I couldn't talk. When they gave me a clipboard with paper and a pen, I wrote in capital letters: *WHY?* My mind was obsessed with the thoughts: *Why did this happen to me? What did I do to cause this to happen?* After thinking those thoughts I became unconscious again.

"When I lost consciousness this time, the doctors discovered that there were still bleeders in me, so I was again returned to surgery. While I was in this second surgery my heart flat-lined, and they had to use the resuscitation paddles to restart it. This whole period, the second surgery, and recovery in Intensive Care were just a fog to me. I was unaware of what was happening.

"Five days after I entered the hospital, at night when the lights were low, I awakened in the Intensive Care unit. The respirator had been removed, and I only had one tube going up my nose and down my throat. My mouth felt as if an army had marched through it with muddy boots. Looking around the room I spotted a bottle of sterile water nearby. I grabbed it and took some long delicious swallows of water. The nurse happened to come into the room as I was drinking the water, and she was horrified.

"Apparently when you have a stomach wound you are not supposed to have water. In my case the water started massive internal bleeding, and I slipped into unconsciousness."

The Savior—An Amazing Valley

"One night, about a week after entering the hospital, while in Intensive Care, I slipped away and they again had to resuscitate me with the paddles. During that night, with my room darkened, I became fully aware of what was going on in my room. Looking around the room I could see everything—and standing by one side of my bed was my Savior. He was as plain to me then as you are now.

"Reaching over to me, He ran His hands up and down my body, and all the tubes, all the staples and other attachments to my body were gone.

His right hand reached out, as if to beckon me; I reached back to touch His hand.

"As my hand touched His, instantaneously we were on the rim of an incredible valley. It was a huge valley, on the order of Yosemite or Zion National Park in size, and it was verdantly green. There was water; there were rivers, there were lakes—and the valley was filled, almost shoulder-to-shoulder, with people.

"Gazing on this astonishing scene, I had the feeling of eager anticipation emanating from the multitude below me. The mood of this enormous crowd, the feeling that I could also feel, was as if in expectation of some marvelous event that would soon happen.

"The breadth of the scene was breathtaking, and I stood there trying to absorb what I was viewing. People were milling about, some of them speaking in soft tones, and there was a calmness about them despite the feeling of anticipation.

"Turning to my Savior, I asked: 'What are we waiting for?' He said something that I've later had to reconstruct, because the moment that He spoke I found myself back in Intensive Care with all the tubes and staples attached to me. My sense, upon returning, was that I would not only survive my physical ordeal but I would be better for it. I was overwhelmed by a glow within me, almost a fire, and a complete feeling of well-being.

"Thinking about the Savior's reply to my question, I had difficulty translating what He said into English. He communicated, and I had a sense of what it meant, but it was a form of communication that English doesn't cover. When He spoke, a number of thoughts were conveyed simultaneously. One thought was that we were waiting for the second coming; another thought was that we were waiting for the resurrection; a third thought was that we were waiting for redemption. And all of those thoughts entered my mind instantaneously."

Recovery

"When I found myself back in Intensive Care, I could hardly wait to tell others what I had seen. Seeing Chris and my father the next day, I wanted to tell them everything—and they believed me when I told them. Some of the people I told, though, thought I was affected by the morphine and demerol that I had been taking. I knew better. It was too real.

"Father Burns, the Catholic Priest who was the chaplain for the hospital, came to see me, and I told him about my experience. His response was that my experience was very special, and it had a reason. He told me that I should take it for what it was, and he said it was not the first time he had heard such a story.

"It took another month and a half in Intensive Care before they moved me to another wing. Then there were another three weeks in a regular care unit before they let me go home. My recovery was truly a miracle, I wasn't supposed to live; or at least that's what the doctors said. One of the doctors told my wife that I only had a one-percent chance to live."

Questions about David's Experience

Dave agreed to some questions, so I began: "On the first incident, when you heard the voice, it was your voice yet it seemed to come from elsewhere—was that it?"

"Yes. There were obviously no vocal cords involved, but I could hear myself say that I wasn't ready yet. It was a real voice coming from outside myself, but it sounded like me."

"On this first event, could you see your body?"

"I could see my body, I could see the bed, I could see the sheet, but I couldn't see my face. The nurses were all clearly apparent and recognizable. Later, I told one of the nurses, for example, that she was reading my blood pressure when the doctor told them to get the clergy. She agreed that my memory of what happened was exactly right, and she wasn't surprised at what I told her. She had apparently been through such incidents previously."

"In the next event, Dave, you said that your Savior was standing near the bed?"

"Yes, He was on my left as I was lying in bed."

"What was He wearing?"

"Exactly as I imagined my Savior would look, with a white robe, and a sash tied in the center of the robe. He had a beard and long hair."

"Was He, or was the room, bathed in light?"

"Not that I noticed—except when He put his hands on me. The sheets seemed to get brighter during that instant."

"What were your feelings when He put his hands on you?"

"It was comforting. There were no feelings of fear or pain."

"It was comforting. There were no feelings of fear or pain."

"How did you know it was your Savior?"

"I know Jesus Christ when I see Him."

"How did you know?"

David chuckled as he thought. Then he said: "Probably it was the sense of goodwill and the sense of comfort that I felt—together with the other events that I witnessed. The fact is, I just knew. I knew!"

"When you found yourself at the rim of the giant valley, and saw the people, how were they dressed?"

"In white."

"Were there any sounds associated with the valley?"

"Only the sounds of nature, and the gentle speaking of some of the people."

"What were the colors like?"

"Vivid blue and green. It was the greenest forest and grass that I had ever seen. The sky was the deepest blue I had seen, and the water was crystal clear. Perhaps the most remarkable thing about the scene was its intense clarity. It was as if someone had cranked the focus up on a remarkable camera or TV screen."

"Did you have any special feelings during this event?"

"Just the overwhelming sense of anticipation; and I was getting that sense from all the people who were present."

"And He communicated with you about that anticipation?"

"Yes, in response to my question: 'What are we waiting for?' Then I was back in my room."

"How did you communicate?"

"I spoke just as I do now, by voice. But His communication was different—it was not English—it was communication of thought. When He spoke, words were used, but I can't tell you what they were. It was more a conveyance of knowledge. Later, I was able to recollect the ideas of the second coming, the resurrection, and the redemption."

"Has this experience affected you?"

"Very much so. People who knew me previously, and who know me now, say that I am two different people. My life changed completely after the event. Prior to the event I was a typical hot-tempered, redheaded Irishman. Since the event I have obtained a new appreciation for people, for my family, and for my associations with people. If you had said before the incident, for example, that I would be teaching college classes, I would have responded that you were out of your mind. Now, I love the interaction I get with the students."

"Has life been easier or harder since your experience?"

"With Post Traumatic Stress Disorder (PTSD) induced by this event, I have been faced with a great number of difficulties since the experience in 1981. Schooling had to be completed while supporting a wife whose health was fragile. There was pressure to support kids and family, and lack of success in finding full-time employment, but despite those and other difficulties, life has been rewarding."

"How has your health been?"

"My current doctor in Utah was completely surprised when he examined me after I told him about the gunshot wound. Since 1981 when I was finally released from the hospital, I've had two instances when I've had to go back in the hospital. The doctors tell me, though, that based on the extent of my injuries I should have had to return to the hospital at least annually. They tell me that scar-tissue, alone, should keep me in a constant state of distress. That hasn't been true; I don't have recurring complications.

"My doctor, the one who operated in Iowa, talks about me as his proudest achievement. Originally, after the operation, he told Christine that I only had a 1 percent chance of living. He said I beat all the odds, and he later wrote a paper on me."

As David told me of his injury and recovery, he opened his shirt and lowered his trousers so that I could see the scar. There was a one- or two-inch-diameter semi-circle of scar-tissue on the lower right abdomen, peppered by surrounding dots of scar-tissue. There was also a scar from the operation, starting at the solar-plexus, running down Dave's center-stomach, skirting around his navel, and ending two inches below his belt-line. The evidences of a massive wound were obvious.

Thoughts on the Meaning of the Experience

"Have you any sense of why you were allowed to come back?"

"That question has plagued me since I was shot. Initially I thought it might be to help my wife and my two sons. Then, after I completed my education and started teaching, I thought it might be because I am able to express myself and to teach others well. Recently, when my daughter was born, I suspected it might be to help nurture and raise her. Maybe it's all of those things."

"Has your religious perspective changed?"

"Very much so. During the '50s and '60s, my generation was filled with doubters. Even though I went to different churches, I still had a skeptical, show-me attitude about religion. About one year prior to my getting shot, Christine and I took the boys and attended The First Christian Church. At that time I was baptized and surrendered myself to Christ.

"When I was shot, therefore, my first thought was for my spiritual well being rather than my physical survival. My prayer was for repentance, not survival. The appearance of my Savior, I think, was in part due to my prayer for repentance.

"Had you read much about near-death experiences when you had yours?"

"Nothing prior to the experience. After it happened I became very curious and searched for material. About two years later I read Raymond Moody's *Life After Life*, and it helped me. Just this year I read *Return from Tomorrow* by George Ritchie."

"Could your experience have been a dream or hallucination?"

"No. It was the most real thing that ever happened to me—more real than being here now in my conscious state."

"Are there any messages you would like to leave for others?"

"My message involves faith. People are often told to have faith; to have faith that there is life after death, to have faith that Jesus Christ is real and is our Savior, and to have faith in a living God. I would like to offer myself, to those who struggle with their faith, as a living testimony that He does exist. I have seen Him, and I know that He is there. If people can't believe based on their own faith, then believe because of my witnessing—it is the truth. Please listen to me as someone who is a first-hand witness that Jesus Christ lives and is our Savior."

Chapter 15

THREE WHO FELT THE LOVE

Mary

Mary was waiting as Carol and I drove up to her home in the Salt Lake City area, on a spring day in 1993. Her two dogs greeted us, and while she seated us, she began to tell us of her background.

She was born in Utah in 1934, in the Salt Lake City region. Her family moved around somewhat as she was growing up so that her stepfather could pursue his occupation as a miner. By the time she reached the sixth grade she had gone to fifteen different schools. When she was in the eleventh grade she quit school and went to work. She had eight brothers and sisters.

Mary and her husband have two daughters, and two grandchildren, all of whom lived in the Salt Lake City area. Mary's husband, John, is a construction foreman, and he also has an interest in rodeos. Mary showed Carol and me many mementos and pictures from the rodeos they attended.

During her youth Mary was exposed briefly to the LDS, Assembly of God and Baptist religions. As an adult she has a very strong Christian belief in Jesus Christ as our Lord and Savior.

A Hunger for Love

Mary began to tell her story: "In 1968 I was very depressed. My life seemed to have no meaning, and I hungered for love, but I didn't seem to know how to get it. Worldly events and material things were all that mattered to me, and there was no spiritual satisfaction in anything that I did.

169

"On one particular day I decided that I had had enough of this life; I wanted out. So I wrote a note asking the Lord to forgive me, and I left the note for my husband to find. Then I took every pill I could find in the house, and I lost consciousness.

"When my husband came into the house, he found me and rushed me to the Cottonwood Hospital in Salt Lake City. The doctors told him they didn't give me much hope. It was especially bleak because there was no fight in me—I didn't want to live."

A Tunnel, and a Rainbow-colored Room

"My first memory after losing consciousness was to awaken and realize that I was speeding down a dark tunnel. There was a light at the end of the tunnel, and I was moving toward it. Suddenly I came to the end of the tunnel. Entering a beautiful room that was filled with a rainbow color, I stood in awe and wonder at the beauty of it all. Then a bright light came down upon me, and I knew it was something special.

"The peace I felt was wonderful, a perfect tranquility and warmth, for I was surrounded by an unconditional love. The love was everything that I had hungered for but seemed unable to find in life. All the anger, hate, pain, and fear that I had previously felt were removed. Pure love and peace were all around me.

"Wanting to stay in the presence of that love forever, I continued to stand in the light. Suddenly, though, I knew I couldn't stay—and I was sent reeling back through the tunnel of darkness. It was not a pleasant feeling coming back. Opening my eyes, I discovered that I was again in the hospital. Leaving that beautiful place of peace left me furious. Instead of a place of peace and love, I was greeted by a nurse who gave me a painful shot. And I was cussing mad.

"When I came home from the hospital, I still had the memory of the wonderful love and peace that I felt in the rainbow-room. Only my husband was aware of what had happened to me. In those days it was not acceptable to talk about what I had experienced or witnessed. People seemed to be afraid to hear me talk about it. So it became my private knowledge."

A Second Experience

"In January 1986 I entered the hospital with pneumonia. It was particularly dangerous for me because I was a heavy smoker, and I had not stopped—despite having been told that I should stop. After being treated for pneumonia and related respiratory illnesses for a week, they talked of releasing me. Things weren't quite right, though, so they kept me somewhat longer.

Finding myself in darkness on one occasion, but conscious, I tried to figure out where I was. Looking down from an elevated position, I saw a lady, in bed, dressed in blue. Medical people were clustered around this poor lady in blue, and they were attempting to put a ventilator on her.

"At first I couldn't imagine who the lady in blue was. The view I was seeing was from the upper corner of a hospital room. I continued to watch the scene, feeling empathy for the patient, when things went dark again. Much later I figured out that the poor lady was I.

"My next conscious memory was to awake in bed, and to see my sister, who had died in 1980 in a car wreck, standing at the foot of my bed. Her hands were folded and she was smiling at me.

"It seemed strange to see my sister, and I wondered what she was doing there. Then I felt the presence of someone else on my right side. Looking in that direction, I saw my Savior, Jesus Christ." Mary paused in her discussion as she attempted to control her emotions.

"Jesus was looking down at me, and I knew that He wasn't too happy with me because I hadn't quit smoking. He was so full of love, though, and He turned to my sister and smiled.

"The moment Jesus smiled at my sister, I knew that I wasn't going to die. He turned back to me, and. . . . Now He didn't talk to me like you and I talk. The message He sent to me, it was. . . . I heard Him in my head.

"As He turned to me, there continued to be this unconditional love, and He said: 'Tell your family about Jesus Christ.' That was the only message. Then He smiled at me and left.

"My sister continued to stand there for a time. She was dressed in a brown dress with a white collar. Her dress, in that environment, seemed to symbolize scholarship.

"After a short period my sister left; and I was back with the nurses, the ventilator, and all the medical equipment. They had me tied to the bed—the ties were to keep me from removing the tubes that they had me plugged into.

Recovery

"My recovery was very fast. My brother, whom I had not seen for some time, came to see me during my recovery period. Because of my experience I felt a necessity to tell my family of Jesus. Also, I wanted my brother to read from the 23rd Psalm. We joined hands as he read it; then we said the Lord's Prayer together.

"The hospital kept me for one week after that. Returning home, I continued to feel the love of my Savior, and I knew that my immediate medical emergency was over. My overall health, though, still suffered from the years of smoking that I had done. Chronic Obstructive Pulmonary Disease (COPD) was a continuing problem. At night, even now, I have to use oxygen because of the limited capacity of my lungs."

Questions About Mary's Experiences

Mary agreed to being questioned about her experiences. I began: "In your first experience, when you went through the tunnel and came out in the room, can you describe the room?"

"It was just like a rainbow. I think the colors were representative of God's promises to us."

"Was there any furniture in the room, or were there other distinguishing features?"

"Nothing. Just the rainbow-colored light. There were pastel colors, and it wasn't exactly like our rainbow, it was just . . . We don't have the kind of beauty that I saw."

"Did you hear anything?"

"No."

"In your second experience, when you were up near the corner of the room, how did you feel?"

"It didn't seem strange to be up there—I didn't even question it. There was no pain, and I felt great."

"When you saw Jesus, what were the circumstances?"

"It was a different place than the hospital. I was in bed, and my sister was there, but I didn't have the ventilator or other equipment on me from the hospital. It was a different dimension, or something. Jesus was standing on the right of the bed."

"How do you know it was Jesus?"

"I just knew. I know Jesus."

"What did He look like?"

"He looked just like Jesus. His robe was in the style of the biblical times, and it seemed to be made of homespun material. There was no question about His identity. When I later tried to tell someone about it, I just broke down and sobbed—from the feeling I got remembering Jesus."

"Did you say anything to Jesus?"

"No. I didn't talk. He just asked me to tell my family about Jesus Christ. That was all, and then I was back."

"Were you angry, this time, when you came back?"

"No, because this time I had something to do. There was an important reason for my being here. And I am telling my family and others about Jesus Christ."

A Serious Illness and a Healing

As Mary finished telling of her second out-of-body experience I asked her if there were any other similar events in her life. She said there were not any others where she left her body, but she did have an unusual experience related to her health. I asked her to tell me about it.

"In 1978 and 1979 I had lots of problems with tumors. The doctor had been trying to get me to stop smoking, but I also had these tumors that kept growing in my breast. He had removed several of them, but they kept coming back. It reached the point where I was completely frustrated.

"One of my friends knew how I was suffering, and she talked to me about having her son give me a blessing. At first I told her no, but she persuaded me that I should do it.

"Her son came and gave me a wonderful blessing. At one part of the blessing, I still remember, he said to keep my faith. Following the blessing I felt an inner warmth.

"The doctor had me scheduled to come in and have a tumor, about the size of a quarter, removed. The operation was scheduled for the following day. When I awoke on the day of the operation, the tumor was gone. I didn't have to go through the operation. The doctor said that I was living proof of a miracle. There was no other explanation."

"Later, the doctor still had me scheduled for a bilateral mastectomy, but I said no. Seeking other medical advice, I finally found an oncology expert who told me that I could avoid a mastectomy and just treat the tumors if and when they appeared. So, after praying about what to do, that is what I did—there was no mastectomy."

Final Thoughts from Mary

"Did you ever quit smoking, Mary?"

"Yes. In 1988 I got to the last cigarette, and I prayed to the Lord to help me. After that I never had the desire to smoke again. Unfortunately, the damage had been done and I got COPD. It's a combination of emphysema, bronchitis and asthma. So I now have to take lots of medicines for it."

"Are there any messages you would like to leave for others?"

"Yes. Life is a beautiful gift from God. Suicide is never the answer to our problems. We should trust in God, and love the Lord with all our heart. We should also love our neighbors. Once I had a question: 'How big is my family?' The answer just came to me: 'My family consists of all the people that Jesus Christ leads into my life.' And we should understand the message given in John 3:16."

Maria

Maria was a friend of Mary's, and Carol and I visited with her at Mary's home. Mary arranged for our meeting after informing us that Maria had also had a near-death experience.

We visited for a while, and then Maria began to tell us about herself. Having been born in 1915 in Salt Lake City, Utah, she and her two brothers were raised in the Salt Lake region. She went to school at the Hawthorne School. Her marriage was in 1936 and she had six children, twenty-seven grandchildren, and six great-grandchildren.

At the time of our visit, Maria and her husband were raising three of her grandchildren. One of her daughters became ill, so Maria and her husband volunteered to raise the grandchildren.

A Ruptured Appendix

Maria began to tell her story: "In 1956 I became ill. One day I got this horrible pain in my left side. It got bad enough that I went to the doctor.

"The doctor thought something could be wrong with my colon, and they said they might have to operate. They sent me home for a period, and when I was walking up some stairs I felt something break. I became very ill and had to go to the hospital.

"My husband took me to the hospital. When the doctors operated on me, they thought it was for a ruptured colon, or something else. In actuality they found that my appendix was on the wrong side, and it had ruptured.

"I was so sick I hardly knew what was going on for a while. The doctors were very concerned about me, and one night I felt so bad I didn't think I would make it."

A Beautiful Experience

"Suddenly I heard the most beautiful music imaginable, and I felt somebody holding me in their arms. There was so much peace and love. It was a tremendously comforting feeling. The pain left, and I felt wonderful.

"I had the sensation of being carried up someplace, until we got to a location that had a veil (like a curtain). A voice said: 'Do you want to go in?' and I asked: 'Is there more for me to do?' The voice then answered: 'Yes.' Immediately afterward I awakened in my bed. That was the end of my experience.

"My recovery, due to peritonitis, phlebitis, and other complications was extended. I was in the hospital for sixteen days."

"May I ask you a few questions about your experience, Maria?" I asked.

"Yes."

"When you were first ill, was it very painful?"

"My, yes. It hurt so much I told my husband to take me out and shoot me. My little girl cried when I did that. She told her daddy not to shoot me." Maria laughed as she thought back on the incident.

"When you went to the hospital, did it still hurt?"

"By that time I was weak, and I felt sick to my stomach."

"Then when you had your experience, how did you feel?"

"There was no illness or pain, and I felt as though someone were holding me. The music was the most marvelous sound I had ever heard."

"What did it sound like?"

"It sounded like a choir singing wonderful church music, and it surrounded me. There was a marvelous feeling of peace that went with it."

"Then you were carried somewhere?"

"I was carried to a veil."

"What did the veil look like?"

"It resembled a white curtain, or a drape. Then they asked me if I wanted to go through."

"When you say *they*, what do you mean?"

"I was carried by someone, and a man was standing by the veil. He asked me if I wanted to go through."

"What did the man look like?"

"He was dressed in white."

"How did you feel when he asked you that?"

"My thoughts went to my children, and I asked: 'Isn't there more that I should do?' At that time, my oldest boy was away; the second boy, Steve, was six years younger; and then there were George, Judy, Nola and Charlotte. They needed me, and I knew it. I had to come back."

"When you came back, did you hurt again?"

"Yes. It hurt all over my body."

"Are there any messages you would like to leave for others?"

"I've heard all my life that Jesus will win. There is so much sin in the world, today, that I worry the devil will win. I want everyone to get on the Lord's side."

Debbie

She was a tall, young blonde woman with a delightful southern accent. She greeted Carol and me graciously when she came to our home in May 1993.

Debbie was born in Chicago, Illinois, in June 1961; she was the oldest of five children. The family moved from Illinois to Ohio, and then back to Alabama, their previous home, where Debbie was raised.

Most of her youth was spent in a backwoods region of Alabama. Despite no tradition of formal education in her family, Debbie graduated from high school. In 1979, before graduation from high school, she enlisted in the Air Force, and she became an active member immediately after graduation. As an adult, at the time of our interview, she was attending college and taking pre-med courses.

Debbie's youth was not entirely happy, since she had an abusive father. Her mother, however, was a spiritual woman, and she took the children to church whenever she could. They attended a fundamental Baptist Church.

After entering the Air Force, and completing basic training in Texas, Debbie was assigned to Hill Air Force Base in Utah. She met her future husband there. When she became pregnant, she obtained a discharge from the Air Force. At the time of our visit, Debbie had two children, and she was divorced.

As Debbie visited with Carol and me, she exhibited some nervousness, typical of many who tell their experience for the first or second time. She informed us that she had not often told her story. She seemed to be under considerable emotional pain.

A Difficult Operation

Debbie began to tell her story. "Before I joined the Air Force, I had braces on my teeth. In order to be allowed in boot-camp I had to remove the braces. The recruiting officer signed a statement, however, that after basic training the Air Force would continue my treatment.

"At my first duty station I visited the military dentist on the base, and he examined me. After the examination he scheduled me for cosmetic surgery, known as malocclusion surgery, to correct a severe overbite problem.

"They flew me to Texas, where the surgery was to take place, on Christmas eve, 1980. My surgery was scheduled for January 3; the delay was so that dentists and doctors could be flown in from other Air Force installations. This was to be a major operation, and it would be filmed for later training purposes.

"The doctors were nice to me, and they gave me a complete physical before the operation, which they said would take six hours. Joking with them to relieve my nervousness, I told them to be sure and wash their hands before they worked on me.

"A number of complications arose during the surgery. They put a tube down me, and that apparently caused severe bleeding of an ulcer in my esophagus. The worst problem, though, was from the anesthetic. It turned out that I was allergic to it, and I went into cardiac arrest during the operation. They were able to restart my heart using resuscitation techniques, but in the process they ruptured my diaphragm."

Cradled by Christ

"While the doctors were having these problems I suddenly felt warmth all around me, and I knew that somebody was holding me. The area I was in was surrounded by light.

"It felt as though I were being cradled by someone, and when I saw all this light, I looked around to see what was happening. As I lifted my head I found myself looking into the eyes of Christ. He was carrying me, as a child would be carried, in a cradling fashion.

"There were no fear and no pain, just a feeling of lightness and security—and I kept staring at Him. He was walking with me; then, strangely, He carried me through a wall, or something, and we went from the light into darkness.

"Christ's lips never moved, but He communicated with me, and He asked: 'Do you know where you are? Look around the room.'

"Looking around, as He directed, I saw that we were in the hospital room and He was carrying me toward my body. The darkness frightened me, and I looked back at Christ's face where there was light. Looking at Him calmed me, and then I noticed that we were again moving toward my body.

"Having a sense that I would have to return to my body, I asked Him repeatedly, 'Why? Why?'

"In a soothing way He told me that it was not my time yet. While He stood there holding me, I could see my body plainly. But at the same time, I knew I had a semblance of a body, or a spirit body, that Christ was holding. And I could feel His strength while He held me.

"When He went to lay me down into my body, I tried to resist by grabbing at Him. Crying desperately, I kept repeating: 'Please don't. I don't want to go back.'

"Struggling with my emotions, and crying continuously, I asked Him what I must do. He smiled at me and responded: 'Shhh, everything will be all right.' My gaze was riveted on Him, and He began backing away.

"Christ was moving slowly in a gentle manner, but, as I cried, I wanted Him to stay and talk to me. He addressed me again, saying: 'Keep focused—stay focused!'

"Then the light sort of followed Him out of my room. He was gone.

"Continuing to look for Christ, I saw a light a short distance away, but it was only the light from the area where the nurses were. One of the nurses saw me look, and she announced to the others that I was conscious."

Questions About Debbie's Experience

Debbie agreed that I could ask her some questions. "Can you describe what Christ looked like?" I asked.

"His hair was long and sandy-blonde, with a nice wave in it. He was bearded with a smooth face, and His eyes . . . His eyes were the bluest blue I had ever seen; they were a clear see-through blue. There was warmth, there was love, there was compassion in his eyes. I couldn't look away from Him—He was the one that told me to look around."

"So you did, then, look around?"

"Yes, and when I did I felt fearful."

"How was Christ dressed?"

"He was wearing a white gown."

"Was there light associated with Him?"

"Oh, yes. There was light all around Him; it actually stood off of Him. It was an energy."

"What color was the light?"

"It was white, with a blue tint."

"When you were carried through the wall, where did you wind up?"

"I don't know; I wanted to ask Him how He walked through the wall." Debbie laughed as she thought back on the event. "I don't know where we were because, at that time, I didn't look around. Gazing into the eyes of Christ, as much as I could, there was just light around us. It was a brilliance that filled everyplace."

"How did you know it was Christ?"

Debbie sighed as she gathered her thoughts. "Knowing that my heart was at that much peace, and that I felt so drawn to Him, it had to be Christ.

If it wasn't Christ, I guess I could say, that's where I want to go. He understood me, and He loved me—it was a love that I had not felt previously nor have if felt it since, anyplace on earth."

"Why did you use the word: *peace*?"

"Perhaps it was because I've had such a lack of it in my life. There's always been turmoil and difficulty. With Christ, I finally found peace."

"You mentioned that when you saw your body, you existed in another body. What was your other body like?"

"That's hard to explain, because I was in full body. There were limbs, and I knew Christ was carrying me. But it was without the bulk I normally felt in my earthly body. I felt light, and I also felt as though I had light around me. When He placed me back in my body, it was as if this light, transparent something was entering a bulky body."

"When you saw your body, did you have any feelings toward it?"

"Yes. I didn't want it."

"Why didn't you want it?"

"I didn't want to leave, and when He put me back into my body, I felt as if I couldn't move in that bulky thing. Trying to grab for Him, I reached out, but I couldn't touch Him anymore. There was no way I could get back in His arms."

"You didn't feel pain when you were out of your body?"

"No. Trying to find words in the English language that express the feeling is impossible—I've tried. All the positive thoughts you've ever had will not explain the feeling that I had. The word that most expresses it is: *peace*. I was deliriously happy while I was there. I never wanted to return here. Later, when I was back, I was ashamed at the way I clung to Christ and cried while He brought me to my body. It must have been hard on Him to have to return me under those circumstances.

"My feelings haven't changed much about this life, since my experience." Debbie began to cry as she attempted to explain her feelings. "In that environment of love, and in my innocence at the time, I was fed up with the world and its mixture of hypocrisy, hate, envy and pain. I still feel that way. My anger at returning to this cruel world spills over at times, and the only relief I get is from prayer. Praying long and hard is my solution."

Debbie's Recovery, and Her Final Thoughts

"The film of my operation was a documentary of medical history. They had to cut my jaw in two places, and my jaw was wired shut after the operation. The wires weren't supposed to come off for at least four to six weeks. They un-wired me in two-and-a-half weeks, and my jaw was healed. During the healing process, I didn't feel pain with my mouth—Christ healed me.

"My jaw healed well, but I did have a relapse. Since my jaw was wired shut, they could only feed me through straws, and they gave me this terrible protein stuff. I hated it, so when they gave it to me I hid it in the closet; I wouldn't drink it. After a few days I passed out, and they found out what I was doing. They put tubes back down me and fed me that way until I recovered."

"How long were you in the hospital?"

"It was the Wilford Hall Medical Center in San Antonio, Texas, and I was there for two months."

"Did you tell others about your experience when you regained consciousness?"

"My mouth was wired shut, so I had to write messages to talk. I wanted to tell my doctor, but he wouldn't let me. He just said: 'Honey, I know you are blessed,' and he kissed me on the lips. After that, I sort of shut the experience inside of me."

"Do you think your experience could have been a dream or a hallucination?"

"No. It was too real—as real as my sitting here next to you."

"Are there any messages you would like to leave for others?"

"Yes. The Bible says not to judge others, and that is the primary message I would like others to have. We can't know the circumstances of others, so we shouldn't judge them."

Chapter 16

A LESSON IN PAIN

DeLynn

DeLynn had stopped off at the University of Utah Medical Center for a brief check-up when I first met him in March 1993. He smiled and shook hands as we sat in the hall to conduct our interview.

Having read a little of DeLynn's experience before meeting him, I knew that he had severe chronic health problems. When he joined me, therefore, I was unprepared for the vigorous, lively man who shook my hand with aggressive good nature. He was shorter than the average man, but his youthful appearance and energetic nature dispelled my preconception.

DeLynn was born in October 1951 at the Utah Valley Hospital in Provo, Utah. Upon his birth the medical people observed that there was something wrong with his body. He was secreting excessive salt, and he was having severe intestinal and pulmonary problems. These problems ultimately led to a diagnosis of cystic fibrosis.

During much of his youth DeLynn was raised in the Orem, Utah area where his family found a physician who could properly treat DeLynn's disease. Until the age of five or six, DeLynn was not able to eat normal foods; he grew up on liver, rice water and fruit. His diet allowed no milk, no greases or fats, and no whole grains. This restricted diet was largely the cause of his short stature.

DeLynn was the oldest of four brothers and one sister. All of the children were adopted so the genetic origin of his disease was unknown.

Both of DeLynn's parents had obtained higher degrees. DeLynn's father had a doctorate in chemistry, and DeLynn's mother had a master's degree. Because of their educational status they actively sought information concerning DeLynn's symptoms in medical journals—at that time, cystic fibrosis was not well understood. It was not discovered as a genetic disease until 1945, and most of the research was in the eastern part of the United States. DeLynn was ten years old before they identified his problem as cystic fibrosis.

After attending high school in Orem, DeLynn went to college where he obtained a Bachelor of Science degree.

During his youth, and later, DeLynn and his parents learned how to minimize problems with the disease. Diet was a prime control factor, and he learned to avoid excessive sun or heat. However, DeLynn believes that there was another factor that contributed to the long-term control of his disease. I will let him tell his story from this point.

A Father's Blessing

"By the time I was five years old my parents had faced many crises with my health. Neither they nor the medical community knew what the real cause was of my recurrent health problems. My parents were concerned about my long-term survival; consequently, one day my father sat me down on the sewing stool in our home and gave me a blessing. In the blessing he promised that if I remained faithful to the Lord, as a little boy, and later as a responsible adult, I would receive all of the blessings of a normal person. He told me that I would live a normal life.

"Had my father known how serious my disease was, he might not have promised all the things that he did. As it was, since he was largely ignorant of the real implications of my illness, the blessing he gave was unrestricted. Subsequently all of the promises in the blessing were fulfilled. I still remember the promises as he gave them. The blessing has had an enormous impact on my life.

"Concerning the promise of marriage, I met a wonderful lady where we were both teaching classes. This young woman was a superb teacher and I was impressed and attracted to her. At the time, we were both dating and engaged to separate fiancés. We were each having trouble with our respective relationships. We used to get together and commiserate over our respective problems. It took me about three years to get my head together and ask my friend to marry me. We were married in July 1977 and have since adopted our two boys, who are now eleven and seven."

Health Crises

"After we were married, I fell ill with pneumonia and other difficulties related to cystic fibrosis, but nothing life-threatening until January of 1985. For one week I couldn't pass anything, and I felt very ill. I was not sure what the trouble was. It turned out that I had a blocked bowel—common with cystic fibrosis—and it was a serious blockage. It got bad enough that I couldn't even stand up.

"My wife took me to the Utah Valley Regional Medical Center after I collapsed on the morning of January 10. The doctor examined me and said that he had to operate immediately or I would die. I doubted that my illness was that serious. He again assured me, with the utmost urgency, that there must be an immediate operation or they could not save me.

"They operated right then, and they found two liters of black sewer water in a gangrenous bowel. They removed the diseased portion of the bowel—and my appendix burst. I was in very serious condition, but I recovered. That was the first major operation that I had.

"Because of the severity of the disease I had in my bowel, and because of scar tissue from the first operation, one-and-one-half years later the bowel became blocked again. I returned to the same hospital and the same doctor, and he operated again. Two days after that operation it abscessed, and they had to operate a third time.

"The third operation was on my hospital bed. They could not put me under anesthesia because that would have killed me."

"Did they use a local anesthetic?" I asked DeLynn.

"They used no anesthetic at all. My surgeon instructed one of the three nurses to lie on my legs and hold me so that I wouldn't move. The other nurse was instructed to hold my hand and tell me when to breathe in order to keep me from hyperventilating. The third nurse was the surgeon's operating assistant.

"After disinfecting the area, the surgeon retrieved a pair of surgical scissors which he plunged into the abscessed area in order to reopen the incision. There was a crunching feeling throughout my body as he slowly cut through the abdominal wall. I was writhing in pain. Finally he stopped cutting and pinched open the abscess. The scene was so gruesome that the nurse lying on my legs passed out. After cleaning out the infected area, he sewed me up with rough, catgut thread. When he tied the knot, the thread broke, upon which he ordered a larger needle and thicker thread. Needless to say, the entire process was extremely painful and emotionally traumatic.

"After that series of operations I recovered and resumed life. In November of 1988 I was admitted to the Utah Valley Hospital with a moderately high temperature, pneumonia, and a severe sinus headache. They let me go home for Thanksgiving dinner; however I felt so bad and my teeth were hurting so much that I couldn't eat. I went back to the hospital. The next day I went to my dentist and had him take X-rays, thinking that I might need root canal work on my teeth.

"My dentist said that I had the worst case of sinusitis he had seen. He urged me to see an Ear, Nose and Throat Specialist. I returned to the hospital and they had an ENT specialist examine me. Upon completing the examination he explained that I must have an emergency operation.

"Three hours later I was on the operating table. They asked me to count backwards from ten as they administered the anesthetic. Before I lost consciousness I remember thinking: *I wonder if I'm going to wake up from this one?*

"When I awakened, my wife, as usual, was waiting for me. She reassured me that I had behaved well and the doctors were pleased. Unlike other operations, however, I noticed that I had many wires attached to me. I was wearing an oxygen mask and there was an urgency about the people as they attended to my needs.

"I asked my wife: 'What's going on?' and she said: 'It was a difficult operation and you bled a lot. They had to give you two units of blood.'

"They put me in the Intermediate Care section of the hospital and for four days I was in and out of consciousness. Blood continued to be lost down my throat, requiring that I receive three more units. This worried me because of the fear of contracting AIDS.

"I remained in IMC until Tuesday, November 29, when they put me in a private room. My doctor came into the room to remove the nose packing that had been tightly packed into my sinuses to minimize bleeding. As he was pulling the packing out of my sinuses through my nostrils, it seemed as if there would never be an end to the packing. The pain was excruciating. I was crying from the intense pain, but he just kept pulling and pulling. My mother left the room because she could not bear to see me suffer such pain.

"When the doctor left I just wanted to go to sleep and forget the pain. I was totally exhausted, both physically and emotionally."

A Trip in a Tunnel

"In the early morning hours of Wednesday, November 30, I woke up to the realization that I was no longer in my body. In fact, I was being drawn down a tunnel. Had it not been for the books I had read about near-death experiences, I would have probably been ignorant of where I was."

I interrupted DeLynn's narration and asked: "You had read books about the near-death experience, then, before you went through this?"

"Yes. For some reason I had a fascination with the subject."

"Okay, so you were in the tunnel. What happened next?"

"I found myself being drawn toward a bright light that was down the tunnel. The tunnel was about seventy-five yards long, and as I was drawn toward the light, I finally realized where I was and I said to myself: *Whoa, stop!* I had to consciously say, stop. My movement wasn't by walking, it was more like floating. But it wasn't floating, either. It was a different process than anything I had experienced in mortal life.

"As I told myself to stop, I stopped moving. I was about half-way down the tunnel with the light at the end I was moving toward. Turning around and looking at the opposite end, I saw my family sitting there. My wife was there with our two boys sitting on her lap. I thought to myself: *This is really strange.*

"Before I had this experience, and knowing how serious my disease was, I told myself that if I ever went through a near-death experience, I would ask a set of questions. My first question was: *If I came into this world naked, how do I leave the world?* I looked down and saw that I was dressed in a white garment, tailored like a jump suit. The material had a thick weave to it, yet it had the softest feel of any material I had ever felt. It was softer than silk and it glowed. The color of the material was the whitest white I had ever seen. The suit covered most of my body. Starting with a snug, but comfortable neckline, it had full sleeves to my wrists, and full legs to my ankles. A curious part of the suit was that it had no openings such as those we need as humans. I wondered briefly about this aspect of the clothing, but then I focused my attention on other questions.

"One amazing aspect of my experience attracted my early attention. Because I had suffered from cystic fibrosis since youth I was not aware that breathing could be a pleasant exercise. I soon noticed, in the tunnel, that I was breathing and it didn't hurt. I could actually fill my lungs and it didn't burn, it didn't sting, it didn't tickle! How exhilarating it was for someone who had never breathed without difficulty. Filling my lungs was such a pleasure that I stayed in the same place for a moment simply enjoying it.

"Not only were my lungs responding without pain, I next noticed that I had no pain throughout my body. Pain had been a constant companion throughout my life; I had learned to accept it as normal. I learned there, however, that pain was not normal. For the first time I realized how intense my pain had been. It was a wonderful feeling—to be without pain—one that I sometimes have to force myself to forget when I am having painful sieges in the hospital.

"A second question that I had puzzled over was: *If I am a spirit when I die, do I really have substance to me?*

"To find out whether I had substance, I rubbed my hands together and I felt my face with my hands. In both cases I found that I had form and substance. I could feel myself. Looking at my hands, I saw that they looked like my hands normally did, except there was a glow to them. My feet weren't visible, I'm not sure why, but I knew that I didn't have shoes or socks on. These discoveries excited me. I remember thinking: *Wow! This is great.*

"Another issue that I had wondered about from reading the near-death literature was the physical characteristics of the tunnel. When that thought entered my mind I found myself at the side of the tunnel. My tunnel was about as wide as this hallway (about 30 feet), and it resembled a half-circle. The texture of the tunnel, which I felt, was rough and undulating. The side of the tunnel was cool. Indeed, it had temperature, texture and form.

"One of my anxieties about death was that of fear. To my delight I found that the emotion of fear was nonexistent. There was absolutely no worry, no concern, no fear. My primary emotion was a feeling of security. I was alone, and yet I knew that I wasn't alone. There was something else there that was encompassing me. I felt warm and serene—fear couldn't exist in that environment. It was a wonderful feeling."

A Familiar Voice

"At this point in my experience I became aware of a voice talking to me. My surroundings, and my analysis of them, had so interested me that I had not paid attention to the voice at first. It was a soft, fatherly voice that kept repeating my name. Facing the light, and then turning 90 degrees to my left and looking up at a slight angle, I looked to see where the voice was coming from. There was no one that I could see—but the voice persisted, not in my ears, but in my mind. I finally responded by asking the voice: *What?*

"The voice didn't immediately respond. I wondered how I could hear with my mind and not my ears, and I learned that it wasn't necessary for me to understand the process just then. My mind next thought the questions: *Why am I here? Why me? I'm a good guy—why did I die?*

"The voice answered: *You are here because you have earned the right to be here based on what you did on earth. The pain you have suffered qualifies you to be here. You have suffered as much pain in 37 years as a normal person might have suffered in 87 years.*

"I asked: *It's pain that gets me here?* and the answer was yes.

"This still puzzled me so I asked: *But why was it necessary for me to suffer so? I was a worthy member of Christ's Church; I kept all the commandments. Why me?*

"Then I received a most startling answer. He said to me: *You chose your disease and the amount of pain you would be willing to suffer before this life—when you were in a premortal state. It was your choice.*

"While I was hearing this voice, I became aware that it was a familiar voice—it was one that I knew. It was a voice that I had not heard during my mortal lifetime. When it was speaking to me, though, there was no question but that I knew who it was. There was enormous love for me in the voice."

"You said, DeLynn, that you knew who the voice was. Who was it?" I asked.

"It was my Father in Heaven."

"It was not Jesus Christ?"

"No."

"And you felt love in the voice?"

"We don't have a word that would describe what I felt from Him toward me. The closest word we have is *love*, but it doesn't begin to describe the feeling. There is no appropriate description in mortal tongue that can explain the feeling—you have to feel it."

A Premortal Choice

"When He told me that it was my choice, in a premortal environment, to suffer when I came to earth, I was both astonished and incredulous. He must have understood my incredulity, because I was immediately transported to my premortal existence. There was a room that I was viewing from above and to the side, but at the same time I was sitting in it. In a sense I was both an observer and a participant. About thirty people were in the room, both men and women, and we were all dressed in the white jump-suit type of garment.

"An instructor was in the front of the room, and he was teaching about accountability and responsibility—and about pain. He was instructing us about things we had to know in order to come to earth and get our bodies. Then he said, and I'll never forget this: *You can learn lessons one of two ways. You can move through life slowly, and have certain experiences, or there are ways that you can learn the lessons very quickly through pain and disease.* He wrote on the board the words: *Cystic Fibrosis*, and he turned and asked for volunteers. I was a volunteer; I saw me raise my hand and offer to take the challenge.

"The instructor looked at me and agreed to accept me. That was the end of the scene, and it changed forever my perspective of the disease that I previously felt was a plague on my life. No longer did I consider myself a victim. Rather, I was a privileged participant, by choice, in an eternal plan. That plan, if I measured up to the potential of my choice, would allow me to advance in mortal life in the fastest way possible. True, I would not be able to control the inevitable slow deterioration of my mortal body, but I could control how I chose to handle my illness emotionally and psychologically. The specific choice of cystic fibrosis was to help me learn dignity in suffering. My understanding in the eternal sense was complete—I knew that I was a powerful, spiritual being that chose to have a short, but marvelous, mortal existence."

A View of Gethsemane

"While I was marveling at this new-found knowledge, or rather, from the reawakened knowledge that I previously had, I was again transported to another era. This time I found myself looking on a different scene—the scene was the Garden of Gethsemane. Looking down from above, I saw Christ undergoing his ordeal of pain with dignified endurance."

"When you were transported to these different scenes in time, DeLynn, did you ask to see them?"

"No, they were completely automatic. The first one seemed to be in response to my astonishment when the voice told me that I chose the disease, cystic fibrosis, in a premortal life. I suspect that the second scene, in Gethsemane, was to teach me more about the value of a dignified endurance of pain."

"Did you feel anything when you saw Christ suffering?"

"I felt bad that he had to go through it, and I felt empathy for him. I also realized why he was doing it; I understood that it was his choice, just as cystic fibrosis had been my choice."

A Familiar Home

"When the scene in Gethsemane closed, I found myself back in the tunnel. At this point I realized that I had come *home*. Everything was familiar—especially God's love. His voice was a familiar voice of unlimited and unconditional love.

"The knowledge I was obtaining, too, was knowledge that I had held before. The events in my experience merely reawakened in me a dormant part of my memory, and it was wonderful. I no longer felt picked on because of my pain and illness. I understood the choices I had made and the reasons for them. And I understood the tremendous love that God had for me to allow me to make those choices—and to suffer pain.

"The realization that this was all by my choice had an enormous rejuvenating effect on me. I was no longer a victim of chance, or worse yet, of some punishment for wrong doing. In the broadest sense I now saw myself as a master of my own destiny—if I lived up to the possibilities of my choices. Instead of looking at cystic fibrosis as a severe disability, I was now able to look on it as my truest mentor.

"It was astonishing, the speed with which I was learning. Knowledge that had somehow slumbered deep in my soul was released, and I was extremely exhilarated by this reawakened knowledge. Light and knowledge were flowing into me from every direction. I could feel it. Every part of my body was reverberating with the light gushing in. Even my fingertips were receptors of light and knowledge. It was as if I were drinking from a fully engaged fire hydrant. I was excited with the thought of going further into this wonderful world of knowledge and love. So I turned, expecting to travel toward the light at the end of the tunnel."

A Decision to Return

"The light was overwhelming. It was at the end of the tunnel, and it lighted the inside of the tunnel. It was pure white and it was the brightest bright I had ever seen. I was drawn to it, and I turned to move in that direction.

"As I turned, I heard my youngest son, who was three at the time, ask: 'Daddy, what are you doing?'

"I asked: 'What?' and he repeated: 'What are you doing?'

"I answered: 'I don't know. What am I doing?'

"The Voice then said: 'What do you want to do?'

"Evidently I was going to have to make another choice, and that choice would involve returning to my family or staying where I was.

"Speaking to the Voice, I asked: 'If I choose to go back to my family, can I go back, and what will be the consequences?'

"The Voice responded: 'You may return, but you may lose your reward.' My reward flashed before me, and I saw that eternal happiness would be mine if I chose to stay.

"The Voice also told me that there were no guarantees if I returned. He said that if I chose to go back to earth I would have greater pain than I had ever felt in life to that point. Puzzling over the risks of returning, I then asked: 'What gives me the right to go back?'

"The Voice said: 'You have learned accountability and responsibility. If you choose to go back you have the obligation to teach those principles to your family and your employees.'

"I wondered about that charge and asked: 'What do my employees have to do with it?' He didn't answer the question. I later learned that my employees were included so that I would, in time, overcome my fear of telling others about this entire experience. They, too, were part of my 'family.'

"When I finished asking questions about returning or staying, I again analyzed the risks and rewards of staying or returning. After I was satisfied that I understood the options, I said: 'I choose to return.'

"The Voice asked me: 'Are you sure?'

"My response was: 'Yes, I'm sure.

"He asked, again: 'Are you sure?'

"My answer, this time, was: 'Yes, I think so.'

"A third time the Voice asked: 'Are you sure?'

"This time it hit me. My answer must be certain—I must not lie to myself or try to conceal my real intent from Him. I looked again at my family. I thought about it, and I said: 'Yes, I choose to return.'

"The next thing I knew, I was back in my hospital room. The pajamas I was wearing and the bed linens were soaked. The doctors and nurses seemed concerned, and one of the nurses asked me what happened. Not wanting to tell her about the experience, I said that I must have choked. She responded: 'You did more than that!'"

Out-of-Body in the Hospital Room

"The night nurse came into my room, to stay the rest of the night with me. I asked her to watch and make sure that I didn't go to sleep—I was afraid to sleep. The experience I had just been through was so traumatic I was afraid to repeat it.

"Settling in a chair behind me, the nurse talked to me for a while. Her chair was far enough behind me that I couldn't see her without twisting to an awkward position in the bed. Suddenly, however, I could see her. Finding myself sitting up in my bed, I waved my arms at her to see what she would do. I was amazed that she didn't see me.

"During this brief period, I was acutely aware of many small events happening around me. It was about 2:00 a.m., and the clock in the room was ticking loudly. I was conscious of people in the hall outside my room and of the light in the hall. It was an increased sensitivity of my complete surroundings. Sounds were much clearer than they normally were.

"Wondering what was going on, I turned my head and saw my body lying in the bed. The real *me*, my spirit self, was partially removed from my body. I was sitting out of my body from the waist up.

"Thinking to myself: *Here I go again*, I wondered what to do. I offered a little prayer in which I said: *Lord, I don't want to leave.* The impression came to me: *Well, then, lie back down in your body.* I lay down—I felt no transition—it was as if I just woke up.

"Without moving a muscle I said to the night nurse: 'You can't just sit there and knit. You've got to help me stay awake.' She responded:

'How do you know I'm knitting? You can't see me.' I told her that I knew everything that was happening in the room.

"The nurse commented that I had scared her enough that night. Six months after the event I asked the same nurse what her experience with me was during this period. She said that when she first came back into the room and found me, I was cold and gray, my mouth was open, my eyes were glassed over, there was no pulse, and my skin was clammy. That's when they called for the crash-cart and the doctor to resuscitate me."

Questions About DeLynn's Experience

In order to better understand some of the events in DeLynn's experience I received his permission to ask questions. I began: "When you first moved into the tunnel you mentioned that breathing was pleasant for you. Were you breathing air, or what?"

"I don't think it was air, but I have no idea what it was. The pleasantness and reality of my breathing, though, is still vividly clear in my memory."

"When you found yourself in a premortal environment, what did the room look like?"

"It was a rectangular room, everything was white, and we were sitting in desk-type chairs. I was assimilating the teacher's instruction as fast as he gave it to us. Notes were unnecessary. I simply absorbed everything I was told instantaneously."

"Did the information you were getting seem as if it were new information?"

"The procedures we were being taught were new, but the principles guiding those procedures, I already knew. The *how to* portions of the earthly experience were new. I remember thinking about it and wondering if I were ready to pay the price, and then deciding that, yes, I was willing to pay the price."

"So, when you saw yourself in the premortal environment, you could actually remember how you felt in that earlier time?"

"Yes. I knew my thoughts from the premortal experience. I could see myself sitting in the room, yet I knew what I had been thinking and feeling when I was in that room. I can remember thinking: *Be careful about that choice—you don't even know what pain is.*"

"So it was as if you were two different people, yet you had the feelings of both?"

"Yes. They were simultaneous feelings."

"When your son talked to you in the tunnel he asked you what you were doing. Have you asked him about the experience?"

"Yes. He is unaware of having talked to me."

"But you are convinced that he did talk to you?"

"Absolutely. He never opened his mouth, but I heard him call my name, and I recognized his voice."

"You mentioned the tunnel as a short one. You didn't feel that you traveled a long distance?"

"No, it was about the length of a football field. There was a drawing power, like a magnet in the center of my chest that drew me into the tunnel and toward the light. I didn't travel far."

"When you returned to your body, did you feel pain again?"

"Most certainly. There was no pain associated with returning to my body. I didn't feel that process; I just woke up. The pain associated with my operation was severe and instantaneous, though. Of course I've had other pain related to my disease since then."

"What was your recovery like?"

"I was out of the hospital within the next few days. My energy was up, and I felt invigorated. That didn't take away the pain, however, I just dealt with it better. The experience has helped me over time to deal with pain better."

"Have you had greater pain than before?"

"I thought when the doctor used scissors—to slice into me without an anesthetic—that I couldn't experience worse pain. This past winter, the winter of 1992-1993, I was in the hospital over ninety days. They almost lost me twice. Again, I had a blocked bowel in which they used barium while X-raying my bowels. I was unsuccessful in cleansing my bowels of the barium, and it set up like rocks in my intestine. Passing those rocks almost killed me. I became allergic to most of the pain killers they were giving me, and I had to pass the barium rocks over a period of four days without pain killer. The pain was so bad that if it hadn't been for my Dad, I don't think I would have made it."

"What did your Dad have to do with it?"

"My father died in March 1992. He came back and gave me a blessing, and that relieved me of the pain."

"What do you mean, your father came back and blessed you?"

"My father and I were very close. He was the one that gave me the blessing when I was five years old. When he died, I became aware of it before the doctor called. The same voice that I heard in the tunnel told me, during the night, that my father had died (Dad died early Monday morning). My father came to me at 1:30 a.m., Tuesday morning, and told me several things, including why he had to go, and what I should be doing. Then Dad said that he would be with me when I had medical emergencies.

"In August 1992, when I was in so much pain from the barium (morphine shots administered every two hours were not helping), one night at three in the morning, I cried out: *Lord, what did I do wrong?* I also cried: *Dad, you promised you would be here!* Suddenly my father was at my bed and I felt him put his hands on my head. Within a few seconds, there was a feeling as if someone were pouring something warm over my body. It cascaded from my head to my toes, and the pain left. My father smiled and then he left. The next day I began passing the stones."

"You said that your choice was to come back to earth despite the knowledge that you would be subjected to greater pain. Do you know why you made that choice?"

"I wanted to be with my family—I would do anything to be with my boys and my wife."

"Did you have a feeling for any mission you might have?"

"Yes. My purpose for being, now, is to teach people accountability and responsibility; to teach them that they are agents with freedom to choose; and to let them know that there is a Father in Heaven who loves them beyond all description."

"Because of this experience, have your feelings about life or death changed?"

"Absolutely. Life has greater meaning, since I no longer look at myself as an unfortunate victim of disease. Nor am I the victim of other circumstances caused by family, parents, neighbors, and others—or of 'accidents.' Instead, I make the choices that decide my fate. That is a wonderfully liberating feeling."

"Has the experience changed your religious perspective?"

"Yes. My priorities have changed. I am more people oriented than I was before. I used to be program oriented, but now I know that people are far more important than programs. My experience taught me that the

Lord has boundless love for *all* people, whether or not they are members of any particular church."

"Is there any message you would like to leave for others?"

"Yes. Despite what the world teaches, there is a loving Father in Heaven who loves *every* person. That love, which I have experienced, is indescribable. We are literally the children of God, and He knows each one of us by name. He is willing to bless us with any righteous desires that we have. All we need to do is ask—and be willing to pay the price."

Chapter 17

CHILDREN'S EXPERIENCES

Eileen and Jennifer

Carol and I visited Eileen in her motel room, where she, her husband, and her children were staying prior to returning to their home after an extended stay in Egypt for her husband's work. Eileen smiled, invited us in, and seated us next to the window where we could watch the February snowfall.

Eileen's even features were accented by large brown eyes, a dazzling smile, and a warm personality. She informed us that she was born in 1952 in California. She had brothers, and Eileen and her brothers were raised by her mother who was divorced. They grew up in Utah, where their grandparents lived.

Jeff, Eileen's husband, was employed in the international arena, and she informed us that he was a wonderful man. Both Eileen and Jeff had previous marriages, and they had seven children between them. Eileen was introduced to Jeff by her brother, and they later married.

Jennifer, the first of Eileen's and Jeff's children, was born in 1981. Eileen said that Jennifer was an active child who appeared to live each minute to the fullest, even as a small child.

Eileen told Carol and me that, for many years, she had often had spiritual warnings concerning events in her life. These warnings usually involved relatives or someone close to her. The spiritual communications, in some instances, were so dramatic, and the later actual events so sure, that her family had come to rely on them. Her husband and children understood that when the warnings came they should pay attention.

197

A Spiritual Warning and a Reassurance

Eileen began her story: "In about 1985 I began to have feelings that something bad was going to happen. It was a panic type feeling; it persisted for months, and it seemed to center around Jennifer. I told my husband about it, and I had him put dead bolts on the door. As the year progressed the feelings became even more pronounced.

"Finally, the feelings got so strong that neighbors, and others of my friends, noticed that something was wrong. I would call them frequently, for example, and ask if my children were there, and I would urge them to check and see if everything was all right. It became almost an obsession, as if I had to know where the children were for each moment of time. Some of my neighbors began to tell me that I needed to settle down and be less obsessive about the children's welfare.

"My husband and I were getting ready to go on a vacation, the first one where I had agreed to leave the children, but I didn't feel good about it. I told my husband about my bad feelings, but he said we needed to go.

"On the day before we were to leave, I was driving to a doctor's appointment, and as I passed through an underpass this strange electrical feeling went through my body. Simultaneous with the electrical feeling the Spirit told me that there was going to be an accident, it would be one of my children, and the child would be okay.

"I asked the Spirit which child would be injured and the answer was: 'Jennifer.' I asked: 'Will she live?' and the Spirit responded, 'Yes.' I asked, again: 'Do you promise that she will live?' and the answer was: 'Yes, I promise.' I then asked, 'Will I be able to raise all of my children to adulthood?' and the Spirit told me yes. At that point I insisted on getting a further commitment by saying: 'Are you sure—do you promise me?' and I could feel someone right there in the car with me—no face, no body, just a presence—and the Spirit again told me: 'Yes, I promise.'

"Our communication was not vocal. It was a mental communication on a spirit-to-spirit level. When I got the final reassurance from the Spirit that Jennifer would live, the tears flowed from my eyes. I continued my trip to the doctor happy in the knowledge that my daughter would live.

"When I got home I told Jeff that we couldn't leave on the trip until he completed the fence in our back yard to protect our children. I insisted that my feelings were still there about the accident, and I wanted to take every precaution. I told him I thought Jennifer was going to be run over, and I wanted the fence completed so she couldn't get out of the back yard.

"Jeff went to one of our neighbors, who was a doctor, and asked for his help in finishing the fence. He told Dave, the neighbor, about my feelings concerning Jennifer, and Dave agreed to help.

"During the morning breakfast, before the children went out to play, I looked at them and said: 'If any of you get hit by a car, *do not die*, because Mom and Dad and the doctors will help you. Promise me that you won't die.' The children looked at me and said: 'Okay, Mom, we won't die.'"

A Terrible Accident

"Jennifer was five years old at the time, and she went over to the neighbor's house to play after promising that she wouldn't go into the street. Jeff and Dave were working on the fence in the back yard, and I was scrubbing the floor trying to get ready for our departure at six. At two-thirty in the afternoon, while I was working on the floor, I had this overwhelming feeling that I should call again to my girlfriend's house, where Jennifer was playing.

"My girlfriend said: 'She's fine, Eileen. I just fed her a hot dog, and they're playing in the cul-de-sac. Nothing's going to happen.'

"I hung up the phone, and I had that electrical feeling again—then the phone rang. My girlfriend was on the phone, and she said: 'Jennifer's been run over.' I said: 'I knew it.'

"Calling to Jeff in the back yard, I told him that Jennifer had been run over. Jeff and Dave, the doctor, ran to my neighbor's and found Jennifer. I got there shortly after them. They were holding my bloodied child in their arms. Her stomach had been mashed flat, and she was all scratched up. She looked at me and said: 'I'm okay Mommy, I didn't die.'

"A one-ton truck with dual wheels on the back had run over her. The driver had been smoking marijuana. Jennifer was on a hot-cycle when the truck ran over her. The driver said he felt something that seemed to be a child's toy, so he stepped on the accelerator to get over it, stopping when he heard a muffled scream. Then he got out and saw a child with the truck's rear wheels on her. He got back in the truck and pulled it off her. Then he picked her up and set her on the grass, thinking she was dead.

"While he was searching for help Jennifer jumped up and started yelling at the truck driver. He was shocked that she was still alive; he picked her up and brought her to my neighbor where my husband and Dave found them.

"Jeff and Dave rushed her to the hospital where they examined her. Her stomach was crushed flat, and they told us that it was unlikely she could live. She was still conscious, and she kept asking for water.

"The policeman who was there and Jeff gave Jennifer a blessing. In the blessing she was told that her mission in life had not yet been completed, and she would live to complete it. She was also told that she would touch many lives, and she was promised that her face, which was badly damaged, would not sustain any scars.

"They transferred her to the McKay Dee Hospital in Ogden where they had better facilities. My husband rode in the ambulance with her, and my girlfriend drove me in her car. When we got to the hospital nine physicians examined her. By then her face had swollen and turned purple, and her eye was bulging out. They said she was probably hemorrhaging and her brain was swelling. One of the doctors told us that she couldn't live through the night.

"I began to doubt myself and my husband's blessing. I turned to him and said: 'You promised she would live!' At that point I remembered what the Spirit had told me the day before, and I offered a silent prayer.

"They did a CAT scan and X-rays, and they found no broken bones. The doctors still didn't offer much hope. They said an aneurysm could be the cause of her death. She was in intensive care for eight days."

A Visit by a Great-grandfather

"While she was in intensive care, and in her greatest pain, she kept calling for her Grandpa Lemmon. We asked her why she called for Grandpa Lemmon whom she had never met. We asked her if she meant her other living grandfather. She insisted it was Grandpa Lemmon—who was actually her great-grandfather on my husband's side—who had died many years earlier.

"During this difficult and painful period for Jennifer I urged her to fight and stay alive, and she kept reassuring me that she wasn't going to die. She said that Jeff and I should go on our trip since she was going to be okay. The hospital physicians still felt that Jennifer would not live, and they had us talk to a psychologist to prepare us for what they thought was inevitable.

"As time progressed, the hospital staff began to talk of a miracle. They observed that it had to be a miracle that she was still alive. They had no explanation as to why she was still with us.

"Jennifer was taken to therapy each day and treated for her injuries. The therapist, whom we got to know, asked who Grandpa Lemmon was. He said that Jennifer kept asking about Grandpa Lemmon. Explaining that he was her great-grandfather, we told the therapist that Jennifer had never met him. We had no idea why she continued to talk about him; we thought she was mixed up over her grandfathers, and we told the therapist that.

"After eight days they released Jennifer because she was so anxious to return home. We did not talk about the accident to ourselves or to Jennifer because it was too painful for us. Jennifer healed well, with no scars on her face, and we resumed life.

"Two years later, when Jennifer was seven, we went to a family reunion in Idaho. Great-grandmother Lemmon was still alive and would be at the reunion, and this would be the first opportunity for Jennifer to meet her. In Great-grandmother's house she had one wall devoted to pictures of relatives—grandchildren, great-grandchildren, children, spouses, and others. Great-grandfather Lemmon was active in athletics during his life, having been a professional ball player when he was young, and his wife had pictures of him on the wall amongst all the others.

"When we arrived my son took Jennifer to the wall of pictures, and she pointed to one of them and said: 'There's Grandpa Lemmon. That's how he looked when he came to me while I was under the truck; only, he was all dressed in white.' We were astonished, and we queried her further about the incident. We asked her if he said anything to her, and she said: 'Yes, he told me that he loved me and everything would be okay, and to tell Grandma that he loved her.'

"The picture that she had selected was taken when Great-grandpa Lemmon was thirty-five years of age. He was in coveralls with the farm as backdrop. I showed her some other pictures when he was older, but she said he didn't look like that. When Great-grandmother Lemmon came in and heard Jennifer, she cried and cried. She told us that she had seen him too, and he looked as he did when he was young."

A Conversation with Jennifer

Shortly after I finished interviewing Eileen, the door opened and a lovely girl with short curly blond hair entered the room. She was a typical eleven-year-old with the bouncy energy of youth. She asked her mother if she could go swimming in the motel pool. Eileen asked her to join us for a moment. She sat next to me, while I positioned the tape recorder, and she displayed the complete trust only possible from the very young.

Our conversation was as follows: "What is your name?"

"Jennifer."

"How old are you, Jennifer?"

"Eleven."

"What grade are you in school?"

"Fourth."

"What other country did you just return from?"

"Egypt."

"How did you like Egypt?"

"It was okay, but I like it here."

"And you will have some new friends, won't you?"

"Yes."

"Jennifer, once, a long time ago you had a truck run over you, didn't you?"

"Yes."

"Can you tell me what happened?"

"I was riding my bike, outside, and this truck was parked over there. I saw it, and no one was in it, so I went over to the other side of the street on the bike. The truck started to go when I was trying to get up the hill. I couldn't get up the hill, and he ran over me."

"Do you remember any of what happened when he ran over you?"

"He stopped on top of me, and he got out of the truck."

"Did you see anybody or hear anything when you were under the truck?"

"Yes, I saw my grandpa," said Jennifer in a matter-of-fact tone.

"What did your grandpa say, and what did he look like?"

"He was in a white robe, and he told me I would be okay and that they would take me to the hospital."

"Did you feel that he was telling you the truth?"

"Yes."

"Had you ever seen your grandpa before?"

"No."

"How did you know it was your grandpa?"

"I don't know, but . . . like a year later we went to my grandma's house. My brother picked me up and asked me which one I saw, and I pointed to my grandpa."

With Eileen's urging Jennifer then showed the scar on her stomach where the truck had run over her. It was an obvious scar, but it had healed nicely. There was no sign of scarring on her face. She was a beautiful eleven-year-old full of the joy of life. She quickly left us and reappeared in her swimming suit. She and her friend bounded from the room toward the swimming pool.

Rocky and Berta

Carol and I visited Rocky and his mother, Berta, on a bright spring day in 1993. Berta was a youthful appearing petite lady with an energetic manner. Rocky and several beautiful children were in and out during our visit, and it was obvious that love and respect were shared by the mother and children.

Berta was born in Kansas in 1950, and her parents moved to New Mexico where she grew up. There were four children in Berta's family, and her father died when she was five years old. She had a loving step-father who helped raise her until she was in the eighth grade, when he died.

Schooling for Berta was accomplished in New Mexico. She completed high school and attended college for one year. Upon reaching the age of twenty-one, Berta and her mother moved to Colorado and opened a wig and clothing business.

In 1978 Berta married her present husband, and in 1984 they moved to Utah. At the time of our visit, they had eight children; three of them were adopted.

Berta was raised Methodist, and her husband was raised Baptist. Neither of them, as they were raising their children, was actively involved with their particular faiths. In 1983 Berta began reading from the Bible and telling the children Bible stories, but church attendance was sporadic.

After visiting with Berta and her delightful children, and absorbing what she had to tell us of her background, Carol and I asked her to tell of the events leading up to the experience. She began the story.

A Bad Fall and a Prayer

"In November 1983, we moved to Oklahoma City where my husband had been transferred for his work. In May 1984, my son, who had turned four years old that February, came in the house soaking wet from a mud-puddle he and his friends had been playing in. I told him to go upstairs and change his clothes.

"His friends were waiting at the front door. My neighbor and I were sitting near a window, and I saw a flash go by the window, but I dismissed it from my mind when I looked over and saw nothing. The neighbor and I continued visiting until the little children came in and asked for Rocky.

"The children went up to Rocky's room when I directed them there, but they returned shortly saying that Rocky wasn't in the bedroom. Instantly I knew that the flash I had seen was my son, so I ran out the door and found Rocky, unconscious, under his window. He had fallen twenty feet from the second floor bedroom to the concrete below and landed on his head. He told me later that he leaned against the screen on the window and it gave way.

"We got the ambulance to take him to the hospital, and at the hospital they contacted the best pediatric surgeon in the area. Because Rocky's brain was swelling so badly, the surgeon told us he would have to operate immediately. To allow for the swelling the surgeon had to open a hole in Rocky's skull about the size of a grapefruit.

"After the operation we waited for three days while he was in intensive care. Tubes were hooked to him in many places, and he was breathing with the aid of a breathing machine.

"Prayer and waiting were my primary activities. There was a chapel in the basement of the hospital, which was a Catholic institution, and I frequented it when I wasn't with Rocky. On one occasion when I was praying, I recalled a passage from the Bible where it said, in effect: *He's not mine, he is your son, you gave him to me;* and I felt like that. My prayer reflected that passage and I asked Heavenly Father if Rocky would remain in a coma or if I would get him back. The pain concerning my son was intense and I was sobbing as I prayed—I asked for a sign. I knew that

Rocky didn't belong to me, he was just lent to me from God, but I needed an answer.

"After completing my prayer I entered the elevator and came back upstairs. Waiting for a moment in a small waiting-room on my son's floor, I attempted to regain my composure. While I was sitting on a chair in the room, my crying ceased, and I felt all the pain leave me. A wonderful feeling of peace came over me. Then a voice . . . a voice with peace and love spoke to me and said, very casually: 'He will be fine.'

"Wondering who was speaking to me, I rose and looked up and down the halls to see who was there. No one was present. There was just that marvelous feeling—I wondered whether it was Jesus or an angel that spoke to me. Entering Rocky's room, my husband who was in the room, said: 'Rocky, give me your hand.' At that moment, for the first time since the accident, Rocky moved—he gave me his hand.

"I took that as the sign I had asked for. Rocky's recovery was still difficult, though. For the next two weeks it was obvious his brain had sustained severe injury. His eyes would roll wildly, and he appeared frightened. We attempted to get 'yes' and 'no' answers from him with hand signals."

Recovery, and a Story of a Visit to Heaven

"After two weeks he was released to go home, with frequent trips to the therapist. When we left the hospital one side was partially paralyzed, but he could walk with a limp. Words did not come for over a month, then Rocky began to speak again, one word at a time.

"Since I was with Rocky most of the time to aid in his recovery, I was present when he began to talk. He kept trying to tell me something. Before the words came he would point. Often he would point up and then he would point at himself. Thinking that he was trying to tell me of his fall I would respond: 'Yes, Rocky, you fell out the window.' That didn't satisfy him, and one day as I was sitting next to him he said: 'Me, heaven!'

"I was startled by his answer, and I asked him: ' What?' He repeated: 'Me, heaven!' at the same time making the motion upward, and then pointing at himself. I asked him if he went to heaven, and he shook his head yes. Musing over what he had said, I dropped the subject.

"As the weeks stretched into months for Rocky's recovery a strange phenomenon occurred. Simple words concerning his everyday activities continued to give him difficulty, but he started quoting things from the Bible. I was not that expert with the Bible, but I would search out what he had been saying. To my surprise, the passages he quoted were accurate replications of similar passages from the King James version of the Bible.

"During this period of Rocky's recovery, he told me that he had seen my father. Dad had been dead since I was five years old, and I didn't remember him myself. There weren't many pictures of my father, and I didn't speak much of him since I was so young when he died. Rocky insisted, though, that he had seen his grandfather. I asked him what grandfather looked like, and he answered: 'He looks like me,' meaning that his grandfather looked like himself. Rocky is the only dark-eyed, dark-skinned, dark-haired, child that we have. He is similar in complexion and features to what my father's pictures show.

"Through the following months, Rocky told me that Jesus had taken him by the hand and taken him to heaven. When I asked him what it was like there, he said that there were homes there, too, only they were kind of cloud-like. People had families, he said, and they live in homes like here.

"Jesus visited Rocky and gave him an apple. Heavenly Father also visited him. Rocky's frequent reference to Heavenly Father and Jesus caused me to ask: 'How do you know the difference between Heavenly Father and Jesus?' He responded: 'Heavenly Father has light hair and Jesus has dark hair.' Explaining how they communicated he said: 'They talk to you but they don't move their mouths.'

"These vignettes continued to come from my son for some months. It was as if he had an inner knowledge of some distant place—a place that I had not taught him about. Once, for example, he told me that Jesus and Heavenly Father had power. I looked up passages in the Bible, such as Mark 12:24, where it referred to God's power, and I wondered how a five-year-old could know that. I certainly didn't teach it to him.

"With time, a rather complete picture emerged of Rocky's visit to another world where Jesus and Heavenly Father dwelled. So, I asked him why he came back. He cried and said: 'I'm sorry, Mom, I liked heaven. It was wonderful there and I didn't want to come home. But Jesus said I had to come back. He told me that my mother needed me.'

"Wondering about this further I asked Rocky: 'How did you get back?' 'Jesus has powers,' he said, and then he put his hand to his lips and motioned outward. When Rocky did that the thought came to me: *It's no more said than it is done.*

"These revelations from a five-year-old child astonished me. Seeking help from clergy and hospital personal, I asked about some of the things Rocky was saying. No one seemed able to help, yet I knew in my heart that I had heard a voice—and that Rocky was telling me of factual events that had happened to him. For years, because of the many doubters, I put it aside. Then I started reading books of people who had gone through near-death experiences. I discovered that their experiences were similar to what Rocky had told me. The discovery that others had shared similar experiences was most comforting.

"Once, after having read some books on the subject, I was explaining to others in the room that Rocky did not remember leaving his body. Rocky happened to be standing nearby, and he looked at me in a stunned way and said: 'I do too remember leaving my body, Mom. When the doctors were working on me, I floated up near the ceiling and I could see them doing something on the side of my head where I got hurt. That's when Jesus came and took my hand.

"As the years have passed Rocky has forgotten much of what he told me. Key elements of what happened to him are retained in his memory, but the details are lost.

"Rocky's recovery has been truly miraculous. There is some residual damage, and recent psychological tests have confirmed that damage—his slowness of speech, for example. Rocky should be able to lead a normal life, though, and we are grateful for that."

A Tragic Accident

"In October 1989, Rocky, his brother, Sage, and his sixteen-year-old brother, Shane, were in a car wreck. Shane had driven to the spa to pick them up from a swimming lesson, and on the way back the car got out of control and struck a pole. Shane was killed instantly.

"Rocky was in the back seat, and he ran the two blocks to home. Running to the accident I found that the police and paramedics were there trying to extract the boys from the car. Shane appeared gone, and Sage was critically injured.

"Watching this scene in agony, the thought came to me: *It's okay. I know he is gone, but Rocky came back to tell me that the soul has a place in heaven.*

"It all seems to me, now, like a puzzle that fell into place." Berta struggled with her emotions as she attempted to continue. "Survival from the loss of one of my children would have been almost impossible if I hadn't known it was okay. Rocky taught me that there was a beautiful place where Heavenly Father and Jesus took care of people like my son."

Questions of Berta

Berta agreed to answer questions I had. I began: "You say you only went to church infrequently. How did Rocky know the scriptures?"

"I have no idea; especially for a four-year-old. When I searched the scriptures out, I found them to be almost word for word."

"Was it from the New Testament, the Old Testament, or both?"

"It was mostly from the New Testament."

"Do you remember the specific scriptures, now?"

"Unfortunately, no. I have never been one to know the scriptural details. Frequently he would cover several scriptures, particularly when he was trying to explain something to me."

"Can you remember some of the subjects you discussed?"

"One subject that surprised me was that Jesus told Rocky it was okay for him to come back, because we are all going to be together as families in heaven. And then Jesus said: 'I promise you.'

"Frequently when Rocky told me something, like the comment about families, in his own words, then he would say something from the scriptures. To be taught by your four- and five-year-old son was unnerving."

"Had you taught Rocky that you would be together as a family when you went to heaven?"

"No. It's not something I was raised with. Rocky knew that my father had died, and I said that he was in heaven, but I didn't talk about being together as a family."

"Are there other subjects you discussed with Rocky?"

"Once I asked him: 'You saw God?' and he said: 'He prefers that we call him *Heavenly Father.*'"

A Visit With Rocky

Rocky, who had been running in and out during our interview with Berta, came over and sat when Berta called him. His dark hair, smiling eyes, and pleasant demeanor were the characteristics of a healthy boy. I began the interview.

"Tell me your name."

"Rocky."

"How old are you?"

"I'm thirteen."

"What grade are you in school?"

"I'm in the sixth."

"Do you like school?"

"Yes, it's okay."

"And you like sports?"

"Yeah."

"Do you remember back when you got hurt?"

"Yes, kind of."

"Can you tell me what happened?"

"I remember being in my room, on the window-sill. I was leaning against the screen, it popped out, and I fell to the ground."

"Do you remember hitting the ground?"

"No. I remember looking down on my body while the doctors worked on me."

"Is there anything else you remember?"

"I remember Jesus and heaven."

"Do you remember anything about Jesus or heaven?"

"No. That's all I remember."

"Can you recall what happened during your recovery?"

"I remember I had to learn everything all over again—I forgot everything I knew."

"Did you tell other people about what happened to you?"

"I think I did, but I don't remember."

"Okay, thanks Rocky." That ended my interview with a charming thirteen-year-old.

Chapter 18

A REMARKABLE EXPERIENCE

Howard Storm

Introduction

In 1991, through the auspices of the International Association for Near Death Studies (IANDS), I received a copy of a tape covering the experience of Howard Storm, a Professor of Art from Northern Kentucky University. The taped experience was so unusual and so extensive that I transcribed it into a written experience. Professor Storm was 38 years old in 1985 when he had his remarkable experience. With Professor Storm's kind permission I have included much of his experience in this book.

After having the experience detailed below, Professor Storm attended the United Theological Seminary in Dayton Ohio where, in 1992, he received a Master of Divinity Degree. After serving, for a time, as a student pastor at Zion United Church of Christ, Norwood, Ohio, he was ordained in the United Church of Christ in 1992 and installed as pastor at Zion United Church of Christ. Having resigned his position as a Professor at Northern Kentucky University, he no longer devotes full time to university-level instructing, but he does still teach in the university as a part-time faculty member in the art department.

Pastor Storm and his wife are the parents of two married children and the grandparents of four grandchildren. They devote much of their time to their personal family and their church family.

The following material is Howard Storm's account of what happened to him.

Background

What I'm about to describe to you is the person that I was and what I thought. It's not pleasant for me to talk about myself this way because, looking back, it's a very unflattering picture. But this is truly who I was.

By society's standards I was doing very well. I didn't break the law, openly, and I had a job. I had a wife, I had a family, I had two cars. Inwardly, I had a lot of trouble being alone—because when I was alone I used to think about killing myself. I didn't find joy in anything. Everything, to me, was an extension of my ego. I basically liked what I could control and had nothing to do with what I couldn't control.

As a consequence of these feelings, my children were under my thumb, and my wife was under my thumb. I had enough intelligence to keep the leash just right so that they had a little slack, but I was ready to pull on the leash at any time and choke them back. The way I would accomplish this was with a rage—where I would take something like the kitchen table and throw it across the room—as a little demonstration of force that would impress them.

Anything that wasn't seen, touched or felt, I had no faith in. I believed in the material world, and I knew with certainty that that was the full extent of everything there was. All belief systems associated with religion I considered to be fantasies for people to deceive themselves with. If people needed those systems to deceive themselves and to survive in the world, that was okay, that was their thing.

What science said and could measure was all that mattered. Beyond what science said, there was nothing else. Science, I believed, was in the process of finishing up its discovery of all known reality, and that science was in a position to control known reality somewhat.

Controlling my environment was one of my goals, so that I could manage things. I was proud of my own physical prowess; I was very strong. I built my own house. I took care of my own life.

When someone crossed me I was quick to cut them off. They were on my list of "dead people." And that's how I felt about them. Rambo wasn't around then, but this was sort of a mythic Rambo-Viking-Superman image I had of myself. There were your buddies, and then there were all the "dead people" who happened to be in your way. That's how I viewed the world.

Getting along in the world was no problem for me. I was convincing.
Most people would have said that I was an okay guy.

A Trip to Europe and a Serious Illness

On June 1, 1985, I was on the second-to-last day of a trip around
Europe with my wife and a few students. We had gone to museums,
galleries, cathedrals, castles—we had been all over Northern Europe. Now
we were completing our trip in France. Things had gone really well.

While viewing the sights, I had experienced a few instances of
indigestion. That's pretty normal for a trip around Europe. There was
some tension associated with trying to keep the group together and
organized. When someone wandered off I would get aggravated—angry.
It was pretty much situation normal.

There was a Saturday morning, and my wife and I had gotten up early
to go to a museum. We had come back to the hotel to get the group and go
to another museum. While talking to a student, suddenly I felt the most
intense stabbing pain in the center of my abdomen. It hurt with such
severity that I crumpled up.

Yelling at the student to get out of the room, I hit the floor. Much of
what was upsetting me was fear and anxiety—I didn't know what was happening.

Thrashing around on the floor, I yelled to my wife to get a physician.
Then I tried to find a position where it wouldn't hurt so much. The best
position was to lay on my side with my knees pulled up.

A doctor came to the hotel room who spoke English. He said that I
had a problem in my small stomach, maybe an ulcer. He gave me a shot of
morphine for the pain, but a small amount, because, he said, I was going
to have an operation within an hour. The doctor said I was in a serious
situation.

The ambulance took me on a wild ride through mid-day traffic in
Paris. At the hospital two young women interns took my medical history,
examined me and did x-rays. They said there was a perforation of the duodenum, the small stomach. They told me I would have the operation right
away.

I asked about going to another hospital and coming back to the United
States. That was impossible, they said, because I needed the operation

immediately. I was wheeled to another building a few blocks away, which was the surgery wing.

They put me in a room with a 66-year-old Frenchman who spoke English. At that point it was about noon. I felt pretty good about the whole situation. I even thought how I would have a story to tell when I got back.

Enormous Pain

Time went by; occasionally a nurse would come into the room, and she always said much the same thing: "How are you doing?" in French. I never saw a doctor, and one o'clock became two o'clock. By three o'clock the morphine was wearing off, and the pain was getting much worse.

I couldn't talk well, because I had a tube in me and a stomach pump going. By four o'clock the pain was back, only it was ten times worse than when it first hit me. With this severe pain the thought that kept coming was: *How come I'm still conscious? Nobody can feel this kind of pain and still be conscious. Why am I conscious?*

All I wanted to do was black-out, and I couldn't. The pain went from a localized event to general pain through the entire abdominal area. Hydrochloric acid, from my stomach, was leaking into other areas. The pain was awful.

I didn't want to cry, but the pain was beyond belief. Telling my French room-mate that if I didn't get pain relief soon, I would die, I asked him to tell the nurses what I said. They came to the room, and he told them in French. Their response was that they could do nothing because the doctor wasn't available. Only a doctor could prescribe medicine.

By six o'clock my wife had been thrown out of the hospital three times. She was physically removed—because she had been trying to get someone to do something to help me. She was also having a terrible day, since she was so ineffectual. She had to watch her husband, who appeared to be dying—and no one would take him or her seriously, except for the patient in the next bed.

By eight o'clock I felt that I was hanging on by my fingernails. Hanging on to life, that is. I had given up going unconscious; I had been hoping for that all day, but to no avail. I was hanging on to life moment by moment.

A Death Sentence

Sometime after eight o'clock the nurse came in and told Beverly, my wife, and me, that the doctor had gone home, and he would operate on me sometime the next day. Not saying anything, I knew that was my death sentence.

Struggling to say goodbye to my wife, I wrestled with my emotions. Telling her that I loved her very much was as much of a goodbye as I could utter because of my emotional distress. She looked awful. She looked better after she had our children than she did then, because of the crying.

Sort of relaxing and closing my eyes, I waited for the end. This was it, I felt. This was the big nothing, the big blackout, the one you never wake up from, the end of existence. I had absolute certainty that there was nothing beyond this life—because that was how the really smart people understood it.

While I was undergoing this stress, prayer, or anything like that, never occurred to me. I never once thought about it. If I mentioned God's name at all it was only as a profanity.

For a time there was a sense of being unconscious or asleep. I'm not sure how long it lasted, but I felt really strange, and I opened my eyes. To my surprise I was standing up next to the bed, and I was looking at my body laying in the bed.

My first reaction was: *This is crazy! I can't be standing here looking down at myself. That's just not possible.*

Not knowing what was happening, I became upset. I started yelling and screaming at my wife, and she just sat there like a stone. She didn't look at me, she didn't move—and I kept screaming profanities to get her to pay attention. Being confused, upset, and angry, I tried to get the attention of my room-mate, with the same result. He didn't react.

An Invitation by Strange People

Then I heard my name. In French there is no equivalent to Howard, and they messed it up when they tried to use it. But someone was saying my name correctly. I heard: *Howard, Howard—come here.*

Wondering, at first, where it was coming from, I discovered that it was originating in the doorway. There were different voices calling me.

I asked who they were, and they said: *We are here to take care of you. We will fix you up. Come with us.*

Asking, again, who they were, I asked them if they were doctors and nurses. They responded: *Quick, come see. You'll find out.*

As I asked them questions they gave evasive answers. They kept giving me a sense of urgency, insisting that I should step through the doorway. With some reluctance I stepped into the hallway, and in the hallway I was in a fog, or a haze. It was a light-colored haze. It wasn't a heavy haze. I could see my hand, for example, but the people who were calling me were 15 or 20 feet ahead, and I couldn't see them clearly. They were more like silhouettes, or shapes, and as I moved toward them they backed off into the haze.

These strange beings kept urging me to come with them. I repeatedly asked them where we were going, and they responded: *Hurry up, you'll find out.* Looking back into the room, I saw my wife and my room-mate, and I decided they had not been able to help me so I would go with these people.

Walking for what seemed to be a considerable distance, these beings were all around me. They were leading me through the haze. I don't know how long . . . there was a real sense of timelessness about the experience. In a real sense I am unaware of how long it was, but it felt like a long time—maybe even days or weeks.

As we traveled, the fog got thicker and darker, and the people began to change. At first they seemed rather playful and happy, but when we had covered some distance, a few of them began to get aggressive. Then, others would seem to caution the aggressive ones. It seemed that I could hear them warn the aggressive ones to be careful or I would be frightened away.

Wondering what was happening, I continued to ask questions, and they repeatedly urged me to hurry and to stop asking questions. Feeling uneasy, especially since they continued to get aggressive, I considered returning, but I didn't know how to get back. I was lost. There were no features that I could relate to. There was just the fog and a wet, clammy ground, and I had no sense of direction.

Attacked by Bizarre Beings

Finally, I told them that I wouldn't go any farther. At that time they changed completely. They became much more aggressive and insisted that I was going with them. A number of them began to push and shove me, and I responded by hitting back at them.

It seemed to be, almost, a game for them, with me as the center-piece of their amusement. My pain became their pleasure. They seemed to want to make me hurt—by clawing at me and biting me. Whenever I would get one off me, there were five more to replace the one.

By this time it was almost complete darkness, and I had the sense that instead of there being twenty or thirty, there were an innumerable host of them. Each one seemed set on coming in for the sport they got from hurting me.

Fighting well and hard for a long time, ultimately I was spent. Lying there exhausted amongst them, they began to calm down since I was no longer the amusement that I had been. People were still picking at me, occasionally, and I just lay there all torn up, unable to resist.

Exactly what happened was . . . and I'm not going to try and explain this. From inside of me I felt a voice, my voice, say: *Pray to God.* My mind responded to that: *I don't pray. I don't know how to pray.* The voice again told me to pray to God. It was a dilemma since I didn't know how. The voice told me a third time to pray to God.

I started saying things like: "The Lord is my shepherd, I shall not want . . . God bless America . . ." and anything else that seemed to have a religious connotation. And these people went into a frenzy, as if I had thrown boiling oil all over them. They began yelling and screaming at me, telling me to quit, that there was no God, and no one could hear me. While they screamed and yelled obscenities, they also began backing away from me—as if I were poison.

I screamed back at them: "Our Father who art in heaven," and similar ideas. This continued for some time until, suddenly, I was aware that they had left. It was dark, and I was alone yelling things that sounded churchy. It was pleasing to me that these churchy sayings had such an effect on those awful beings.

Lying there for a long time, I was in such a state of hopelessness, and blackness, and despair, that I had no way of measuring how long it was. I was just lying there in an unknown place—all torn and ripped. And I had no strength; it was all gone. It seemed as if I were sort of fading out, that any effort on my part would expend the last energy I had. My conscious sense was that I was perishing, or just sinking into the darkness.

A Rescue by the Light

Then a most unusual thing happened. I heard very clearly, once again in my own voice, something that I had learned in nursery Sunday School. It was the little song: "Jesus loves me, yes I know, . . ." and it kept repeating. I don't know why, but all of a sudden I wanted to believe that. Not having anything left, I wanted to cling to that thought. And . . . and I, inside, screamed: *Jesus, please save me.* That thought was screamed with every ounce of strength and feeling left in me.

When I did that, I saw, off in the darkness somewhere, the tiniest little star. Not knowing what it was, I presumed it must be a comet or a meteor, because it was moving rapidly. Then I realized it was coming toward me. It was getting very bright, rapidly.

When the light came near, its radiance spilled over me, and I just rose up—not with my effort—I just lifted up. Then I saw—and I saw this very plainly—I saw all my wounds, all my tears, all my brokenness, melt away. And I became whole in this radiance.

What I did was to cry uncontrollably. I was crying, not out of sadness, but because I was feeling things that I had never felt before in my life.

Another thing happened. Suddenly I knew a whole bunch of things. I knew things . . . I knew that this light, this radiance, knew me. I don't know how to explain to you that I knew it knew me, I just did. As a matter of fact, I understood that it knew me better than my mother or father did.

The light conveyed to me that it loved me in a way that I can't begin to express. It loved me in a way that I had never known that love could possibly be.

I knew that this radiant being was powerful. It was making me feel so good all over. I could feel its light on me—like very gentle hands around me. And I could feel it holding me. And we, I and this light, went up and out of there.

We started going faster and faster, out of the darkness. Embraced by the light, feeling wonderful and crying, I saw off in the distance something that looked like the picture of a galaxy, except that it was larger and there were more stars than I had seen on earth. There was a great center of brilliance. It was off in the distance.

Then I . . . I didn't say it, I thought it. I said: *Put me back.* What I meant by telling the light to put me back, was to put me back into the pit. I was so ashamed of who I was, and what I had been all of my life, that all I wanted to do was hide in the darkness. I didn't want to go toward the light anymore—I did, yet I didn't.

For the first time, my friend, and I will refer to him in that context hereafter, said to me: "You belong here."

My response was: "No, you've made a mistake, put me back." And he said: "We don't make mistakes. You belong."

Beings of Glory

Then my friend called out in the darkness, and a number—because they came to us—a number of brilliantly illuminated beings surrounded us. I was still crying. One of the first things these marvelous beings did was to ask, all with thought: "Are you afraid of us?" I told them I wasn't. They said that they could turn their brilliance down and appear as people, and I told them to stay as they were. They were the most beautiful, the most . . .

As an aside, I'm an artist. There are three primary, three secondary, and six tertiary colors in the visible light spectrum. Here, I was seeing a visible light spectrum with at least 80 new primary colors. I was also seeing this brilliance. It's disappointing for me to try and describe, because I can't—I was seeing colors that I had never seen before.

What these beings were showing me was their glory. I wasn't really seeing them. And I was perfectly content. Having come from a world of shapes and forms, I was delighted with this new, formless, world. These beings were giving me what I needed at that time.

A Life's Review

Next, they wanted to talk about my life. To my surprise my life played out before me, maybe six or eight feet in front of me, from beginning to end. The life review was very much in their control, and they showed me my life, but not from my point of view. I saw *me* in my life—and this whole thing was a lesson, even though I didn't know it at the time. They were trying to teach me something, but I didn't know it was a teaching experience, because I didn't know that I would be coming back.

We just watched my life from the beginning to the end. Some things they slowed down on, and zoomed in on, and other things they went right through. My life was shown in a way that I had never thought of before. All of the things that I had worked to achieve, the recognition that I had worked for, in elementary school, in high school, in college, and in my career, they meant nothing in this setting.

I could feel their feelings of sorrow and suffering, or joy, as my life's review unfolded. They didn't say that something was bad or good, but I could feel it. And I could sense all those things they were indifferent to. They didn't, for example, look down on my high school shot-put record. They just didn't feel anything towards it, nor towards other things which I had taken so much pride in.

What they responded to was how I had interacted with other people. That was the long and short of it. Unfortunately, most of my interactions with other people didn't measure up with how I should have interacted, which was in a loving way.

Whenever I did react during my life in a loving way they rejoiced. Most of the time I found that my interactions with other people had been manipulative. During my professional career, for example, I saw myself sitting in my office, playing the college professor, while a student came to me with a personal problem. I sat there looking compassionate, and patient, and loving, while inside I was bored to death. I would check my watch under my desk as I anxiously waited for the student to finish.

I got to go through all those kinds of experiences in the company of these magnificent beings. When I was a teenager my father's career put him into a high-stress, twelve-hour-a-day job. Out of my resentment because of his neglect of me, when he came home from work, I would be cold and indifferent toward him. This made him angry, and it gave me a further excuse to feel hatred toward him. He and I fought, and my mother would get upset.

Most of my life I had felt that my father was the villain and I was the victim. When we reviewed my life I got to see how I had precipitated so much of that, myself. Instead of greeting him happily at the end of a day, I was continually putting thorns in him—in order to justify my own hurt.

I got to see, when my sister had a bad night one night, how I went into her bedroom and put my arms around her. Not saying anything, I just lay there with my arms around her. As it turned out that experience was one of the biggest triumphs of my life.

The Therapy of Love

The entire life's review would have been emotionally destructive, and would have left me a psychotic person, if it hadn't been for the fact that my friend, and my friend's friends, were loving me during the unfolding of my life. I could feel that love. Every time I got a little upset they turned the life's review off for awhile, and they just loved me. Their love was tangible. You could feel it on your body, you could feel it inside of you; their love went right through you. I wish I could explain it to you, but I can't.

The therapy was their love, because my life's review kept tearing me down. It was pitiful to watch, just pitiful. I couldn't believe it. And the thing is, it got worse as it went on. My stupidity and selfishness as a teenager only magnified as I became an adult—all under the veneer of being a good husband, a good father, and a good citizen. The hypocrisy of it all was nauseating. But through it all was their love.

Questions to the Friends

When the review was finished they asked: "Do you want to ask any questions?" and I had a million questions. I asked, for example, "What about the Bible?" They responded: "What about it?" I asked if it was true, and they said that it was. Asking them why it was that when I tried to read it, all I saw were contradictions, they took me back to my life's review again—something that I had overlooked. They showed me, for the few times I had opened the Bible, that I had read it with the idea of finding contradictions and problems. I was trying to prove to myself that it wasn't worth reading.

I observed to them that the Bible wasn't clear to me. It didn't make sense. They told me that it contained spiritual truth, and that I had to read it spiritually in order to understand it. It should be read prayerfully. My friends informed me that it was not like other books. They also told me, and I later found out this was true, that when you read it prayerfully it talks to you. It reveals itself to you. And you don't have to work at it anymore.

My friends answered lots of questions in funny ways. They really knew the whole tone of what I asked them, even before I got the questions out. When I thought of questions in my head, they really understood them. I asked them, for example, which was the best religion. I was looking for an answer which was like: "Presbyterians." I figured these guys were all Christians. The answer I got was: "The best religion is the religion that brings you closest to God."

Asking them if there was life on other planets, their surprising answer was that the universe was full of life. Because of my fear of a nuclear holocaust I asked if there was going to be a nuclear war in the world, and they said no. That astonished me, and I gave them this extensive explanation of how I had lived under the threat of nuclear war. That was one of the reasons I was who I was. I figured, when I was in this life, that it was all sort of hopeless; the world was going to blow up anyway, and nothing made much sense. In that context I felt I could do what I wanted, since nothing mattered.

They said: "No, there isn't going to be any nuclear war." I asked if they were absolutely sure there wasn't going to be a nuclear war. They reassured me again, and I asked them how they could be so sure. Their response was: "God loves the world."

They told me that at the most, one or two nuclear weapons might go off accidentally, if they weren't destroyed, but there wouldn't be a nuclear war. I then asked them how come there had been so many wars. They said that they allowed those few to happen, out of all the wars that mankind tried to start. Out of all the wars that humans tried to create, they allowed a few, to bring people to their senses and to stop them.

Science, technology, and other benefits, they told me, had been gifts bestowed on mankind by them—through inspiration. People had literally been led to those discoveries, many of which had later been perverted by mankind to use for its own destruction. These friends of my friend wanted war, because of the level of our technology, to be put aside. We could do too much damage to the planet. And by the planet, they meant all of God's creation. Not just the people, but the animals, the trees, the birds, the insects, everything.

Love for all People

They explained to me that their concern was for all the people of the world. They weren't interested in one group getting ahead of other groups. They want every person to consider every other person greater than their own flesh. They want everyone to love everyone else, completely; more, even, than they love themselves. If someone, someplace else in the world hurts, than we should hurt—we should feel of their pain. And we should help them.

Our planet has evolved to the point, for the first time in our history, that we have the power to do that. We are globally linked. And we could become one people.

The people that they gave the privilege of leading the world into a better age, blew it. That was us, in the United States.

When I spoke with them about the future, and this might sound like a cop-out on my part, they made clear to me that we have free will. If we change the way we are, then we can change the future which they showed me. They showed me a view of the future, at the time of my experience, based upon how we in the United States were behaving at that time. It was a future in which a massive worldwide depression would occur. If we were to change our behavior, however, then the future would be different.

Asking them how it would be possible to change the course of many people, I observed that it was difficult, if not impossible, to change anything on earth. I expressed the opinion that it was a hopeless task to try.

My friends explained, quite clearly, that all it takes to make a change was one person. One person, trying, and then because of that, another person changing for the better. They said that the only way to change the world was to begin with one person. One will become two, which will become three, and so on. That's the only way to affect a major change.

A World of Peace and Love

I inquired as to where the world would be going in an optimistic future—one where some of the changes they desired were to take place. The image of the future that they gave me then, and it was their image, not one that I created, surprised me. My image had previously been sort of like "Star Wars," where everything was space age, plastics, and technology. The future that they showed me was almost no technology at all.

What everybody, absolutely everybody, in this euphoric future spent most of their time doing was raising children. The chief concern of people was children, and everybody considered children to be the most precious commodity in the world. And when a person became an adult, there was no sense of anxiety, nor hatred, nor competition. There was this enormous sense of trust and mutual respect.

If a person, in this view of the future, became disturbed, then the community of people all cared about the disturbed person falling away from the harmony of the group. Spiritually, through prayer and love, the others would elevate the afflicted person.

What people did with the rest of their time was that they gardened, with almost no physical effort. They showed me that plants, with prayer, would produce huge fruits and vegetables. People, in unison, could control the climate of the planet through prayer. Everybody would work with mutual trust—and the people would call the rain, when needed, and the sun to shine. Animals lived with people, in harmony.

People, in this best of all worlds, weren't interested in knowledge; they were interested in wisdom. This was because they were in a position where anything they needed to know, in the knowledge category, they could receive simply through prayer. Everything, to them, was solvable. They could do anything they wanted to do.

In this future, people had no wanderlust, because they could, spiritually, communicate with everyone else in the world. There was no need to go elsewhere. They were so engrossed with where they were and the people around them that they didn't have to go on vacation. Vacation from what? They were completely fulfilled and happy.

Death, in this world, was a time when the individual had experienced everything that he or she needed to experience. To die meant to lie down and let go; then the spirit would rise up, and the community would gather around. There would be a great rejoicing, because they all had insight into the heavenly realm, and the spirit would join with the angels that came down to meet it. They could see the spirit leave and knew that it was time for the spirit to move on; it had outgrown the need for growth in this world. Individuals who died had achieved all they were capable of in this world in terms of love, appreciation, understanding, and working in harmony with others.

The sense I got of this beautiful view of the world's future was as a garden, God's garden. And in this garden of the world, full of all beauty, were people. The people were born into this world to grow in their under-standing of the Creator. Then to shed this skin, this shell, in the physical world, and to graduate and move up into heaven—there, to have a more intimate and growing relationship with God.

What Happens at Death

I asked my friend, and his friends, about death—what happens when we die? They said that when a loving person dies, angels come down to meet him, and they take him up—gradually, at first, because it would be unbearable for that person to be instantly exposed to God.

Knowing what's inside of every person, the angels don't have to prove anything by showing off. They know what each of us needs, so they provide that. In some cases it may be a heavenly meadow, and in another, something else. If a person needs to see a relative, the angels will bring that relative. If the person really likes jewels, they will show the person jewels. We see what is necessary for our introduction into the spirit world, and those things are real, in the heavenly, the divine sense.

They gradually educate us as spirit beings, and bring us into heaven. We grow and increase, and grow and increase, and shed the concerns, desires, and base animal stuff that we have been fighting much of our life. Earthly appetites melt away. It is no longer a struggle to fight them. We become who we truly are, which is part of the Divine.

Judgment of Others is Wrong

This happens to loving people, people who are good and love God. They made it clear to me that we don't have any knowledge or right to judge anybody else—in terms of that person's heart relationship to God. Only God knows what's in a person's heart. Someone whom we think is despicable, God might know as a wonderful person. Similarly, someone we think is good, God may see as a hypocrite, with a black heart. Only God knows the truth about every individual.

God will ultimately judge every individual. And God will allow people to be dragged into the darkness with like-minded creatures. I have told you, from my personal experience, what goes on in there. I don't know from what I saw any more than that, but it's my suspicion that I only saw the tip of the iceberg.

I deserved to be where I was—I was in the right place at the right time. That was the place for me, and the people I was around were perfect company for me. God allowed me to experience that, and then removed me, because he saw something redeeming in putting me through the experience. It was a way to purge me. People who are not allowed to be pulled into the darkness, because of their loving nature, are attracted upwards, toward the light.

Did Not Want to Leave

I never saw God, and I was not in Heaven. It was way out in the suburbs, and these are the things that they showed me. We talked for a long time, about many things, and then I looked at myself. When I saw me, I was glowing, I was radiant. I was becoming beautiful—not nearly as beautiful as them—but I had a certain sparkle that I never had before.

Not being ready to face the earth again, I told them that I wished to be with them forever. They said: "No, you have to go back." Responding that I couldn't go back, I tried to argue with them, and I observed that if I went back I would become what I was before. Telling them that I couldn't bear that thought—the thought that I might wind up in the pit again—I pled with them to stay.

My friends then said: "Do you think that we expect you to be perfect, after all the love we feel for you, even after you were on earth blaspheming God, and treating everyone around you like dirt? And this, despite the fact that we were sending people to try and help you, to teach you the truth? Do you really think we would be apart from you now?"

I asked them: "But what about my own sense of failure? You've shown me how I can be better, and I'm sure I can't live up to that. I'm not that good."

They advised me to recognize it when I made a mistake and to ask for forgiveness. Before I even got the words out of my mouth, I would be forgiven—but, I would have to accept the forgiveness. My belief in the principal of forgiveness must be real, and I would have to know that the forgiveness was given. Confessing, either in public or in private, that I had made a mistake, I should then ask for forgiveness. After that, it would be an insult to them if I didn't accept the forgiveness. I shouldn't continue to go around with a sense of guilt, and I should not repeat errors—I should learn from my mistakes.

Final Arguments and the Return

"But," I said, "how will I know what is the right choice? How will I know what you want me to do?" They replied: "We want you to do what *you* want to do. That means making choices—and there isn't necessarily any right choice. There are a spectrum of possibilities, and you should make the best choice you can from those possibilities. If you do that, we will be there helping you."

Presenting my biggest argument against coming back into the world, I told them that it would break my heart, and I would die, if I had to leave them and their love. Coming back would be so cruel, I said, that I couldn't stand it. I mentioned that the world was filled with hate and competition, and I didn't want to return to that maelstrom. I couldn't bear to leave them.

My friends observed that they had never been apart from me. I explained that I hadn't been aware of their presence, and if I went back I, again, wouldn't know they were there. Explaining how to communicate with them, they told me to get myself quiet, inside, and to ask for their love; then that love would come, and I would know they were there.

After that explanation I ran out of arguments, and I said I thought I could go back. And, just like that, I was back. Returning to my body, the pain was there, only worse than before. It was around nine o'clock, and the nurse came in and said the doctor was back, and they were going to do the operation.

Medical Procedures and the Aftermath

They wheeled me by my wife on the way to the operating room. Filled with pain, and half groggy from the preparatory medications, I said to her: "I'm going to be okay." I said it cheerfully, and I'm sure she thought I was out of it, but I meant it. My knowledge was that I was going to be okay.

The next day, in the intensive care recovery room, I saw my wife again. With tubes in me and staples across my stomach, I didn't feel very good, physically. But I remembered my experience of light.

Beverly told me that she loved me and that other people loved me also. Muttering that all there was was love, that love was everything, I tried to tell her something of the experience, but I got emotional and could only cry.

Beverly had a hard time understanding me. She tried to stop me from talking about it, because every time I did I would cry. It took me about a week, but I finally managed to tell her most of the story.

After the experience I did a lot of thinking about what had happened to me. The experience was real, more real than this life is real, and I knew it. Yet my skeptical nature caused me to wonder if it weren't some sort of hyper-hallucination that seemed real. I wondered about that possibility until other things began to happen that made me know of the reality of the experience.

A Spiritual Message and Return to the U.S.

One of the things that helped assure me of the reality of my experience had to do with my physical condition after the operation. The operation was Saturday night. On Tuesday I was taken back to a room for recovery. While I was laying there, about noon, waiting for my wife to come I heard a voice say: "Buy tickets and go home on Monday." I literally asked: "Who said that?" but no one was there. The voice repeated the message, and I said to myself that I didn't believe what was happening, but the voice told me to believe.

My wife came to visit me. Beverly is an attorney, a strong-willed lady who never takes a command from me. Moreover, I had just been taken out of intensive care, and I was supposed to remain in the hospital recovering for three weeks. When Beverly walked in, I said: "Buy tickets; we are going home Monday." Her answer was an agreeable: "Yes, Dear."

Turning around, she made arrangements for the return trip, and by four o'clock that afternoon, despite numerous obstacles which should have prevented it, she had two airplane tickets for home. She said that she felt under some sort of compulsion to get the tickets.

Later, on Saturday, I felt in my mind that I was too sick to go home. The voice came again and said: "Believe." Sunday morning when I woke up, I felt great. After the staples were removed from my stomach by the nurse, I got up, shaved, cleaned up, and got dressed. A doctor came and signed me out—after I explained that I needed to return to America—without a complaint. That would normally have been an unthinkable thing.

Monday morning we got on the plane. We got home late, and the next day I checked with my doctor. He sent me, immediately, to the hospital.

There, the diagnosis was extreme peritonitis, and non-A, non-B hepatitis (now called hepatitis C). The hepatitis was an especially virulent one; I had essentially no liver function. My SGOT, which measures liver function, was three thousand or so. Normal range is under 50. I also had double pneumonia and a collapsed lung.

What had happened was that the little voice, in the French hospital, knew I was desperately ill. It knew I wasn't being treated properly, and it knew that, in order to get well, I had to get to a place where I would get proper treatment.

Resting in critical condition for three weeks at St. Luke's Hospital, I began to mend, and the doctors kept telling me it was a miracle that I was recovering. Trying to tell them about angels, and Jesus, and other parts of my experience, they were mostly amused. My wife said to me: "Did you notice how everybody who comes into your room is always smiling?" I told her that I did—I thought it was nice. She said: "It's because you are the laughing stock of the hospital."

A Changed Man

After getting out of the hospital in June and returning to normal activities, I became a different person. Desiring to make up for all of the years I had been less than what I should have been, I wanted everyone to feel as I did. Reading the Bible, at night, for example, I thrilled to the messages and wished for Beverly to share in this new-found joy.

Beverly, who sometimes works long hours, ten to twelve, was exposed to my zeal. One night in September after a hard day's work, Beverly was lying in bed while I read to her from the Bible. It was about two o'clock in the morning, and she was exhausted and crying. Producing tears in her was enjoyable because I assumed it was from the thrill of my message. On this occasion she was getting some of my best Bible instruction, when suddenly she said: "I can't take it anymore. I'm leaving you."

I was dumb-struck. Here, I was giving this woman the word of God, and she couldn't take it. As a result of that experience I went into a full retreat. Keeping silent for a few weeks, I evaluated my approach to people. One of my friends talked to me during this period. He said: "I love you, but somebody has to lock you up for a year or two until you cool down."

Finally finding a balance in life that was appropriate for me, for my family, and for my friends, life returned to normal. But I know, because of the things that happened to me, that the experience was real. Those happenings were to teach me what I needed to know. God was helping me to be a better person.

Final Thoughts

What I have said about the experience is the unvarnished truth. You may think that I have exaggerated—just the opposite is true. If I had the eloquence to explain what really happened you would find it even more difficult to believe. The really good stuff, the love that I felt, the goodness, the trust, the warmth, the acceptance, I can't begin to explain.

Part of what I want to get across is, when anyone reaches out to God He will be there for him. The struggle that I went through to find God was worth it. Knowing what I now do, I would suffer much worse in order to find what I did. One of the most important things we can do is to spread the good news that God loves us.

Chapter 19

ARE THE STORIES TRUE?

Reasons for This Chapter

Questions about the reality and truth of NDE stories have plagued researchers since Raymond A. Moody, Jr.'s pioneering effort, *Life After Life*, first published in 1975.[1] Since beginning our research in 1990, my wife, Carol, and I have also been asked about the reality and truth of the experiences. Because of the persistence of numerous questions on this subject I have decided to devote a chapter to this important topic.

Commonly Asked Questions

But Arvin, how do you know they were telling you the truth? Maybe they thought it was a real experience, but couldn't it have been some type of dream or hallucination? Couldn't their experience have been from the effects of the medication they were taking? Why in the world would anyone tell you a story like that—what was their motivation? Did you offer to pay them money for their stories? Do you really believe all of these stories? Aren't there a lot of nuts who call you with screwy stories—how do you separate them from the authentic experiences? Why do some people have near-death out-of-body experiences, and others with equally serious injuries or illnesses, do not? Why do individuals have such varied experiences—doesn't that prove that they are just figments of the mind? Do you think that these experiences prove that there is a life after death? Could reincarnation explain some of the experiences?

These are some of the questions I am repeatedly asked. Interestingly, they are most often asked by people who have not taken the trouble to read much, if anything, on the subject of near-death experiences. Those who have read extensively on the subject are equally curious, but their questions are centered more on what our research findings show. It is clear from these, and other questions, that the subject has created substantial interest with the public. Although a comprehensive review of all of these questions is beyond the scope of this book, I will attempt to respond to the most commonly asked ones.

Authenticity of the Experiences

Research by Others
The question of whether the experiences are truly out-of-body, and not some psychological or other phenomenon, is of considerable interest to the research community as well as the public. Many studies have been done in an attempt to explain the NDE as some phenomenon other than a spiritual out-of-body experience. Dr. Kenneth Ring, a professor of psychology at the University of Connecticut, and one of the founders of the International Association for Near Death Studies (IANDS), has studied a number of possible explanations, including: depersonalization, wishful thinking, psychological expectations, dreams or hallucinations, anesthetics, other drugs, temporal lobe involvement, cerebral anoxia, and other physiological or neurological explanations. He concludes that none of these possibilities can satisfactorily account for all of the NDEs that he has researched.[2]

Dr. Melvin Morse, a physician involved in pediatrics in Seattle, and one who has done extensive research on NDEs for children, examined the following possible explanations that others had proposed: Lysergic Acid (LSD)-induced hallucinations, morphine and heroin hallucinations, "recreational drug" hallucinations, anesthetic agents, ketamine, transient depersonalization, memories of birth (as suggested by Dr. Carl Sagan), autoscopic hallucinations, endorphin-induced hallucinations, and hypoxia. He concludes from the research in his book that: "None of these mimics the powerful experiences revealed in this book."[3]

Dr. Raymond Moody, a psychiatrist whose classic book *Life After Life* started much of the research in NDEs, said in his book *The Light Beyond:*

For more than twenty years I have been working on the cutting edge of NDE research. In the course of my studies, I have listened to thousands of people tell about their deeply personal journeys into. . . what? The world beyond? The heaven they learned about from their religion? A region of the brain that reveals itself only in times of desperation?

I have talked to almost every NDE researcher in the world about his or her work. I know that most of them believe in their hearts that NDEs are a glimpse of life after life. But as scientists and people of medicine, they still haven't come up with 'scientific proof' that a part of us goes on living after our physical being is dead. This lack of proof keeps them from going public with their true feelings. . . .

I don't think science can ever answer the question. It can be pondered from almost every side, but the resulting answer will never be complete. . . .

In the absence of firm scientific proof, people frequently ask me what I believe: Do NDEs provide evidence of life after life? My answer is 'Yes.'[4]

No Scientific Proof for Life after Death

In the process of performing our own research Carol and I have interviewed approximately one-hundred people who have undergone NDEs or analogous spiritual experiences. In addition to that first-hand research work, I have read essentially all of the available literature on NDEs, and I am actively involved in a local chapter of IANDS.

As to the question, Can science provide proof of life after death?, I share Dr. Moody's skepticism. Most other near-death researchers hold an equally skeptical view, and I agree with that position. If it were possible to prove life-after-death through the near-death experience, then the need for faith taught by most Christian religions would be compromised. As a Christian, I believe that it is a necessary part of our development that we move through this life with faith: faith in the ultimate goodness of our Father in Heaven, faith in the Lord Jesus Christ, faith that there is a life after death, faith that it does matter how we live.

Patterns of Evidence Discerned

Despite the inability through scientific methods to *prove* the existence of a life after this life, the NDE does offer substantial evidence that there *could* be something beyond this life. Indeed, in many instances the NDE evidence is best explained by a form of life after life. The evidence comes in several forms.

One of the most fascinating forms of evidence is that provided by the witnesses themselves. Most of those who have had an NDE, when they tell of their experience (especially if they have not told it frequently before), are extremely moved by the experience. There is an awe about them that is obvious to anyone observing them. In many instances they tend to relive the experience, their emotions overcome them, and they are unable to continue with their discussion for a time. This is true whether or not the experience was negative or positive, whether or not they are male or female, and independent of their cultural and educational background. The only exceptions that Carol and I observed seemed to be small children. They simply told their experiences in a matter-of-fact manner, as if to say: *Of course I saw Jesus—doesn't everybody?*

Another form of evidence involves patterns of behavior by those being interviewed. Although the stories, by their very nature, are anecdotal and therefore not subject to the rigor of repeatability that characterizes most scientific research, there are certain aspects that are repeatable. In the next chapter, for example, I point out how certain words were used by the respondents repeatedly, almost as if the respondents were programmed to use them. Words such as *peace, warmth, love,* and *light* were used with such frequency—and with a scriptural context or meaning—that they clearly represented a significantly high pattern of usage.

A subtle form of evidence derives from the method I used to create the final written version of the experiences. After each experience was taped and transcribed into a computerized printed version, I forwarded that version to the respondents for their corrections. Invariably, they would return the copy with what to me were trivial corrections that had nothing to do with the substance of their stories. Yet, the respondents were adamant that the changes needed to be made in order for the stories to be correct. Typical of these changes was a recent one by a lady who said: "When I told you the story, I got the order of two events wrong. That wasn't the way it was. The first thing that happened was . . ." These kinds of small corrections, and the insistence of the respondents that I make the changes, gave further evidence that they, at least, had a sense of the reality and order of the events.

Other Significant Forms of Evidence

Many of the experiences, because of the circumstances involved, offered opportunities for partial corroboration.

The two little children I interviewed (reported in Chapter 17) told their stories with complete candor and innocence. And their mothers related—with awe and reverence—their memories of the same events. I was fascinated to listen to Berta explain how her son—five-year-old Rocky, as he began to recover—described his experience on the other side by quoting scriptures from the King James version of the Bible, scriptures that he had not previously been taught.

When Bill told of his two-stage experience (Chapter 12), he explained how one of his cousins gave him a special blessing, while Bill was comatose, which Bill witnessed from out of his body. The physical details of what he saw were later confirmed by his cousin, and I obtained a written account of the record from the cousin as it was recorded shortly after the event.

In the books *In Search of Angels*, and *Glimpses of Eternity*, I described an NDE and subsequent miraculous healing by DeAnne Anderson Shelley.[5,6] Some years after DeAnne's experience I met the physician who attended her, Doctor Parkinson, and heard him explain that there was no medical explanation for why DeAnne was alive, nor for the healing that subsequently happened to her. The only explanation he could offer was her own account of the experience.

Three of the individuals I interviewed suffered grievous gunshot wounds. In each case they showed me the scars from the wounds. It was obvious from these scars, and from the scars of the subsequent operations, that they had suffered immense damage to their persons. Although such evidence does not confirm the NDE, it does confirm that something significant happened to the individuals.

Several individuals told of visiting, during their out-of-body events, locations where they were later able to confirm physical evidences that could not have been seen from the location of their physical selves. One lady, for example, later (after her NDE) verified the presence of a frail old man in a hospital bed whom she saw while out of her body in an adjacent room, a location that could not have been seen from where she was being treated. There were several such instances described by the people we interviewed.

Some individuals were able later to discuss with medical personnel the details of their treatment—details they should not have been able to see while they were under anesthetic. In fact, one lady that I interviewed told me that after her NDE she made arrangements to visit the home of the anesthesiologist who attended her during her medical emergency. At first he was reluctant to tell her the details of what happened to her during the crisis—until she told him what she saw the medical personnel doing. She told him that the doctors and nurses appeared to be out of control during the worst of her crisis. He confirmed what she saw and said that the hospital had instituted changes in their procedure as a result of what happened to her.

A fascinating experience was reported by Professor Kimberly Clark of the University of Washington, Seattle, concerning a patient called Maria who suffered a cardiac arrest. Maria described an out-of-body experience that was typical of many undergoing an NDE. She saw the medical personnel working on her, and as is often the case, she floated out of the hospital. While in this spirit body state, she happened to observe an object on the third floor ledge on the north wall of the hospital. The object was a tennis shoe. During her recovery she described her NDE and told Professor Clark what she had seen. She asked Professor Clark to search for the tennis shoe—she wanted to satisfy herself that she had really seen it.

Professor Clark said of the event:

> With mixed emotions I went outside and looked up at the ledges but could not see much at all. I went up to the third floor and began going in and out of patients' rooms and looking out their windows, which were so narrow that I had to press my face to the screen just to see the ledge at all. Finally, I found a room where I pressed my face to the glass and saw the tennis shoe! My vantage point was very different from what Maria's had to have been for her to notice that the little toe had worn a place in the shoe and that the lace was stuck under the heel and other details about the side of the shoe not visible to me. The only way she would have had such a perspective was if she had been floating right outside and at very close range to the tennis shoe. I retrieved the shoe and brought it back to Maria; it was very concrete evidence for me.[7]

The Varied Nature of the Experiences

Which People Have NDEs?

A frequently asked question is why do some people have NDEs and others do not. There is no really good answer to that question, but there have been studies that examine which people, and what percentage of the population, are likely to have NDEs.

Kenneth Ring summarized the pertinent research with these words:

Taking into account all the relevant research so far published then, and allowing for the possibility that Gallup's own figure may reflect a minimum value for the population, I would propose that somewhere between 35 and 40 percent of those who come close to death would report NDEs.[8]

In summarizing the research about whether one group of people is more likely to have an NDE than another, at least in western societies, Dr. Ring said the following:

Demographic characteristics such as age, sex, race, social class, educational level, occupation, and the like seem to have no particular relationship to NDE incidence. . . . I found no relationship for such demographic variables as social class, race, marital status, or religious affiliation.

. . . There is, in fact, no difference in either the type or incidence of NDEs as a function of one's religious orientation—or lack of it. To be sure, an agnostic or an atheist might—and actually appear to—have a more difficult time coming to terms with the experience and may be less likely to interpret it in conventional terms than a believer, but the form and content of the NDE will not be distinctive.[9]

Why Such Varied Experiences?

A recent article in the *Journal of Near-Death Studies* (an IANDS publication), by Professor John Wren-Lewis of the University of Sydney, argued that the varied nature of the NDE was proof that the experiences were not real. Professor Wren-Lewis said:

But even among those NDE reports that do involve visions, the great majority could not be literal glimpses of the undiscovered country beyond the grave for the simple reason that they contradict each other in significant ways. Some, for example, depict the heavenly landscape as a pastoral scene, others as an insubstantial cloudy space, others as a science-fiction-style Celestial City, and still others as human scenes almost justifying the Monty Python spoof. The long-dead relatives encountered in certain much-publicized experiences sometimes appear the age they were when they themselves died, sometimes as the age they would have been had they lived on, sometimes miraculously rejuvenated, and sometimes totally transfigured into shining angelic forms that are somehow recognizable.[10]

My own perspective was just the opposite from that of Professor Wren-Lewis. Howard Storm (Chapter 18), in a research conference after his NDE, said this about why people have different experiences:

The angels told me that when a good person died, and that's all we talked about, the angels go and meet the person. The angels' concern is not to impose anything on people, but to first help them over the transition. That transition is traumatic for individuals when they die. Our training in this world is not good training for the transitional state.

Many people, when they die, are very confused, upset and disturbed, so the angels create a reality for them in order to make the transition. The reality might be a palace, a garden, a seashore—anything that might ease the transition for the one experiencing death. The angels know these people intimately—better than the people know themselves. They create a state that will help the people through the transition.

The angels can create things and situations, easily, because they are one with God. They have that kind of power. They can create simply by wanting it to be, and it is. So any epiphany that a person experiencing an NDE says that he or she has had, I would be willing to accept at face value, because the angels can create those situations for them.

It's hard for us to understand people who are not selfish. The angels are not selfish. They are not interested in proving anything to anyone. They only want to provide what is best for us. And if what is best for us when we die is to lie in a swimming pool, and relax, then we will get a swimming pool.

From my own research work I would add the following to what Professor Storm said:

These different experiences stem from the Lord's knowledge of us, and his understanding of our needs. John Stirling commented after his experience that we see through a glass darkly in this life, but in the next we are known by Jesus Christ, and we know him. John said it was a comfortable feeling, one which he was familiar with. He was amazed at the review of his life, and at the complete knowledge of him shown in the review—in the presence of himself and his God.

Thus we are known by Jesus Christ far better than we know ourselves. When individuals leave this earth, even temporarily from some sort of trauma, the Lord understands them. He is able to tailor a view of the spirit world according to their particular needs. What to one person might be complete nonsense, to another is a tremendous spiritual experience.

And these experiences, in my view, are real. It is a real world that those having NDEs are visiting, albeit a spiritual one. Many whom we interviewed said that the other world was more real to them than this one.

Motivation of Those Telling Their Stories

People responded to our advertisements and came to see us for several reasons, but none of the reasons had anything to do with money. Of the hundred or so people we interviewed, only three or four asked if there were a fee involved. When I explained to those few that such a fee would make the story itself suspect, they understood and dropped the subject.

The reasons that most people came were: to talk to someone who was sympathetic to what they had to say; to find out about others who had had similar experiences; and to help others by sharing what the respondent knew about death. Many of them, after the interview was completed, questioned Carol and me for an hour or more about others we had interviewed. They were thrilled that we accepted their stories for what they were—a profound spiritual experience—and they were extremely curious about others. Equally important to those we interviewed was the possibility of having their stories published in a manner that would help others. In many instances they felt an obligation to bear witness to what they had seen and heard.

With regard to whether or not some people might fabricate stories for a variety of reasons, that possibility exists, of course. In a research study of the size that Carol and I performed, there were a few individuals who professed to have had experiences that were quite possibly untrue. One man attempted to explain the details of his encounter with a UFO. The number of such instances, however, was remarkably small, perhaps three percent of the total. Those few individuals were identified within the first few minutes of the conversation, usually while the contact was still in the telephone stage. Upon being identified, I thanked them for their trouble and excused them from further discussion.

Although there is no absolute assurance that a fabricated story could not have found its way into this book, I believe that all included accounts are true and valid for the reasons discussed in the previous material. The evidences were overwhelmingly in favor of those telling their experiences, even those stories that fell somewhat out of the norm.

What About Reincarnation?

Surprisingly, questions about reincarnation continue to come up. In *Glimpses of Eternity* I explained some of the pitfalls for this point of view, and why certain groups continued to be enamored with it.[11] Since completing *Glimpses* I have discussed the issue with two clinical psychologists, both of whom have used hypnotherapy in their work.

Doctor Lynn Johnson discussed three cases that he was personally familiar with, where the patients who were subjected to hypnosis were regressed into presumably previous lives. He was able to show that the one patient claiming to speak in Spanish and German, from her previous lives, was in fact "producing random combinations of consonants mixed with the vowels O and E." His conclusion, based on his own and other research work, was: "It would appear that the specific cases which 'prove' reincarnation can be explained as confabulation [made-up stories], especially when a desire to believe that is combined with hypnosis which allows for vivid fantasies to be experienced as reality."[12]

Marian Bergin is a clinical psychologist who has engaged in hypnotherapy in her own practice. She is convinced that work which reveals previous lives in hypnotized subjects is false. She has given me a number of papers, of the type discussed below, in which researchers show the extreme culpability of the patients to suggestions by the hypnotherapists. Hypnotherapy may be used, with care, for treatment of specific psychic disorders, but not for accurately reclaiming historic information.

Marian sent me the paper: *Secondary Identity Enactments During Hypnotic Past Life Regression: A Sociocognitive Perspective.* Despite its ponderous title, it is an excellent work. It relates to the reincarnation hypothesis that is so popular among New Age adherents and some near-death researchers.

Researchers for this study, led by Nicholas Spanos of Carleton University in Ottawa, Canada, conducted a series of controlled experiments on 175 subjects at the university. The subjects were selected for their hypnotizability and separated into three control groups. The groups differed in the specificity of suggestions made before and during hypnosis by the hypnotist. Individuals in all groups were led by the hypnotist back in time to presumably earlier lives.

Results of the study showed that subjects in all three groups were significantly affected by what they thought was wanted of them by the hypnotist. The more information that was transmitted to them by the hypnotist, the more detailed their past life regressions became. The researchers also showed that the subjects confabulated, or made-up, their previous lives' histories from books they had read, plays they had seen, newspapers they had read, or travels they had taken. Where information was lacking about a topic the researcher was asking about the subjects' imagined fictitious stories and represented them as real. Some of the subjects were, in fact, convinced that their stories were real.

The researchers deliberately led the subjects into increasing detail about the geopolitical history from their so-called previous lives. These histories were checked later and found, universally, to be faulty.[13]

Perhaps the best argument against reincarnation, however, is that it is contrary to the scriptures. Paul, in the New Testament, said: "It is appointed unto men once to die . . . ."[14] Reincarnation doctrine is, of course, that we die many times; each time that we are reincarnated. When Christ was on the cross he said to the thief on the adjacent cross: "Verily I say unto thee, To day shalt thou be with me in paradise.[15] Jesus did not say to the thief that he would meet him in the next incarnation on earth.

What Do Carol and Arvin Gibson Believe About NDEs?

Carol said of her part in interviewing the people: "I saw tears running down the face of a man, as he relived the experience of a life's review, who told me his family thought he was not an emotional man. Another lady we interviewed was angry about returning to life. She knew that no one could love her like the love she felt in Christ's presence—and she wanted that love again. Yes, I believe the people were telling the truth, and they were describing real experiences from beyond the veil of this earthly life."

Do I, Arvin Gibson, believe that they were telling us the truth about real experiences, and do I believe that these experiences are evidence of life after death? The answer is unequivocally, *yes*. I further believe that the lessons learned from these experiences can aid us in this life, not with the strength that the scriptures aid us, but aid us nevertheless. These stories provide windows, in today's language, of a spiritual realm where a loving God reigns supreme.

Chapter 20

PATTERNS AND PARALLELS

Statistical Summary

Introduction

While performing the research for the various books I was working on, it became apparent that certain patterns were appearing. Particular words kept showing up in the vocabulary of the subjects being interviewed, for example, and the people were unaware that they were repeating words used by others. The word *peace* was used so often that I began to look for it in the vocabulary of the candidates. It was almost as if they were programmed to repeat the word.

I asked one fourteen-year-old girl, Tracie, why she used the word *peace* in describing how she felt during her NDE. Her response was: "I don't know. It just seems like the right word."

Most of those using the word peace did not think of it in the normal sense of the word (lack of conflict); rather, they thought of it in the scriptural sense, the sense that Christ used it as reported in the New Testament: "Peace I leave with you, my peace I give unto you: Not as the world giveth, give I unto you. Let not your heart be troubled, neither let it be afraid."[1]

Paul described the Lord's peace in this manner: "And the peace of God, which passeth all understanding, shall keep your hearts and minds through Christ Jesus."[2]

Other interesting patterns and parallels developed as the interviewing process continued. Some showed a remarkable consistency with numerous scriptural references, particularly those of the New Testament.

Tabular Data

In order to systematically examine some of the patterns that were becoming apparent, certain repeating characteristics that the subjects spoke of in their experiences were tabulated. A total of 31 parameters have been identified for the purposes of this book. These parameters are tabulated in their completeness for each of 68 different subjects in the Appendix. A summary of a portion of that data is shown in the following table.

Tabular Summary of Research Findings

	Total People	No. of Experience	Out of Body	Saw Body	Spirit Had Form	Tunnel
Totals	68	83	71	44	49	18
Percent	58.8 Female	20.5 Multiple	85.5	53.0	59.0	21.6

	Light	Landscape	Saw People	Knew People	Relatives	Voice
Totals	50	18	46	33	23	53
Percent	60.2	21.1	55.4	39.8	27.7	63.8

	Deity	Saw Deity	Life's Review	Buildings	Knowl-edge	Energy
Totals	22	15	9	6	28	6
Percent	26.5	18.1	10.8	7.2	33.7	7.2

Tabular Summary of Research Findings, Cont'd.

	Peace	Love	Warm	Pure	Remorse
Totals	38	39	17	4	5
Percent	45.7	47.0	20.5	4.8	6.0

	Fear	Music	Sense of Mission	Second Healing	Saw Pre-mortal
Totals	10	9	52	10	3
Percent	12.0	9.6	62.6	12.0	3.6

Multiple Experiences by People

It is seen from the table that several subjects had more than one experience. Of the 68 people whose experiences were included (58.8% female), 20.5% of them had multiple experiences.

A large fraction of the experiences were out-of-body (85.5%), and in 53% of the experiences the people saw their physical bodies lying beneath them. Most (59%) felt that their spirit-bodies had form—or they were able to see those forms, sometimes as energy fields, shaped similarly to their physical bodies.

Light, Color and Landscapes

The NDE literature is filled with descriptions of people who went through a tunnel and saw a light. A relatively modest 21.6% of the experiences tabulated here included a tunnel, but 60.2 % involved some aspect of the bright light. The bright light dominated much of the discussion concerning what the subjects saw and felt during their NDEs.

Twenty-one percent of the experiences involved some type of landscape feature. In most of these cases the people said that they saw plants, trees, shrubs, flowers and gardens with colors that were more vivid and alive than anything they had seen on earth. In a few cases animals were also seen.

A statistical review of those who saw the light is insufficient to illustrate the enormous impact that the light had on those witnessing it.

The feelings of awe, love and peace that the subjects expressed can be partially portrayed by repeating the words of two people I interviewed who witnessed the light. These examples could be repeated many times.

Elane Durham's Description of the Light

"Looking about me, I turned toward the right, and I saw a distant light that resembled a bright star. The light began to move toward me at an incredible rate of speed; at the same time, I had a sense of moving toward the light.

"As the light got closer to me I realized that it had a personality to it. Love and understanding were emanating from the light. It was the most immense amount of love that you could imagine. It was as though you were in the presence of the one person in your life who had loved you beyond anything, despite what you might have done, and that love was magnified many times. That's how it was, in a way.

". . . At that point the light spoke to me—only not in language as here on earth. It spoke to me from everything that it was into everything that I was. I not only heard it, but I understood it with every fiber of my being. There was total communication between that being and my being."

Derald Evans's Description of the Light

". . . the beautiful bright-white light. It gave me a feeling like . . . almost like soft music, or something that was one-hundred percent pure. It's hard to describe in words. I had never seen nor heard anything like it before. It was not frightening, though. More softening. And it kept coming closer, getting brighter and brighter. . . . I will never forget the feeling I got from the light."

Scriptural References to the Light

Descriptions of the light, such as these, and the obvious sublime feelings that ensued, caused me to look in the scriptures for parallels. In general, the light is associated with God and with Jesus Christ as expressed in the New Testament.

The First Epistle of John says of God:

This then is the message which we have heard of him, and declare unto you, that God is light, and in him is no darkness at all.[3]

James says:

Every good gift and every perfect gift is from above, and cometh down from the Father of lights . . . .[4]

From John, in the New Testament, the mission of John the Baptist is described as a forerunner of Jesus Christ. In this discussion Christ is referred to as the Light.

There was a man sent from God, whose name was John. The same came for a witness, to bear witness of the Light, that all men through him might believe. He was not that Light, but was sent to bear witness of that Light. That was the true Light, which lighteth every man that cometh into the world.[5]

Spirit People and Families

A large fraction of the experiences (55.4%) involved other spirit people, and in 39% of the cases the individuals undergoing the NDEs understood that they knew the spirit people whom they saw. Often, however, unless the other spirit people were relatives, the subjects could no longer recall who the people were that they saw. They just knew that at the time of their NDE the other people were known to them.

If the spirit people were relatives (27.7% of the time), then the subjects were able to recall many details about the people they saw. In most cases the relatives were delivering a particular message to the subjects involved. Some of these messages were delivered under dramatic circumstances. Julie saw a cousin who had been a soldier in Vietnam as he communicated with her, shortly after he had been killed, and before the military had discovered that he was missing or dead. Rocky and Jennifer were two children who saw their grandparents during their NDEs. Bill, whose NDE occurred when he broke his neck (and became paralyzed) during an ATV accident, saw his father in a beautiful garden and was told that he would have peace. Renee had an extensive NDE where she saw hundreds of people in a strange environment, all related to each other.

Communication and Deity

It was interesting to hear the people discuss the voices that they heard. Sixty-three percent of the experiences included some memory of voice communication. In some instances the subjects said that communication was as it is on earth, by voice in a person-to-person manner.

These were the minority of the cases, though. Most felt that the *voice* was transmitted into their mind without the benefit of vocal cords. Usually, the voice could be recognized as male, female, or from a particular person. In a few instances the subjects actually heard their own voices delivering a message to themselves. Where deity was involved, they recognized the voice as coming from Heavenly Father or from Jesus Christ, and, often with great emotion, they said that it was a familiar voice—one that they had known from before.

Deity (God the Father, or His son, Jesus Christ) was involved in a surprising twenty-six percent of the cases, and in eighteen percent of the experiences Deity was actually seen. In these instances the subjects were emphatic about whom and what they saw. For those who reported having seen Christ, the most common elements were: seeing a being who transmitted light, or energy; seeing brilliantly bright white clothes in the form of a robe that covered Him from his neck to his ankles and wrists, usually with a sash; having a feeling of love, peace and joy that emanated from Him; noticing His long hair and beard, colored either sandy-brown, or sandy-blonde (and in one case, white); looking into His penetrating blue eyes; receiving intense knowledge communicated from Him without its being spoken; observing a muscular feeling of strength coming from Him; and having innate knowledge that it was Him.

Concerning the last element, several people were asked how they knew it was Christ. Their responses were engrossing. The conversation with David went in this manner:

"How did you know it was your Savior?"

"I know Jesus Christ when I see Him."

"How did you know?"

He chuckled as he thought. Then he said: "Probably it was the sense of goodwill and the sense of comfort that I felt—together with the other events that I witnessed. The fact is, *I just knew. I knew!*"

Life's Reviews—Buildings

A life's review occurred in only eleven percent of the cases, but when it did it was usually under striking circumstances. Four of the nine cases, for example, happened while the subjects were in space and just after they had been traveling through the stars. Their stellar journeys were interrupted so that they could learn something about themselves through a review of their lives. In these particular cases they were able, after the reviews, to decide whether or not they wanted to continue with their lives on earth.

Few, only seven percent of the experiences tabulated, involved people who saw buildings. In some of these, little detail was seen of the buildings. Others, such as Jean's view of the "libraries," included detailed descriptions of exterior and interior features.

Knowledge

One-third of the experiences included people who said that unusual knowledge was theirs while they were undergoing the NDEs. After the NDE they forgot most of what they had known, but they still remembered the remarkable feeling they got when the mere hint of a question resulted in a fountain of information flowing into them.

DeLynn's Experience Concerning Knowledge

It was astonishing, the speed with which I was learning. Knowledge that had somehow slumbered deep in my soul was released, and I was extremely exhilarated by this reawakened knowledge. Light and knowledge were flowing into me from every direction. I could feel it. Every part of my body was reverberating with the light gushing in. Even my fingertips were receptors of light and knowledge. It was as if I were drinking from a fully engaged fire hydrant.

Roger's Description of the Knowledge He Got

Pure knowledge seemed to pour into me from Him. The knowledge was transmitted by . . . energy. Energy flowed into me and with it was knowledge. It was as if my entire being was a receptor of knowledge. And it was knowledge that I seemed to have known before. Everything that was communicated to me made sense.

Words Concerning Feelings During the Experiences

Several words were repeated often enough in the interviews that they attracted attention. These were words that the candidates used in their attempts to describe what they felt. The words were: *Energy* (7.2%), *Peace* (45.7%), *Love* (47.0%), *Warmth* (20.5%), and *Pure* (4.8%). In many instances, as with the word *love*, the individuals said that this was an improper word to describe what they felt. DeLynn put it this way:

"We don't have a word that would describe what I felt from Him toward me. The closest word we have is *love*, but it doesn't begin to describe the feeling. There is not an appropriate description in mortal tongue that can explain the feeling—you have to feel it."

These repeated references to love again call to mind scriptural references. The third chapter of Ephesians expresses it this way: "And to know the love of Christ, which passeth knowledge, that ye might be filled with all the fulness of God."[6]

Remorse and Fear

Remorse and fear were two emotions suffered by those whose experience included some negative features. It was not necessary for the entire experience to be negative, as with Howard's extensive experience which included both positive and negative aspects, or as with Jack's view of Hell. In some cases, as with Dee's bout with an evil spirit, it was terrifying. Remorse played a part in most cases where an individual had a life's review. Sometimes remorse was a major factor in helping the individuals decide that they needed to come back for a second try at life, as with Elizabeth Marie.

Music

Music was mentioned as a factor in only 9.6% of the cases, but where it was mentioned, it was a major factor.

Katrina's Experience with Music

Katrina told how she spent months listening to various classical pieces in an attempt to find what she had heard in the other world. She finally settled on Daniel Kobialka's version of "Pachelbel's Kanon" as a poor (too loud) substitute for what she had heard.

Elane Durham's Description of Music

There was a sound in the air that completely defies description. It was as if there were a multitude of voices, and a multitude of instruments, blended and playing soft music. The twittering of birds, and other beautiful sounds, were all melodically instrumented into the music which wafted through the air. The sounds just flowed into me in a soft, soft manner.

Sense of Mission

An amazingly high 62.6% returned from the other world with a strong sense of mission. In most of those instances they were not aware of exactly what they were supposed to accomplish, just that it was an important part of their lives from thenceforth forward.

Elizabeth Marie's Sense of Mission

Elizabeth Marie, for example, remembered that she was told she should help others who had lost their way to come to Christ. She forgot the details, however, and she said this about it:

> Since my experience, though, I haven't known who it was that I was supposed to help. I've wondered if it was one person, or many persons. I understood that it was to help someone, or several people, who had lost their way, to return to His presence, but I still don't know who they are.

David's Feelings of a Mission

David, who was shot in the lower abdomen by a drunken uncle, said the following when I asked him if he had any sense about why he was allowed to come back:

> That question has plagued me since I was shot. Initially I thought it might be to help my wife and my two sons. Then, after I completed my education and started teaching, I thought it might be because I am able to express myself and to teach others well. Recently, when my daughter was born, I suspected it might be to help nurture and raise her. Maybe it's all of those things.

Dallas's Understanding of His Mission

Dallas, who shot himself in a suicide attempt, said this:

> The Lord called me by name and told me that I had done a foolish thing, and it was not my time to be there. He said that there was a lot of work on the earth that I must do for Him. There were certain things I must accomplish with my family before I would be allowed to return to the Lord. If I did what he asked, he said that my life would be great—not great in an earthly sense, but great in a spiritual sense, and I would be richly rewarded on the other side.

Dallas was still puzzling over exactly what it was he was supposed to do when I interviewed him.

This sense of mission, but not necessarily an exact sureness of what the mission was to be, was fascinating to observe. As seen from the statistical summary, this characteristic was one of the more common features of the experiences of those I interviewed.

Second Healings

In *Glimpses of Eternity* I observed: "A totally unexpected pattern concerned healings. I expected to find people who had returned to this life after an NDE more-or-less healed after their bout with death. And this was the case. Indeed, with several, in addition to the miracle of the NDE, there was a miraculous healing upon their return to this life."

There were four individuals who went through this particular pattern of experiences as recorded in *Glimpses*. Each of the experiences was spectacular in its own right and involved a second, serious, life-threatening event that was miraculously removed. I watched with interest, during the research period for *Echoes From Eternity*, therefore, to see if there were repeats of the pattern. And repeats there were—six more. The percentage of these unusual healings totalled at twelve percent of all experiences.

As a result of the original work (four cases), I suggested a tentative model and hypothesis.[7] Quoting from that work:

"The pattern that became evident from these experiences was the following:

• The individuals were good people, who, as the result of an illness or an accident had an out-of-body experience.

• They came back to this life with an even firmer resolve to live a righteous life. They were more spiritually attuned than they previously had been. They had a sense of purpose about life.

• An illness or injury developed (or lingered) which threatened their ability to carry out their perceived purpose.

• A healing occurred which defied medical knowledge. . . ."

From the observed experiences I reached a tentative conclusion—or hypothesis. The hypothesis was:

When an individual undergoes an NDE and returns to this life, that return is for a purpose. If the individual, after return, has some illness or injury that threatens to thwart the person's life purpose, then the Lord intervenes and removes the threat.

I said, at the time, that "this hypothesis should be tested by further research of persons having NDEs." Additional tests have now been made that tend to confirm the hypothesis—usually in a spectacular manner. Further work should be done to establish the statistical correlations. To be useful, this work should also attempt to identify individuals who do not meet the conditions of the hypothesis. That is, were there those who—after experiencing an NDE and returning *with a sense of mission*—then promptly died? None of the sixty-eight persons whose experiences are tabulated in this book (including follow-up studies on them) failed to comply with the hypothesis.

The very fact that a person has an out-of-body experience and comes back gives evidence of the Lord's interest in the person. I have already discussed how the majority of the people felt that they came back for a purpose. To allow the person to return to this life and then not be able to fulfill his or her purpose would seem a fruitless exercise.

This is not to suggest that all persons return with a strong and healthy body. Just the opposite is often true—and the people having had an NDE understand that they may have to live under difficult circumstances when they return.

Saw Themselves in a Premortal Environment

One of the more interesting patterns was the experience of three individuals I interviewed who saw themselves during their NDE (or related experience) in a premortal environment. Their experiences were similar to an experience described by Betty Eadie in her book *Embraced by the Light*.[8] The pattern of the experiences was as follows:

• The subjects were in the midst of an NDE or unusual spiritual event when they saw themselves in a premortal environment.

• They recognized and felt the emotions they had previously felt in that environment.

• The subjects were making choices concerning their life to come on earth.

DeLynn's Premortal Experience

On the issue of the choices they were making, DeLynn described a fascinating series of events. He had an extensive NDE as the result of the disease cystic fibrosis. During his life he had undergone enormous pain from the disease, and while he was having the NDE he asked a familiar voice why he had to suffer so. He said of that experience:

Then I received a most startling answer. He said to me: *You chose your disease and the amount of pain you would be willing to suffer before this life—when you were in a premortal state. It was your choice.*

While I was hearing this voice, I became aware that it was a familiar voice—it was one that I knew. It was a voice that I had not heard during my mortal lifetime. When it was speaking to me, though, there was no question but that I knew who it was. There was enormous love for me in the voice.

DeLynn was then transported to a time and place in a premortal environment where he saw himself making particular choices of his life to come. As a result of that experience DeLynn said:

That scene changed forever my perspective of the disease that I previously felt was a plague on my life. No longer did I consider myself a victim. Rather, I was a privileged participant, by choice, in an eternal plan. That plan, if I measured up to the potential of my choice, would allow me to advance in mortal life in the fastest way possible. True, I would not be able to control the inevitable slow deterioration of my mortal body, but I could control how I chose to handle my illness emotionally and psychologically. The specific choice of cystic fibrosis was to help me learn dignity in suffering. My understanding in the eternal sense was complete—I knew that I was a powerful, spiritual being that chose to have a short, but marvelous, mortal existence.

Conclusions Concerning the Tabulated Data

These were the majority of the data that I tabulated, and they are sufficient to show the existence of some interesting patterns. It was exciting to interview a person and witness that person attempting to explain a situation with the same stumbling words, and with the same surging emotions, as another individual who had been through a similar situation.

Many of the patterns that became evident during the interviews were patterns that others performing NDE research had previously discovered. The out-of-body experience, the tunnel, the light, and the life's review have all been documented by Raymond Moody (1975),[9] Kenneth Ring (1980),[10] Maurice Rawlings (1978)[11] and others.

Some patterns were reinforced by the present work. The sense of mission or purpose—without knowing exactly what the purpose was—had previously been reported by Kenneth Ring in *Life at Death* (1980).[12] The current work showed that a surprising 63% returned with this sense of mission or purpose. Similarly, others have documented NDEs where the subjects claimed to have seen deity (Ritchie and Sherrill, 1978).[13] The present work documented a strong 18% of all experiences where detailed descriptions of deity were given.

Some apparently new patterns were also divulged by the present work. The second healing phenomenon discussed above was an interesting finding, and the hypothesis generated as a result of the finding should be tested by further research. Perhaps the most unusual new pattern, though, was the premortal experience finding. Although this was a small percentage of the total (3.6%), the three cases identified were consistent with each other. They were also consistent with the experience reported by Betty Eadie in her book *Embraced by the Light* (1992).[8] It will be interesting to watch for further reports of this type in future NDE research.

Note: Much of the material in this chapter originally was submitted for publication in the "Journal of Near-Death Studies," published by Human Sciences Press, New York, N.Y. under the title *Near-Death Experience Patterns from Research in the Salt Lake City Region*, by Arvin S. Gibson. The material is included in this book by permission of Human Sciences Press, Inc.

Chapter 21

UNIVERSAL MESSAGES

Finding the Truth

Incomplete Knowledge

In a previous work involving NDE research I observed that Carol and I, in our search for the truth, had drunk briefly from the river of knowledge that we found.[1] I noted that our drink, though refreshing, had not quenched our thirst for knowledge. Light had illuminated some truths—truths that we had dimly understood—but ultimate knowledge eluded us. Sir Isaac Newton said it better when he stated: "I do not know what I may appear to the world, but to myself I seem to have been only like a boy playing on the seashore, and diverting myself in now and then finding a smoother pebble or a prettier shell than ordinary, whilst the great ocean of truth lay all undiscovered before me."[2]

As with those we interviewed, it was thrilling when we recognized some bit of knowledge that had previously been buried from our sight, but it was frustrating to recognize the incomplete nature of that knowledge. It appears that we, like Paul, can in this life only see through a glass darkly, abiding in faith, hope and charity.[3]

Sin, Faith and Repentance

We are all sinners in the sight of the Lord. Since we are all sinners and fall short of living a perfect life, the Lord has made possible our return to him through the principle of repentance. When Christ was questioned by the Pharisees concerning his eating with publicans and sinners, he said: "They that are whole have no need of the physician, but they that are sick: I came not to call the righteous, but sinners to repentance."[4]

255

By recognizing that we are sinners, by repenting of those sins, by prayer, by reading the scriptures, and by having faith in the Lord Jesus Christ, we may approach the truth through the author of all truth. Paul, in looking at our times, said this about it:[5]

This know also, that in the last days perilous times shall come.

For men shall be lovers of their own selves, covetous, boasters, proud, blasphemers, disobedient to parents, unthankful, unholy,

Without natural affection, trucebreakers, false accusers, incontinent, fierce, despisers of those that are good,

Traitors, heady, highminded, lovers of pleasures more than lovers of God;

Having a form of godliness, but denying the power thereof: from such turn away.

For of this sort are they which creep into houses, and lead captive silly women laden with sins, led away with divers lusts,

Ever learning, and never able to come to the knowledge of the truth.

Now as Jannes and Jambres withstood Moses, so do these also resist the truth: men of corrupt minds, reprobate concerning the faith.

But they shall proceed no further: for their folly shall be manifest unto all *men*, as theirs also was.

But thou hast fully known my doctrine, manner of life, purpose, faith, longsuffering, charity, patience,

Persecutions, afflictions, which came unto me at Antioch, at Iconium, at Lystra; what persecutions I endured: but out of *them* all the Lord delivered me.

Yea, and all that will live godly in Christ Jesus shall suffer persecution.

But evil men and seducers shall wax worse and worse, deceiving, and being deceived.

But continue thou in the things which thou hast learned and hast been assured of, knowing of whom thou hast learned *them*;

And that from a child thou hast known the holy scriptures, which are able to make thee wise unto salvation through faith which is in Christ Jesus.

Can anyone doubt that we live in perilous times, and that men have become lovers of pleasures more than lovers of God? Paul reminds us that even those who live a godly life in Christ Jesus shall suffer persecution, but evil men and seducers shall wax worse. He further observes that we may become wise by studying the scriptures and by having faith in the Lord Jesus Christ.

This particular passage of scripture, in which the folly of men and women in our time—who do not follow the teachings and example of the Lord Jesus Christ—is particularly pertinent to some of the lessons learned by those having had an NDE. The improper use of drugs; despair, leading to suicide; surrender to feelings of hate and depression; lust and greed—all of these characteristics and emotions can lead us in paths that make us easy prey to the Adversary and his followers. In so doing, we deviate from the source of light and truth.

Examples of Some Who Got a Lesson in Truth

Several of those whom we interviewed appeared to be basically good people who, by their own accounts, became vulnerable to evil spirits. Their resulting experiences taught them important lessons that brought them closer to the truth.

A Teaching Experience for Elizabeth Marie

Elizabeth Marie had her experience when fourteen years old. As a result of taking drugs, she was transported to a place where other spirits laughed at her, following which she met Christ. She said this about her experience:

". . . He put his arms around me and asked me if I had known that what I did was wrong. I told Him that yes, I had known it was wrong.

"The amount of remorse I had, I'd never felt before. It was remorse over what I had done. I felt so sorry; there was a deep disappointment over my previous activities. The feelings of remorse and disappointment were pure feelings that permeated my body.

"I was asked if I had known what was right and wrong—and I had. My knowledge, in the presence of Him, was that I couldn't progress from the place I had positioned myself. Knowing that I was stopped in my progression, and feeling great remorse, I asked if I could return and help others to come back to Him. There was an intense desire within me to amend for the pain and suffering that I had caused others.

"The love I felt from Him during this period was extremely intense. Love traveled from my toes to my head, filling my entire body. There are no words that can adequately describe that love. It was a fatherly type of love, and I knew that He was pleased when I acknowledged my sins and asked if I could amend for them.

"He held me in His arms the whole time, and . . . and the feelings were so intense. The love I felt was beyond belief. And while I was embraced by Him and felt of His great love, He asked me if I would help others to come back to Him. I said I would."

Howard Storm's Changed Life

In Howard Storm's extensive NDE, he first encountered evil spirits and then saw marvelous beings of light. He learned much about the truth. As a result of his experience he changed completely—and those changes were not especially easy on those around him. When asked how his family reacted to his changed nature, he said this:

"It was traumatic for them. At the time my son was fifteen and my daughter was twenty years old. I had raised them as materialistic, hedonistic people, just like I was. There were the traumas of a strong father image, and the upset that came with me being sick and my wife having to spend so much time at the hospital with me—and not with them.

"Even more importantly, as my wife has said, I died on June 1 and the guy that came back was a complete stranger. I was not the person she married and lived with for twenty years. She has had to rediscover this totally different person.

"I used to curse all the time. A good night for me, in the past, was to watch a horror movie on TV, drink beer, and curse. After I came home from the hospital, if I heard any swearing at all I would scream in pain. I felt physical pain with any kind of blasphemy. Words that used to be fun words, now, I would go nuts when someone used them.

"Any kind of violence on TV, after the hospital, would repulse me. I couldn't watch horror movies. I didn't approve of many of the things that I used to find unobjectionable. To a fifteen-year-old kid, trying to figure me out, this was difficult stuff."

As noted previously, Howard is now a minister in the United Church of Christ. Howard's dramatic NDE taught him much about the truth—and in the process changed his life completely. As with many who have had an NDE, the changes did not come easily.

The Ultimate Source of Truth

The great universities of the world are repositories of much knowledge, and a great deal can be learned by attending them. Their knowledge, though, is but as a firefly in a dark night compared with the light of Christ. John says this about light and truth:[6] "But he that doeth truth cometh to the light, that his deeds may be made manifest, that they are wrought in God."

The ecstatic feelings of those who saw the light and drank from the fountain of knowledge therein act as a further witness as to the power of the light of Christ. He, the source of all truth, will not lead us astray.

Love

A Universal Message

If there was a universal message that Carol and I learned from interviewing the many people who had gone through an NDE, it was that the other world, for righteous beings, is a world of love. Even for those who are not righteous, the Savior's love extends unconditionally. The love of God knows no bounds.

David Herard's Experience with God's Love

David, the Vietnam veteran who felt God's hand on his shoulder, then felt as if he were embraced by God, said: "When I was embraced, I felt a warmth all through me. And there was a feeling of love. It was all the love there is. . . . it was like that was all the love there was, everywhere. It was like . . . I can't explain the feeling. It's beyond words."

Janet McClellan Explains Her Feelings of Love

Janet, a critical-care nurse who had her experience during childbirth, said this about love: "He [Jesus Christ] wants me to love everybody. It doesn't matter what religion they profess, what their race or politics are, what their skin color is—I must love everybody."

Katrina's Understanding of Christ's Love

Katrina, who had a difficult life, attempted suicide and was transported into Christ's presence during her NDE, said of the experience: "I was amazed at the mercy, understanding and love given to me while in the Savior's presence. There was such total acceptance and love—no condemnation whatsoever.

"Standing in His presence I received a new perception of myself and of my worth. I had left the earth thinking of myself as human garbage. In a few moments in His presence, and feeling for myself what he felt for me, I totally reevaluated my worth. I *did* matter; He *did* care. Even more than that—he loved me, he forgave me.

"I was so overwhelmed by the utter love and peace and mercy that I did not want to leave."

A Therapy of Love for Howard Storm

Howard Storm's life's review exposed him to the emotional trauma of seeing his life unfold in its previous self-centered manner. What he said about it was: "The entire life's review would have been emotionally destructive, and would have left me a psychotic person, if it hadn't been for the fact that my friend, and my friend's friends, were loving me during the unfolding of my life. I could feel that love. Every time I got a little upset they turned the life's review off for awhile, and they just loved me. Their love was tangible. You could feel it on your body, you could feel it inside of you; their love went right through you. I wish I could explain it to you, but I can't. . . . The therapy was their love."

Scriptural References to Love

Paul, in his epistle to the Romans, said this about the love of Christ:[7]

Who shall separate us from the love of Christ? *shall* tribulation, or distress, or persecution, or famine, or nakedness, or peril, or sword?

As it is written, For thy sake we are killed all the day long; we are accounted as sheep for the slaughter.

Nay, in all these things we are more than conquerors through him that loved us.

For I am persuaded, that neither death, nor life, nor angels, nor principalities, nor powers, nor things present, nor things to come,

Nor height, nor depth, nor any other creature, shall be able to separate us from the love of God, which is in Christ Jesus our Lord.

And what should be our response to this great love? When asked by the Pharisees which is the great commandment in the law, Matthew records Jesus's answer in this manner:[8]

Thou shalt love the Lord thy God with all thy heart, and with all thy soul, and with all thy mind.

This is the first and great commandment.

And the second *is* like unto it, Thou shalt love thy neighbour as thyself.

On these two commandments hang all the law and the prophets.

These scriptural references illustrate both the durability and strength of the Lord's love for us, and of the need for our love to be reciprocated to the Savior and to our fellow beings. The experiences of those we interviewed dramatically emphasized the validity of these scriptures.

The Resurrection

The Importance of the Resurrection

There is nothing more central to the message of Christianity than the message of the Resurrection. Christ was resurrected as the great paradigm for us all—in a corporeal, physical way he lived again. It was not just as an ethereal spirit that he survived death, although it certainly included that, but as a resurrected physical being—and in so doing he set the pattern for all humankind. C.S. Lewis, in his book *Miracles*, put it this way:

. . . the Resurrection was not regarded [by the New Testament writers] simply or chiefly as evidence for the immortality of the soul. It is, of course, often so regarded today: I have heard a man maintain that 'the importance of the Resurrection is that it proves *survival.*' Such a view cannot at any point be reconciled with the language of the New Testament. On such a view Christ would simply have done what all men do when they die: the only novelty would have been that in His case we were allowed to see it happening. But there is not in Scripture the faintest suggestion that the Resurrection was new evidence for something that had *in fact* been always happening. The New Testament writers speak as if Christ's achievement in rising from the dead was the first event of its kind in the whole history of the universe. He is the 'first fruits,' the 'pioneer of life.' He has forced open a door that has been locked since the death of the first man. He has met, fought, and beaten the King of Death. Everything is different because He has done so.

This is the beginning of the New Creation: a new chapter in cosmic history has opened.[9]

Who Will be Resurrected and When?

Each of us who have lived on the earth will be resurrected with a new physical body—because of the redemptive power of Jesus Christ. Paul, in writing to the Corinthians put it this way: "For as in Adam all die, even so in Christ shall all be made alive. But every man in his own order: Christ the firstfruits; afterward they that are Christ's at his coming."[10]

Matthew tells us that immediately after Christ's resurrection: "the graves were opened; and many bodies of the saints which slept arose, and came out of the graves after his resurrection, and went into the holy city, and appeared unto many."[11]

From these and other scriptures, it is clear that for the majority of us, because of the Savior's sacrifice, we will ultimately (after the second coming of Christ) be resurrected as he was. Some few others have already been resurrected (as indicated by Matthew), but most of us must await the second coming. In the interim period after our death we will live as spirits but without physical bodies.

Near-death Experiences Concerning Spirits

The near-death literature is filled with accounts of individuals existing in another realm as spirit beings—both those who have undergone an NDE and those who met and interacted with them. Many of those interviewed by Carol and me spoke of having a spirit body that had form and, as some described it, consisting of an energy field. A few during their NDE spoke of being able to feel other spirits while they, themselves, were out of their bodies. It is doubtful, in my view, that these spirit beings were resurrected.

Joy Melvin Feels Deceased Spirit Relatives

Joy Melvin was one lady we interviewed who was able to feel, and even smell, the spirit persons she saw. She said of her experience:

I rounded a corner and there stood my dad, my brother, and my first husband. I remember running to them. I ran up to my brother, I ran my hands down his body and . . . and down his legs where the mortician wouldn't let me look. He lifted me up and he said: 'I'm whole here, Joy, I'm whole here.'

Then, I remember . . . I grabbed my dad and I could feel him, and I could smell him . . . smell his smell. My dad used to call me 'Sis.' He didn't say a lot to me, there wasn't a lot said, only he said that he was okay, it was wonderful, and it was beyond his dreams.

It's almost like I saved my husband for last. He had long blonde hair, and I remember I buried my face in it—I could smell it, and it felt like it did before. And there was this love between all three of us. There was this love.

NDE Accounts Bearing on the Resurrection

Despite these rather elaborate accounts of spirits by those having NDEs, there are relatively few events in the near-death literature that either confirm or reject the validity of the Resurrection. Two individuals I interviewed did say something about it. Both events occurred under dramatic circumstances.

David Chevalier Learns of Resurrection

David Chevalier, who was horribly injured by a shotgun blast to the abdomen, described his experience in this manner:

One night, about a week after entering the hospital, while in Intensive Care, I slipped away and they again had to resuscitate me with the paddles. During that night, with my room darkened, I became fully aware of what was going on in my room. Looking around the room I could see everything—and standing by one side of my bed was my Savior. He was as plain to me then as you are now.

Reaching over to me, He ran His hands up and down my body, and all the tubes, all the staples and other attachments to my body were gone. His right hand reached out, as if to beckon me; I reached back to touch His hand.

As my hand touched His, instantaneously we were on the rim of an incredible valley. It was a huge valley, on the order of Yosemite or Zion National Park in size, and it was verdantly green. There was water; there were rivers, there were lakes—and the valley was filled, almost shoulder-to-shoulder, with people.

Gazing on this astonishing scene, I had the feeling of eager anticipation emanating from the multitude below me. The mood of this enormous crowd, the feeling that I could also feel, was as if in expectation of some marvelous event that would soon happen.

The breadth of the scene was breathtaking, and I stood there trying to absorb what I was viewing. People were milling about, some of them speaking in soft tones, and there was a calmness about them despite the feeling of anticipation.

Turning to my Savior, I asked: 'What are we waiting for?' He said something that I've later had to reconstruct, because the moment that He spoke I found myself back in Intensive Care with all the tubes and staples attached to me. My sense, upon returning, was that I would not only survive my physical ordeal but I would be better for it. I was overwhelmed by a glow within me, almost a fire, and a complete feeling of well-being.

Thinking about the Savior's reply to my question, I had difficulty translating what He said into English. He communicated, and I had a sense of what it meant, but it was a form of communication that English doesn't cover. When He spoke, a number of thoughts were conveyed simultaneously. One thought was that we were waiting for the second coming; another thought was that we were waiting for the resurrection; a third thought was that we were waiting for redemption. And all of those thoughts entered my mind instantaneously.

Mike Sees Nail Prints in the Savior

The other individual whom I interviewed, and whose experience bore on the resurrection, was Mike. He was adamant in insisting that he had seen and felt the Lord. When I asked him how he knew that it was the Savior, he said: "There were the love and the comfort that He gave. He was radiantly beautiful, dressed in a white robe, and He had long brown hair. His dress and appearance were that of the Lord—He showed me the nail prints in his hands."

"Where were the nail prints?" I asked.

"They were on his wrists."

The New Testament is explicit in using the nail prints as evidence that the Savior was resurrected. Thomas, the original doubter, explained his doubts about the resurrection in this manner: "Except I shall see in his hands the print of the nails, and put my finger into the print of the nails, and thrust my hand into his side, I will not believe."[12]

Although these two NDE incidents, by themselves, certainly do not demonstrate the reality of the resurrection, they are, together with the scriptures, a further witness to that reality. As for my own belief, I, like Job "know that my redeemer liveth, and that he shall stand at the latter day upon the earth: And though after my skin worms destroy this body, yet in my flesh shall I see God."[13]

Final Messages

Messages From Those Who Had NDEs

As some final thoughts in this book I shall quote from a few of those who saw what, in my view, we are all destined to share to varying degrees upon the completion of this life—depending upon how we lived.

In many instances these thoughts were expressed by the people with tears in their eyes and with voices choked by emotion—and in one case with hands trembling from fear. Carol and I were privileged thereby to be vicarious participants in their experiences.

Ann's Sublime Feelings

"I felt thoroughly refreshed, enlivened and spiritually rejuvenated. I was filled with a zest for life. It is impossible to explain what it felt like to be lighter than air, with no pain, and totally at peace with everyone and everything around."

Stephanie LaRue—Had Total Knowledge

"About this time I had an experience that I'll never forget . . . a feeling of total, total knowledge without asking. It's like you and me sitting here, now, and wondering how far the universe expands, or . . . just questions we have on earth about the geography of the earth, craters, or anything. This feeling I had of total knowledge was just that, I knew everything without asking. It was an incredible feeling."

Pauline—Discovered What Matters Most

"I've seen a lot of people in my life who have everything in a material sense, and in a split second they have nothing. My experience showed me it's not what you have which matters, but what you've done for other people. . . .

"I think we should talk about death—people should not be afraid of it. It's a personal experience, a very choice experience, so much like opening up, sort of like a panoramic view. Death is more of a beginning than an ending."

Dee—The Dreadful Reality of an Evil Spirit

"When I first became aware of the presence of the thing, . . . it was the most terrible feeling that I've ever had in my life. It was like I was going to die, or worse.

"I thought that it was the Devil, or a spirit that was trying to get my body. That's what I thought. . . . As soon as I felt this presence behind me I knew that this was ugly, this was terror, this was the worst . . . it was the most ugly, the most horrible thing that I had ever encountered. It was going to get me—it was going to destroy me—it was after my body.

"The terror was awful. I could feel myself wanting to scream. I was flailing my arms, grasping for something to pull me back, but there was nothing to hold onto. I was fighting to go back, and I flailed my arms to try and get the thing away from me. It was the most horrible experience I had ever had."

Jean—Learned That Life Is a School

"My experience showed me that there is a life after death. I also learned that this life is a testing period, kind of a school. And that the people in the spirit world are concerned about us and care about us."

Joy Melvin—Understands that Life Has Many Risks

"It's just that there are no guarantees in life. Things can change in a split second. I mean, it just took a phone call to tell me that my dad, my brother and my husband were dead. Life goes so fast you can't take anything for granted. You don't forget the 'I love yous' and the flowers, and the letters. And you should try to be the best you can to people around you."

Marcia Anderson—Found Answer to Prayer

"My hope is that people will develop the love for our Father in Heaven and for his son Jesus Christ, the kind of love that they have for us. You see, he loved me, he loved my children. . . . He loved me enough, as involved as he is, to find us in our desperate time of need. And to extend that love to us in a very practical way. . . .

"I asked God to please help us. I asked him and he listened. I knew it was from him—absolutely."

Julie—There is no Time

In Julie's experience she saw the spirit of her cousin who was killed in Vietnam. As she communicated with him, she recalls saying: "Now, Allen, remember everything I've told you. It's true. You are going to a place where there is no time. We will all be together again, and I want you to be happy. This is wonderful."

Joe Swick—God Knew His Name

"I haven't shared this experience with many people. It is too sacred to me. But whenever I have shared it, I have always told people that the experience has taught me that God is willing to reach out and talk with us. I'm nobody special, I don't have a . . . all I do is translate languages. Nobody knows my name—but I do know that God knows my name. And that he was willing to reach out and talk with me. If he would talk to somebody like me, then he would do it for anybody."

Carol and Arvin Gibson—Final Thoughts

This, then, is the testimony that Carol and I leave with you. Our testimony is of a life beyond this one that is marvelous to behold. It is a life, if we live righteously now, where we will exist with Jesus Christ and his Father in an eternal adventure of growth, development, creation, joy, peace, love and happiness.

The life to come will be a life of truth and knowledge, where uncertainty, doubt, fear and pain will evaporate as the morning dew. Our present earthly life will seem but a short—but immensely important—interlude in the reality of forever. Earthly death will be presented for what it is; namely, birth back into the presence of the Lord Jesus Christ where we may await the glorious resurrection.

Appendix

Research Data Statistics

BookStats	A	B	C	D	E	F	G	H	I	J	K
1		Age at	Age at	Male or	Educa.	One or	Out of	Saw	Spirit		
2	Name	Interview	Exper.	Female	at Exper.	Mult Exp.	Body	Body	Had Form	Tunnel	Light
3	Gibson, Marshall	62	36	M	2.3	1	1	1	1	0	1
4	Evans, Derald	60	22	M	2.2	1	1	1	1	0	1
5	Muecke, Karl	72	59	M	2.3	1	1	0	1	0	0
6	McClellan, Janet	31	27	F	4	1	0	0	0	0	0
7	Ruth	63	36	F	3	1	1	0	1	1	1
8	Shelley, DeAnne	59	32	F	2.4	1	1	0	0	0	1
9	Clark, Lois	57	31	F	2	1	1	1	1	0	1
10	Ann	42	4/28	F	0/2.5	2	1/1	1/1	1/1	1/1	1/1
11	Lucy	34	25	F	2.2	1	1	1	1	0	1
12	Jennette	49	46	F	2	1	1	1	1	1	1
13	Pauline	51	29/43	F	2.4	2	0/1	0/1	0/1	0	0
14	Hansen, Forrest	35	18/20	M	2.2	2	1/1	1/0	0	0/1	1/1
15	Amodt, Bob	33	22	M	2.4	1	?	0	0	0	0
16	Amodt, Margaret	29	20	F	2	1	1	0	1	0	1
17	Norma	37	26	F	2.3	1	1	1	1	0	1
18	Kerry	41	14	M	1.6	1	1	0	1	0	1
19	Herard, David	45	22	M	2.4	1	1	0	1	0	1
20	Walker, Chris	19	10	M	0.8	2	1/1	1/1	0	0	0
21	Kim	15	14	F	1.6	1	1	0	0	1	1
22	Niitsuma, James	26	21	M	2.3	1	1	1	1	0	1
23	Fry, Nyk	26	23	M	2.5	2	0	0	0	0	0/1
24	Vonwaller, Eliz.	30	25	F	2.4	1	1	0	1	0	0
25	LaRue, Stephanie	40	29	F	4	1	1	1	0	0	0
26	Melvin, Joy	31	27	F	2	1	1	0	1	0	1
27	Anderson, Marcia	42	29	F	3	1	1	1	1	0	1
28	Jones, Joanne	61	54	F	2	1	1	1	0	0	0
29	Jackie	32	22	F	2	1	1	1	0	0	1
30	Berg, Ray	51	26	M	2	1	0	0	0	0	0
31	Doris	70	22	M	2.4	1	1	1	0	0	0
32	Katrina	36	35	F	2	1	1	0	1	0	1
33	Dee	42	22/24	F	2	2	1/1	0/1	1/1	0	0
34	Tracie	16	15	F	1.8	1	1	1	1	1	1
35	Daniels, Maureen	31	23	F	2.5	1	1	0	0	0	1
36	James, Shirley	57	31	F	2	1	0	0	0	0	1
37	Martinez, Kathy	45	21	F	2	1	1	1	1	1	0
38	Jean	45	40	F	2.5	1	1	0	1	0	0
39	Stirling, John	38	25	M	2.4	1	1	1	1	0	0
40	Gillum, Gary	47	19	M	2.8	1	1	0	0	0	1
41	Swick, Joe	30	9	M	0.3	1	1	0	1	1	1
42	Storm, Howard	–	38	M	4	1	1	1	0	0	1
43	Weaver, Eloise	50	10/48	F	0.5/2	2	0/1	0/1	1/1	0	1/1
44	Prueitt, Cynthia	34	7	F	0.2	1	1	1	1	0	1
45	Kirk, Barry	42	23	M	2.8	1	1	1	1	1	1
46	Swanson, Vern	48	30	M	4	1	1	0	1	0	1
47	Julie	42	17/19	F	1.9/3.2	2	1/0	0	1/1	0	1/1
48	Durham, Elane	48	32	F	2.4	1	1	1	1	0	1
49	Bill	42	41	M	3	1	1	1	1	0	1
50	Louise	36	24	F	3	1	1	1	0	1	1
51	Joyce	47	36	F	2	1	1	0	1	1	1
52	Pitcher, Jennifer	11	5	F	0	1	0	0	0	0	0
53	Rocky	13	4	M	0	1	1	1	1	0	0
54	Jack	40	5/21	M	0/2.6	2	1/1	1/1	0	0	0/1
55	DeLynn	42	37	M	3	1	1	1	1	1	1
56	Karen	37	20	F	2.3	1	1	1	1	1	0
57	Dallas	54	40	M	2.3	1	1	0	0	1	1
58	Chuck	50	25	M	2.4	1	1	1	0	1	0
59	Mike	31	9	M	0.3	1	1	1	1	1	1
60	Allen, Lavor	81	56	M	1.5	1	1	1	1	0	1
61	Barbara	41	15	F	1.5	1	1	1	1	0	1
62	Patricia	37	13/25	F	1.3/2.5	2	1/0	1/0	1/0	0	0
63	Elizabeth Marie	29	14/28	F	1.3/2	2	1/1	1/0	1/0	0	1/0
64	Lori	29	16/25/29	F	1.8/2.5	3	1/1/1	1/0/0	1/1/1	0	1/0
65	Mary	59	34/52	F	1.8	2	1/1	0/1	0	1/0	1/0
66	Maria	78	41	F	2	1	1	0	0	0	0
67	Debbie	32	21	F	2.2	1	1	1	1	0	1
68	Chevalier, David	40	28	M	2.8	1	1	0	1	0	0
69	Zamora, Renee	32	31	F	2.1	1	1	1	1	0	0
70	Smith, Roger	49	24/29	M	2.5	2	1/0	0	0	0	1/1
71											
72	Totals			68		83	71	44	49	18	50
73				40F 28M							
74	Percentages			58.8F		20.5 Mult	85.5	53	59	21.6	60.2

268

APPENDIX—RESEARCH DATA STATISTICS

BookStats	A	L	M	N	O	P	Q	R	S	T	U	V
	Name	Landscp	People	Knew People	Relatives	Voice	Deity	Saw Deity	Life's Review	Buildings	Knowldg	Energy
3	Gibson, Marshall	1	1	1	0	1	1	1	1	1	1	0
4	Evans, Derald	0	1	1	0	1	0	0	0	0	1	0
5	Muecke, Karl	1	0	0	0	1	1	0	0	0	1	0
6	McClellan, Janet	0	0	1	0	1	0	0	0	0	0	0
7	Ruth	0	1	1	0	0	0	0	0	0	0	0
8	Shelley, DeAnne	0	0	0	1	1	0	0	0	0	0	0
9	Clark, Lois	0	1	0	0	1	0	0	0	0	0	0
10	Ann	1/0	1/0	0	0	1/1	0/1	0/1	0	0	0	0
11	Lucy	0	1	0	0	1	1	1	0	0	0	0
12	Jennette	0	0	0	0	1	1	1	0	0	1	0
13	Pauline	0	0	0	0	1	1	1	0	0	1	0
14	Hansen, Forrest	0	1/0	0	0	0	0	0	0	0	0	0
15	Amodt, Bob	0	0	0	0	1/0	0	0	0/1	0	0	0
16	Amodt, Margaret	0	0	0	0	0	0	0	0	0	0	0
17	Norma	0	0	0	0	0	0	0	0	0	0	1
18	Kerry	0	1	0	0	0	0	0	0	0	0	0
19	Herard, David	1	1	1	1	1	0	0	0	0	0	0
20	Walker, Chris	0	0	0	0	1	1	0	0	0	1	0
21	Kim	0	1	0	0	0	0	0	0	0	0	0
22	Niitsuma, James	0	1	0	0	1	0	0	0	0	0	0
23	Fry, Nyk	0	0	0	0	1	0	0	1	0	0	0
24	Vorwaller, Eliz.	0	1	1	0	0	0	0	0	0	0	0
25	LaRue, Stephanie	0	0	0	0	1	0	0	0	0	0	0
26	Melvin, Joy	1	1	1	1	1	0	0	0	0	1	0
27	Anderson, Marcia	0	1	0	0	0	0	0	0	0	0	0
28	Jones, Joanne	1	0	0	0	0	0	0	0	0	1	0
29	Jackie	0	0	0	0	1	1	1	0	0	0	0
30	Berg, Ray	0	0	0	0	0	0	0	0	0	0	0
31	Doris	0	0	0	0	0	0	0	1	0	0	0
32	Katrina	1	1	0	0	0	0	0	0	0	0	0
33	Dee	0	0	0	0	1	1	0	0	0	1	0
34	Tracie	0	1	1	0	1	0	0	0	0	0	0
35	Daniels, Maureen	0	1	1	1	1	0	0	0	1	1	0
36	James, Shirley	0	1	1	1	1	0	0	0	0	1	0
37	Martinez, Kathy	0	1	1	1	1	0	0	0	0	0	0
38	Jean	1	1	1	1	1	0	0	0	0	0	0
39	Stirling, John	0	0	0	0	1	0	0	0	1	1	0
40	Gillum, Gary	1	1	1	1	1	1	0	1	0	1	1
41	Swick, Joe	0	0	0	0	1	0	0	0	0	1	0
42	Storm, Howard	0	1	0	0	1	0	0	0	0	0	1
43	Weaver, Eloise	0	1/1	1/1	0/1	0/1	1/0	1/0	1	0	1	0
44	Pruitt, Cynthia	0	0	0	0	1	1	1	0	1	1	1
45	Kirk, Barry	0	1	1	1	0	0	0	0	1	1	1
46	Swanson, Vern	0	1	1	1	1	0	0	0	0	0	0
47	Julie	0	1/1	1/0	1/0	1/0	0	0	0	0	1/1	0
48	Durham, Elane	1	1	1	1	1	1	0	1	0	1	0
49	Bill	1	1	1	1	1	1	0	0	1	0	1
50	Louise	0	1	1	0	1	0	0	0	0	0	0
51	Joyce	0	0	0	0	1	0	0	0	0	0	0
52	Pitcher, Jennifer	0	1	1	1	1	0	0	0	0	1	0
53	Rocky	0	1	1	1	1	1	1	0	0	1	0
54	Jack	0/1	1/1	1/0	0	1/0	1/0	1/0	0	0	1	0
55	DeLynn	0	1	0	1	1	1	0	0	0	1/0	0
56	Karen	0	0	0	1	1	1	0	0	1	1	0
57	Dallas	1	0	0	0	1	0	0	0	0	1	0
58	Chuck	0	1	1	0	1	1	1	0	0	1	0
59	Mike	1	1	1	1	1	0	0	0	0	1	0
60	Allen, Lavor	1	1	1	1	1	1	1	0	0	1	0
61	Barbara	0	1	1	1	1	0	0	0	0	0	0
62	Patricia	0	0	1	1	1	0	0	0	0	0	0
63	Elizabeth Marie	0	1/1	0/1	0	1	1/0	0	1/0	0	0	0
64	Lori	0/0/1	1/0/0	0	0	1	1/0	0	1/0	0	1/0	0
65	Mary	0	0/1	0/1	0/1	0/1	0/1	0/1	0	0	0	0
66	Maria	0	0	0	0	1	0	0	1/0	0	0	0
67	Debbie	0	0	0	0	1	1	1	0	1	0	0
68	Chevalier, David	1	1	0	1	1	1	1	0	0	0	0
69	Zamora, Renee	1	1	1	1	0	1	1	0	0	1	0
70	Smith, Roger	0	0	1/0	0	1/1	1/0	1/0	1/0	0	1/1	1/0
72	**Totals**	18	46	33	23	53	22	15	9	6	28	6
74	**Percentages**	21.1	55.4	39.8	27.7	63.8	26.5	18.1	10.8	7.2	33.7	7.2

BookStats	A	W	X	Y	Z	AA	AB	AC	AD	AE	AF
1									Sense of	Second	Saw
2	Name	Peace	Love	Warmth	Pure	Remorse	Fear	Music	Mission	Healing	Premortl
3	Gibson, Marshall	1	1	0	0	0	0	0	1	0	0
4	Evans, Derald	0	0	0	1	0	0	1	1	0	0
5	Muecke, Karl	0	1	0	0	0	0	0	1	0	0
6	McClellan, Janet	0	0	0	0	0	0	0	1	0	0
7	Ruth	1	1	0	1	0	0	0	1	1	0
8	Shelley, DeAnne	0	0	0	0	0	0	0	1	1	0
9	Clark, Lois	1	0	0	0	0	0	1	1	1	0
10	Ann	1/1	1/1	0	0	0	0	0	0/1	1	0
11	Lucy	0	1	0	0	0	0	0	1	1	0
12	Jennette	1	1	0	0	0	0	0	1	0	0
13	Pauline	1/0	0	1/1	0	0	0	0	0	0	0
14	Hansen, Forrest	0	0	0	0	0	0	0	0	0	0
15	Amodt, Bob	0	0	0	0	0	0	0	0	0	0
16	Amodt, Margaret	1	0	0	0	0	0	0	1	0	0
17	Norma	1	0	0	0	0	0	0	1	0	0
18	Kerry	1	1	0	0	0	0	0	1	0	0
19	Herard, David	1	1	1	0	0	0	0	1	0	0
20	Walker, Chris	1/1	0	0	0	0	0	0	0	0	0
21	Kim	1	0	1	0	0	0	0	0	0	0
22	Niitsuma, James	0	0	1	0	0	0	0	0	0	0
23	Fry, Nyk	0/1	0	0	0	0	1/0	0	1	0	0
24	Vorwaller, Eliz.	0	0	0	0	0	0	0	1	0	0
25	LaRue, Stephanie	1	1	0	0	0	0	0	1	0	0
26	Melvin, Joy	0	1	1	0	0	0	1	0	0	0
27	Anderson, Marcia	1	1	0	0	0	0	0	1	0	0
28	Jones, Joanne	0	1	0	0	0	0	0	0	0	0
29	Jackie	0	0	0	0	0	0	0	1	0	0
30	Berg, Ray	0	0	0	0	0	0	0	0	0	0
31	Doris	0	0	0	0	0	0	0	0	0	0
32	Katrina	1	1	0	0	0	0	0	1	0	0
33	Dee	0	0	0	0	0	0/1	0	0	0	0
34	Tracie	1	1	1	0	0	0	0	1	0	0
35	Daniels, Maureen	1	1	0	0	0	0	1	1	0	0
36	James, Shirley	0	1	1	0	0	0	0	0	0	0
37	Martinez, Kathy	0	0	0	0	1	1	0	1	0	0
38	Jean	1	0	0	0	0	0	0	1	0	0
39	Stirling, John	1	1	0	0	0	0	0	1	0	0
40	Gillum, Gary	1	1	0	0	0	0	0	1	0	0
41	Swick, Joe	0	1	0	0	0	0	0	1	0	0
42	Storm, Howard	1	0	0	0	1	1	0	1	0	0
43	Weaver, Eloise	0/1	1/1	0/1	0	0	0	0/1	0/1	0	0
44	Prueitt, Cynthia	0	1	1	0	0	0	0	1	0	0
45	Kirk, Barry	1	0	1	0	0	0	0	1	0	0
46	Swanson, Vern	1	1	0	0	0	0	0	0	0	0
47	Julie	0	1/0	0	0	0	0	0	0	0	0/1
48	Durham, Elane	1	1	0	1	0	0	1	1	1	1
49	Bill	1	0	1	0	0	0	0	1	0	0
50	Louise	1	0	0	0	0	0	0	0	0	0
51	Joyce	0	1	0	0	0	0	0	1	0	0
52	Pitcher, Jennifer	0	0	0	0	0	0	0	0	0	0
53	Rocky	0	0	0	0	0	0	0	1	0	0
54	Jack	1	0	0	0	0	0/1	0/1	1/1	0	0
55	DeLynn	1	1	1	0	0	0	0	1	0	1
56	Karen	0	0	0	0	1	1	0	1	1	0
57	Dallas	0	1	1	0	1	0	0	1	1	0
58	Chuck	0	0	1	0	0	0	0	1	1	0
59	Mike	1	1	1	0	0	1	1	1	0	0
60	Allen, Lavor	1	0	0	0	0	0	0	1	0	0
61	Barbara	0	1	0	0	0	0	0	1	0	0
62	Patricia	0	0	0	0	1/0	1/1	0	0	0	0
63	Elizabeth Marie	0	1/1	0	1/0	1/0	0	0	1/1	0	0
64	Lori	1/0/0	0	0	0	0	0	0	0	0	0
65	Mary	1/1	1/1	1/0	0	0	0	0	0/1	1	0
66	Maria	1	1	0	0	0	0	1	1	0	0
67	Debbie	1	1	0	0	0	0	0	0	0	0
68	Chevalier, David	0	0	0	0	0	0	0	1	0	0
69	Zamora, Renee	0	0	0	0	0	1	0	1	0	0
70	Smith, Roger	0	1/0	0	0	1/0	0	0	1/1	0	0
71											
72	Totals	38	39	17	4	5	10	9	52	10	3
73											
74	Percentages	45.7	47	20.5	4.8	6	12	9.6	62.6	12	3.6

Legend for Statistical Data

Name: As it appeared in research work.

Age at Interview: Reported age at time of interview.

Age at Experience: Calculated age at time of experience.

Male or Female: As stated.

Education at Experience: Less than Grammar School=0; Grammar School=1; High School=2; BS or BA=3; Graduate Degree=4.

One or Multiple Experiences: The number of experiences, on different days, for the individual.

Out of Body: 0 if not out of body; 1 if out of body.

Saw Body: 0 if individual did not see his or her own body; 1 if he or she did see body.

Spirit Had Form: 1 if individual had a sense that his or her body had form; 0 if individual didn't know or if it did not have form.

Tunnel: 1 if individual described something like a tunnel; 0 if individual did not.

Light: 1 if individual saw an unusual bright light; 0 if individual did not.

Landscape: 1 if individual saw landscape features in another world; 0 if he or she did not.

People: 1 if individual saw people; 0 if he or she did not.

Knew People: 1 if individual felt he or she knew people, even if he or she later forgot; 0 if individual did not.

Relatives: 1 if individual knew the people as relatives; 0 if not.

Voice: 1 if individual heard or knew a voice was communicating; 0 if not.

Deity: 1 if individual identified the presence of Deity; 0 if not.

Saw Deity: 1 if individual said that he or she saw Deity; 0 if not.

Life's Review: 1 if individual had a life's review (or analogous event); 0 if not.

Buildings: 1 if individual spoke of being in or seeing buildings; 0 if not.

Knowledge: 1 if individual spoke of receiving unusual knowledge, even if later forgotten; 0 if not.

Energy: 1 if individual spoke of energy as part of experience; 0 if not.

Peace: 1 if individual spoke of peace as part of experience; 0 if not.

Love: 1 if individual spoke of love as part of experience; 0 if not.

Warmth: 1 if individual spoke of warmth as part of experience; 0 if not.

Pure: 1 if individual spoke of pure as part of experience; 0 if not.

Legend for Statistical Data, Cont'd.

Remorse: 1 if individual appeared to have remorse related to what he or she experienced; 0 if not.

Fear: 1 if individual experienced fear at some part of experience; 0 if not.

Music: 1 if individual spoke of music or music-like sounds during experience; 0 if not.

Sense of Mission: 1 if individual returned from experience with a sense of mission; 0 if not.

Second Healing: 1 if individual later had life-threatening illness that was miraculously cured; 0 if not.

Saw Premortal: 1 if individual saw himself or herself in a premortal environment; 0 if not.

Notes

Introduction

1. Moody, Raymond A., Jr., *Life After Life*. New York, N.Y.: Bantam Books, 1988.
2. Ritchie, George G. with Sherrill, Elizabeth, *Return from Tomorrow*. Old Tappan, New Jersey: Spire Books, Fleming H. Revell Co., 1978.
3. Wilson, Ian. *The After Death Experience*. New York, N.Y.: William Morrow and Company, Inc., 1989.

   Grey, Margot. *Return from Death*. London and New York: Arkana, 1987.

   Murphet, Howard. *Beyond Death*. 306 West Geneva Road, Wheaton, IL 60187: Quest Books, The Theosophical Publishing House, 1990.
4. Zaleski, Carol. *Otherworld Journeys*. N.Y., Oxford: Oxford University Press, 1987.

   Grosso, Michael. *The Final Choice*. Walpose, New Hampshire: Stillpoint Publishing, 1985.
5. Ring, Kenneth. *Heading Toward Omega*. N.Y.: William Morrow, Inc. 1985.

   Gallup, G., Jr. *Adventures in Immortality*. N.Y.: McGraw Hill, 1982.
6. Wilson, Ian. *The After Death Experience*. N.Y.: William Morrow and Company, Inc., 1989.
7. Babb, Raymond C. *Hypnotic Induction of Experiences (Letter to the Editor)*, "Journal of Near-Death Studies," Vol 8, Number 1, Fall 1989. 233 Spring Street, N.Y. 10013-1578: Human Sciences Press, Inc., pp. 65-70.
8. Siegel, Ronald K. *Antimatter—Remembering Rogo*. "Omni" Magazine, Jan. 1991, p. 73.
9. Rawlings, Maurice, *Beyond Death's Door*. N.Y.: Bantam Books, 1979.
10. Ring, Kenneth. *Life at Death*. New York, N.Y.: Quill, 1982, pp. 23, 24.
11. Storm, Howard. Unpublished document in possession of author; transcribed from taped experience recorded in 1989 at The NDE Research Institute, Fort Thomas, Kentucky.

Chapter 19: Are the Stories True?

1. Moody, Raymond A., Jr., *Life After Life.* New York, N.Y.: Bantam Books, 1976.
2. Ring, Kenneth, *Life at Death—A Scientific Investigation of the Near-death Experience.* New York, N.Y.: Quill, 1982, pp. 206-17.
3. Morse, Melvin, *Closer to the Light—Learning from the Near-Death Experiences of Children.* New York, N.Y.: Villard Books, 1990, pp. 183-93.
4. Moody, Raymond A., Jr., *The Light Beyond.* New York, N.Y.: Bantam Books, 1988, pp. 151-54.
5. Gibson, Arvin S., *In Search of Angels.* Bountiful, Utah: Horizon Publishers and Distributors, Inc., 1990, pp. 157-73.
6. Gibson, Arvin S., *Glimpses of Eternity.* Bountiful, Utah: Horizon Publishers and Distributors, Inc., 1992, pp. 44-47.
7. Wilson, Ian, *The After Death Experience—The Physics of the Non-Physical.* New York, N.Y.: William Morrow and Company, Inc., 1987, pp. 132-33.
8. Ring, Kenneth, *Heading Toward Omega—In Search of the Meaning of the Near-Death Experience.* New York, N.Y.: Quill, 1985, p. 35.
9. Ring, Kenneth, *Heading Toward Omega, op. cit.,* pp. 45-46.
10. Wren-Lewis, John, "Avoiding the Columbus Confusion: An Ockhamish View of Near-Death Research," *Journal of Near-Death Studies*, Vol. 11, No. 2, Winter 1992. 233 Spring St., New York, N.Y. 10013: Human Sciences Press, Inc., p. 78.
11. Gibson, *op. cit., Glimpses of Eternity,* pp. 302-06.
12. Johnson, Lynn D., *Letter to Author*, February 7, 1993.
13. Spanos, Nicholas P.; Menary, Evelyn; Gabora, Natalie J.; DuBreuil, Susan C.; and Dewhirst, Bridget; "Secondary Identity Enactments During Hypnotic Past-Life Regression: A Sociocognitive Perspective," *Journal of Personality and Social Psychology*, 1991, Vol. 61, No. 2., pp. 308-20.
14. *The Bible.* Hebrews 9:27.
15. *The Bible.* Luke 23:43.

Chapter 20: Patterns and Parallels

1. *The Bible.* John 14:27.
2. *The Bible.* Philippians 4:7.
3. *The Bible.* 1 John 1:5.

4. *The Bible.* James 1:17.
5. *The Bible.* John 1:6-9.
6. *The Bible.* Ephesians 3:19.
7. Gibson, Arvin S., *Echoes From Eternity.* Bountiful, Utah: Horizon Publishers and Distributors, Inc., 1993, pp. 269-71.
8. Eadie, Betty J., *Embraced by the Light.* Placerville, CA: Gold Leaf Press, 1992, pp. 48, 49, 67.
9. Moody, Raymond A., Jr. *Life After Life.* Covington, GA: Mockingbird, 1975.
10. Ring, K. *Life at Death: A Scientific Investigation of the Near-Death Experience.* New York, NY: Coward, McCann and Geoghegan, 1980. Ring, K. *Heading Toward Omega: In Search of the Meaning of the Near-Death Experience.* New York, NY: William Morrow, 1984.
11. Rawlings, M. *Beyond Death's Door.* Nashville, TN: Thomas Nelson, 1978.
12. Ring, K. *Life at Death: A Scientific Investigation of the Near-Death Experience.* New York, NY: Coward, McCann and Geoghegan, 1980, pp. 147-53.
13. Ritchie, G. G., with Sherrill, E. *Return from Tomorrow.* Old Tappan, NJ: Fleming H. Revell, 1978, p. 66.
14. Gibson, Arvin S., "Near-Death Experience Patterns from Research in the Salt Lake City Region," Journal of Near-Death Studies, Winter 1994 (Anticipated). New York, N.Y.: Human Sciences Press.

Chapter 21: Universal Messages

1. Gibson, Arvin S., *Echoes From Eternity.* Bountiful, Utah: Horizon Publishers and Distributors, Inc., 1993, pp. 14, 15.
2. Moore, L.T., *Isaac Newton.* 1934, p. 664.
3. *The Bible.* 1 Corinthians 13:12-13.
4. *The Bible.* Mark 2:17.
5. *The Bible.* 2 Timothy 3:1-15.
6. *The Bible.* John 3:21.
7. *The Bible.* Romans 8:35-39.
8. *The Bible.* Matthew 22:37-40.
9. Lewis, C. S., *Miracles—A Preliminary Study.* New York: Collier Books, 1947, p. 145.
10. *The Bible.* 1 Corinthians 15:22, 23.

11. *The Bible.* Matthew 27:52, 53.
12. *The Bible.* John 20:25.
13. *The Bible.* Job 19:25, 26.

Selected Bibliography

Scriptures

The Holy Bible. Authorized King James Version.

Near-Death Literature

Almeder, Robert, *Beyond Death.* Springfield, Illinois: Publisher, Charles C. Thomas, 1987.

Atwater, P.M.H., *Coming Back to Life.* New York, N.Y.: Ballantine Books, 1988.

Atwater, P.M.H., "Is There A Hell? Surprising Observations About the Near-Death Experience." *Journal of Near-Death Studies*, Vol. 10, No. 3, Spring 1992.

Brinkley, Daniel, with Perry, Paul, *Saved by the Light—The True Story of a Man Who Died Twice and the Profound Revelations He Received.* New York, N.Y.: Villard Books, 1994.

Crowther, Duane S., *Life Everlasting.* Salt Lake City, Utah: Bookcraft, Inc., 1967.

Eadie, Betty J., *Embraced by the Light.* Placerville, CA: Gold Leaf Press, 1992.

Flynn, Charles P., *After the Beyond—Human Transformation and the Near-Death Experience.* New York, N.Y.: Prentice Hall Press, 1986.

Gallup, G., Jr., *Adventures in Immortality.* N.Y.: McGraw Hill, 1982.

Gibson, Arvin S., *Echoes From Eternity.* Bountiful, Utah: Horizon Publishers and Distributors, Inc., 1993.

Gibson, Arvin S., *Glimpses of Eternity.* Bountiful, Utah: Horizon Publishers and Distributors, Inc., 1992.

Gibson, Arvin S., "Near-Death Experience Patterns from Research in the Salt Lake City Region," Journal of Near-Death Studies," Winter 1994 (Anticipated). New York, N.Y.: Human Sciences Press.

Grey, Margot, *Return from Death.* London and New York: Arkana, 1987.

Grosso, Michael, *The Final Choice.* Walpose, New Hampshire: Stillpoint Publishing, 1985.

Harris, Barbara, *Full Circle.* Pocket Books, 1991.

Kübler-Ross, Elisabeth, *On Children and Death.* New York, N.Y.: Collier Books, MacMillan Publishing Company, 1983.

Kübler-Ross, Elisabeth, *Questions and Answers on Death and Dying.* New York, N.Y: Collier Books, MacMillan Publishing Company, 1974.

Lundahl, Craig R., *A Collection of Near-Death Research Readings*. Chicago, Ill.: Nelson-Hall Publishers, 1982.

Millett, Larry R, *A Touch of Here and Beyond*. Salt Lake City, Utah: Hawkes Publishing, Inc.

Moody, Raymond A., Jr., *Life After Life*. New York, N.Y.: Bantam Books, 1988.

Moody, Raymond A., Jr., *The Light Beyond*. Bantam Books, New York, N.Y., 1988.

Moody, Raymond A. Jr., M.D., *Reflections on Life After Life*, New York, N.Y.: Bantam Books, 1983.

Morse, Melvin with Perry, Paul., *Closer to the Light*. New York, N.Y.: Villard Books, 1990.

Morse, Melvin with Perry, Paul, *Transformed by the Light*. New York, N.Y.: Villard Books, 1992.

Murphet, Howard., *Beyond Death*. Wheaton, Illinois: Quest Books, The Theosophical Publishing House, 1990.

Nelson, Lee, *Beyond the Veil—Volume I*. Orem, Utah: Cedar Fort Inc., 1988.

Nelson, Lee, *Beyond the Veil—Volume II*. Orem, Utah: Cedar Fort Inc., 1989.

Rawlings, Maurice, *Beyond Death's Door*. N.Y.: Bantam Books, 1979.

Rawlings, Maurice, *To Hell and Back*. Nashville, Tennessee: Thomas Nelson Publishers, 1993.

Ring, Kenneth, *Heading Toward Omega*. N. Y.: William Morrow Inc., 1985.

Ring, Kenneth, *Life at Death*. New York, N.Y.: Quill, 1982.

Ritchie, George G. with Sherrill, Elizabeth, *Return from Tomorrow*. Old Tappan, New Jersey: Spire Books, Fleming H. Revell Co., 1978.

Ritchie, George G., *My Life After Dying—Becoming Alive to Universal Love*. Norfolk, Virginia: Hampton Roads Publishing, 1991.

Sorensen, Michele R.; Willmore, David R., *The Journey Beyond Life, Vol. One*. Orem, Utah: Family Affair Books, 1988.

Storm, Howard. Unpublished document in possession of author; transcribed from taped experience recorded in 1989 at The NDE Research Institute, Fort Thomas, Kentucky.

Wilson, Ian, *The After Death Experience*, William Morrow and Company, Inc., N.Y., 1987.

Wren-Lewis, John, "Avoiding the Columbus Confusion: An Ockhamish View of Near-Death Research;" *Journal of Near-Death Studies*, Vol. 11, No. 2, Winter 1992. 233 Spring St., New York, N.Y.: Human Sciences Press, Inc.,

Zaleski, Carol. *Otherworld Journeys*. N.Y. and Oxford: Oxford University Press, 1987.

Other Literature

Lewis, C.S., *Miracles—A Preliminary Study*. New York: Collier Books, 1947.

Moody, Raymond A. Jr. *Coming Back—A Psychiatrist Explores Past-Life Journeys*. N.Y., London: Bantam Books, 1991.

Moore, L.T., *Isaac Newton*. 1934.

Spanos, Nicholas P.; Menary, Evelyn; Gabora, Natalie DuBreuil, Susan C.; and Dewhirst, Bridget; "Secondary Identity Enactments During Hypnotic Past-Life Regression: A Sociocognitive Perspective;" *Journal of Personality and Social Psychology*, 1991, Vol. 61, No. 2.

INDEX